LACE

Virginia Churchill Bath served on the staff of the Art Institute of Chicago from 1952 to 1971 as a lecturer for museum education and as conservator and assistant curator of the Textile Department. She resigned in 1971 to devote more time to writing, exhibiting, and teaching. A painter, needleworker, designer, teacher, and lecturer, she is the author of the widely acclaimed *Embroidery Masterworks: Designs and Techniques for Contemporary Application.*

Virginia
Churchill
Bath

PENGUIN BOOKS

Penguin Books Ltd, Harmondsworth,
Middlesex, England
Penguin Books, 625 Madison Avenue,
New York, New York 10022, U.S.A.
Penguin Books Australia Ltd, Ringwood,
Victoria, Australia
Penguin Books Canada Limited, 2801 John Street,
Markham, Ontario, Canada L3R 1B4
Penguin Books (N.Z.) Ltd, 182–190 Wairau Road,
Auckland 10, New Zealand

First published in the United States of America by
Henry Regnery Company 1974
Published in Penguin Books 1979

LIBRARY OF CONGRESS CATALOGING IN PUBLICATION DATA
Bath, Virginia Churchill.
Lace.
Reprint of the 1974 ed. published by Regnery, Chicago.
Bibliography: p. 313.
Includes index.
1. Lace and lace making.   I. Title.
[TT800.B25 1979]   746.2   78-23354
ISBN 0 14 046.378 X

Printed in the United States of America by
Command Web Offset, Inc., Jersey City, New Jersey
Set in Melior

Contents

First came bands of Italian work, tough pieces with drawn threads, in which everything was repeated over and over, as distinctly as in a cottage garden. Then all at once a whole succession of our glances would be barred with Venetian needlepoint, as though we had been cloisters or prisons. But the view was freed again, and one saw deep into gardens more and more artful, until everything was dense and warm against the eyes as in a hothouse: gorgeous plants we did not know opened gigantic leaves, tendrils groped for one another as though they were dizzy, and the great open blossoms of the point d'Alençon dimmed everything with their pollen. Suddenly, all weary and confused, one stepped into the long track of the Valenciennes, and it was winter and early morning, with hoar frost. And one pushed through the snow-covered bushes of the Binche, and came to places where nobody had been yet; the branches hung so strangely downward, there might well have been a grave beneath them, but we concealed that from each other. The cold pressed ever closer upon us, and at last, when the very fine pillow laces came, Maman said: "Oh now we shall get frostflowers on our eyes," and so it was too, for inside ourselves it was very warm.

Over the rolling up again we both sighed; it was a lengthy task, but we were not willing to entrust it to anyone else.

Rainer Maria Rilke, in The Notebooks of Malte Laurids Brigge

"*Marchesa Brigida Spinola Doria,*"
Peter Paul Rubens. c. 1606. Courtesy:
National Gallery of Art, Washington,
D.C. Samuel H. Kress collection.

It is difficult for us, the inhabitants of a utilitarian society, to imagine a world in which lace was a prized possession and to understand the noblemen of the sixteenth, seventeenth, and eighteenth centuries, who went so far as to sell their land, the basis of their wealth and power, to buy lace.

Today most lace is machine made and relatively inexpensive, and much of it is not even especially beautiful. It certainly is not a status symbol. Few of us understand the craft of hand lacemaking. When we read that Charles I of England required 994 yards of lace edging for a dozen collars and cuffs and 600 yards of bobbin lace for his nightwear, we are amazed, but it is only when we realize the enormous amount of time and labor that such an order required that we fully understand why the Puritan leaders forbade the wearing of lace in the New England colonies.

Still, men seem compelled to ornament themselves and their possessions, and even in the early years of the United States, buying and selling lace was a brisk business.

Fragmentary evidence exists to prove that techniques that are the basis for lacemaking as it has been practiced from the fifteenth century until the present were known in very ancient times. Prehistoric people made nets and snares. The ancient Chinese made netting, as did the Egyptians, whose tombs also contain examples of bobbin-like twisted nets, drawnwork, and cutwork.

Gold and other metals were used for early laces, as were colored silks. Techniques and materials arrived in Venice via Ragusa, in Genoa from Cyprus, and in Spain from the east, brought by the Moors, but no one place or time has an undisputed claim to the origin of any of the primary lace techniques. Venice was the greatest of the early needle lacemaking cities; bobbin laces flourished in Flemish towns a few years later.

From the needle lace centers of Italy and the bobbin lace regions of Flanders, lacemaking spread throughout Europe. When she went to France in 1535 to marry Henry II, Catherine de Medici took along Federico Vinciolo, one of the best Italian lace designers, as well as laces from her native Florence. Copies of Venetian laces were made in Spain, England, and France. A great industry developed in Flanders. Lace became an important item of export, and each country passed laws to protect its product.

Collerette
à fraise.

Ruff.

Stiff upright collar with frill.

Falling collar.

Stiff upright
collar with frill.

1

At first the use of lace was restricted to the clergy and nobility. In England, for example, Henry VIII issued the Acts of Apparell, which forbade the wearing of "garded and pynched shirts and partlets" to anyone with a rank lower than that of knight. (According to Cotgrave, to gard means "to trim with lace.") Queen Mary allowed no one under the rank of baron to wear imported cutwork ruffles. Wives of men under the rank of knight were not allowed to wear lace, gold passementerie, or imported cutwork. Laces were used lavishly by the court of Elizabeth I, the first English monarch to wear a great deal of lace, but they continued to be forbidden to the lower ranks.

In the seventeenth century men's clothing in England and on the Continent included yards of metal and linen lace, which were used for instep rosettes, boot-top flounces, and hat ornaments as well as for collars, cuffs, and stripes of decoration on coats, nightshirts, and other garments.

In the sixteenth and seventeenth centuries the most spectacular of the lace collars was the ruff, which evolved from the small ruffled trimming on earlier close-fitting neckbands into a large cartwheel, the millstone collar. Worn for a long period in England and on the Continent by both men and women, this fantasy required the use of poking sticks, careful starching, and weights for the maintenance of its precise arrangement. Both needle and bobbin laces were used for these collars. Some were made entirely of lace, and others were of linen edged with fine points.

In 1623 the *golilla* originated in Spain. A rigid semicircle of linen over stiffening, it

Falling collar.

Golilla.

Falling band.

Open ruff.

Falling ruff.

2

was edged with lace and held up under the chin on a neckband. Sometimes a ruff was laid over it. The ruff also was worn over a falling band (a turned-down collar), which in the second half of the seventeenth century was worn alone. At about the same time the unstarched, falling ruff was also popular.

The *col rabat*, a square-tabbed collar, usually with lace edging about four inches wide and tied in front with decorative, tasseled cords, appeared about 1660. This was also the period of the cravat, introduced simultaneously with the fashion of long wigs for men and worn from 1685 until 1735. When made of heavy Venetian needlepoint lace, the cravat was worn flat; softer lace was used for ruffled versions.

A popular type of cravat emerged in 1690, when Princes of the Blood hastily left for the battle at Steinkirk, having only time enough to fling their cravats carelessly about their necks. The casually arranged *steinkirk*, fashionable until 1730, was loosely twisted around the neck and secured with a long pin or passed through a buttonhole of the coat.

In the eighteenth century men wore first long, then shorter, jabots, full-sleeved shirts with ruffles at the wrists, and sash garters. Cloaks, hats, and gloves were trimmed with gold, silver, and colored silk laces as well as with white linen lace. A combination of laces was usual. Soft yardages were made for women's dresses. The earlier stiff, lace-trimmed open ruff and the multilayered falling collars with their matching, décolleté-filling frontpieces, were succeeded by neckerchiefs (whisks) and soft lace scarves extending to the waist or below. Dresses were trimmed with sets of flounces: *quilles*

Ruff over falling band.

Cartwheel.

Gentleman wearing stockings with deep flounces called canons.

Décolleté filled with front piece.

Whisk.

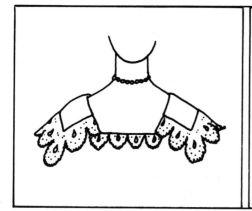

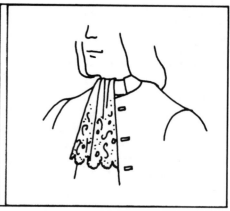

Collar with scalloped lace.

Lace collar for a
deep-cut neckline.

Cravat.

(tapered vertical flounces from neck to hem), *tournantes* (horizontal flounces sewn down at both sides), and multilayered *engageantes* or *pagodes* (tapered sleeve flounces.) Bibless lace aprons were worn. Caps with lappets or flounces were made of especially fine lace. In 1770 the introduction of printed India muslin encouraged laces with small-sprigged or spotted designs, and sometimes white embroidery was used instead of lace.

In the early nineteenth century men began to wear the stock, a high, stiff collar shaped over cardboard, and with it, a large neckerchief. Neither stock nor neckerchief was lace-trimmed. The end of lace fashions for men was at hand.

Clothing styles were reflected in the designs of the laces themselves. The earliest laces were worked in fairly simple, geometric designs. But as needle and bobbin lace techniques became more sophisticated, lacemakers were no longer limited to geometric forms. As fashion changed, so did lace design. Heavy, almost sculptural, needle laces suited the embossed floral stylizations of Renaissance silks and velvets. With the advent of dainty, naturalistic patterns on softer, pastel silks, bobbin laces gained in popularity. In the eighteenth century lace design sometimes bordered on the fantastic, echoing the development of Bizarre design. Motifs included classical themes: rosettes, garlands of stylized leaves, columns, urns, Olympian dieties, nymphs, and fountains. There were biblical themes and rococo motifs: shells and musical instruments. Industrial themes appeared.

The handmade lace industry dwindled after the French Revolution, reviving only weakly as the result of post-war efforts to reestablish the manufacturers. The business in Chantilly and blonde laces was the most thriving. With the invention of machine-made net, talent was diverted to the making of mixed and appliquéd laces. Great amounts of entirely handmade lace were no longer made.

The nineteenth century saw a reworking of many old lace formats, usually adaptations used as make-work projects for the indigent.

Although the quality of workmanship was high, lace design degenerated as it imitated the past. Left to its own devices, the nineteenth century produced compositions of gentle and sentimental subject matter.

In the early twentieth century a few designers brought contemporary ideas to lacemaking, and schools like the Bauhaus included lace design among their experiments.

Lacemaking potentially offers artists as much freedom of personal expression as do painting and drawing, but traditional lace patterns were almost always copied from another lace or from someone else's pattern. The lacemaker was not the creator of the design, and the designer did not make lace. A poor lacemaker could ruin a sensitive design, but a good one, who was in tune with the emotional drift of the designer, could, by delicacy of touch, make the pattern sing as it came to life in thread.

Great lace designers (some of them also painters) achieved great laces, just as Rubens composed great paintings without actually painting them himself. Sometimes Rubens was reduced to banality by uninspired painters or a crew of uncaring tapestry weavers, but at other times he was helped to magnificence by the assistance of Jordaens and others. Of course, the greatest Rubens paintings were those entirely from the master's hand.

Unfortunately there is no analog in lacemaking—as far as we know, until modern times no designer of note ever actually made lace. In fact, most of the designers are, themselves, anonymous; the great Berain, whose designs turned lace patterns away from all-over, large-flowered compositions and toward more tectonic design, is a notable exception.

Square-tabbed collar.

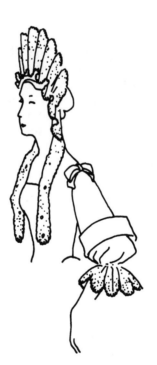

Fontange.

Steinkirk.

The names of actual lacemakers are unknown, but records of their work exist. There are fine books in libraries and exquisite laces in museums. The contemporary lacemaker can use their time-honored methods to experiment, expand, and innovate.

The craftsman may disagree with Elisa Ricci's opinion that lacemaking is not subject to individual caprice. Laces are susceptible to change as work progresses, and often the needs of the technique suggest an alteration of design that no one could foresee. The process of work triggers the imagination as nothing else can.

Lace may be defined as an openwork fabric in which the pattern is achieved with threads that are basic to the structure of the fabric. Needle and bobbin laces fit this definition, but decorated knotted nets and embroidery on machine-made net do not. By tradition and usage, however, embroidered networks are laces. Often they were made as substitutes for more expensive laces and were designed in imitation of them.

Lacy objects can also be made by weaving, knitting, crocheting, tatting, twining, and various other procedures that are not handled in this book. Each of these techniques, with the possible exception of tatting, has a great range of construction and design possibilities. Although from a strict standpoint of construction some of these techniques may more deservedly be called lace than some of the techniques included, they are given less attention here because a great deal of material already has been made available on these crafts.

Categorizing the arts is always difficult. For example, there is no clear line of demarcation between needle lace and embroidery. Bobbin lace is one of the forms now being called off-loom weaving. Many of the mixed laces of the nineteenth century are forms of appliqué or collages of fabric. Similarly, few modern textile artists use traditional lace techniques exclusively. The crafts merge imperceptibly, a fact that vexes writers and catalogers and delights artists.

Crochet can be used effectively for open, lacelike constructions. Crocheted lace was a favored technique in Ireland in the nineteenth century. Irish workers made fine designs of considerable size. Crochet in traditional design continues to be made by hand and can be purchased.

Knitting has also enjoyed an upsurge of popularity in recent years. Designers have innovated in several ways. Large needles have been used with fine threads to produce open, irregular patterns. Patterns are changed at random across the width of a panel, mixed in a seemingly offhand way. Knitting is used to make wall panels and lacy, hanging objects. Sometimes the elasticity of the knit is exploited by stretching a tube of knitting at intervals with inserted hoops. Room dividers, so much in use at present, can be knitted lace panels stretched in a frame. For experienced knitters, as for bobbin lacemakers, fascination comes with the making of an intricate design without bulky joins.

A basic weaving technique is called *gauze* or *leno* weave, a process by which threads of the warp are twisted so that the wefts cannot be pushed closely together. Variations of this and other techniques make lacelike weaving possible. Outstanding among the weavers who produce openwork fabrics with weaving techniques is Peter Collingwood. His term for his wall hangings, monumental in feeling and in comparison to the concept of design in most laces, is *macrogauze*. As Collingwood engineers his threads, warps move sideways, cross, and twist. Threads may enter the weaving as wefts and change to warps and then back to wefts. In making these maneuvers, weaving on the loom gains much of the flexibility of bobbin lacemaking.

In this book traditional laces are surveyed, designs that proved to be appropriate for each method shown, and detailed instructions for making stitches provided. I hope that contemporary readers will recombine ideas and create their own pieces. For additional ideas and inspiration each chapter includes work done by today's textile artists. I hope that readers will discover that lacemaking provides fascination, challenge, and amazing freedom of expression.

Virginia Churchill Bath

Machine-made lace. Late 19th-early
20th century. Plaited and twisted
mesh.

Machine-made lace, embroidered type.
20th century.

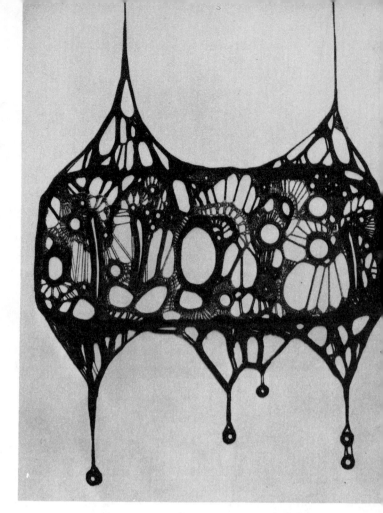

"Pendant," Eta Ingham-Mohrhardt.
Crochet. Lurex, cotton, silk, nylon,
rayon. 4 by 4 feet. Courtesy: Artist.

"Crystal Palace," Jack Lenor Larsen.
Machine-made lace. Courtesy: Artist.

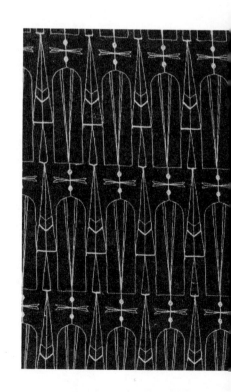

Doily. French, 20th century. Crochet.

Doily. French, 20th century. Crochet.

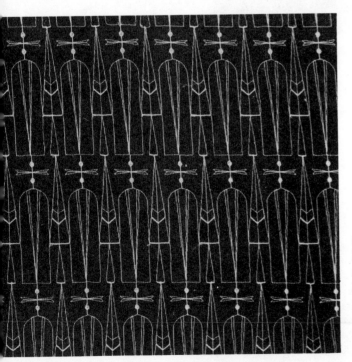

Curtain made in Germany at the Bauhaus, about 1920. Machine-made net with darned pattern. Courtesy: Art Institute of Chicago. Gift of Robert Allerton.

Parasol cover. Irish, Mid-19th century.
Crochet. Courtesy: Victoria and Albert
Museum, London.

Shawl by Dorothy Reade. Copy of Or-
renburg shawl (Russia, c. 1850-60).
Knitted. Courtesy: Artist.

Photo by A. C. Reade

10

Photos by A. C. Reade

"Scrolls" (detail), Dorothy Reade. Courtesy: Artist.

"Phoenix," Dorothy Reade. Knitted. Qivuit and silk. Courtesy: Artist.

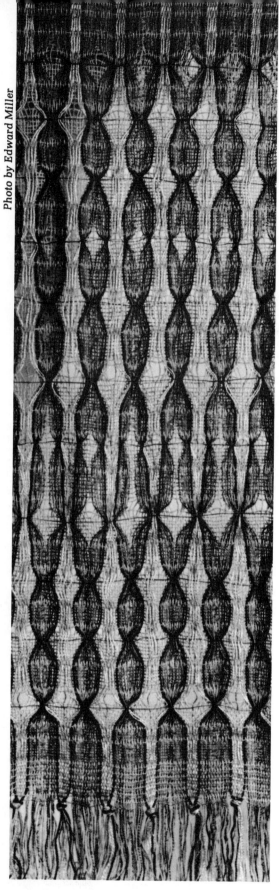

Lace hanging by Jane Redman. Double weave. Courtesy: Artist.

"Macrogauze 29," Peter Collingwood. Linen. 84 x 25 inches. Courtesy: Artist.

"Macrogauze 3D.1," Peter Collingwood. Bleached and natural linen. 60 x 24 inches. Courtesy: Artist.

Network

Netting is the oldest of the techniques of lacemaking. Fish and animal snares made of knotted reeds and grasses were among the earliest human inventions. Many widely scattered and divergent peoples, from Swiss lake dwellers to ancient Chinese and Peruvians, made netting. The sturdy character of network made it useful for battle dress as well as for making traps. Later, dramatic African tribal costumes made use of net as a groundwork for feathers and other ornaments.

In Egyptian art hairnets and bird snares appear as early as the Twelfth Dynasty (2130 B.C.). Knotted mesh from the Seventeenth Dynasty has also been found in Egypt. By the Eighteenth Dynasty, a pattern that seems to indicate network appears frequently in the dresses of Egyptian women. An Egypto-Roman hairnet was found at Fayoum; it has meshes of various sizes and dates from the third to seventh century B.C. The tombs at Antinöe yielded Coptic net headcoverings dated from the third to the sixth century B.C. These nets were knotted in a circle and bordered with fringe. A Bronze Age hairnet was found in a grave at Borum Eshöi in Denmark.

In England, gold network with decorations in lozenge patterns was found in a Danish barrow at Wareham. Many ancient Peruvian nets, some knotted and others having woven grounds decorated with designs in stitches often identical to European network, are also extant.

Insertion of lacis with designs in cloth stitch. Italy, first half of 17th century. 9 1/2 inches wide. Courtesy: Art Institute of Chicago.

The earliest networks were frequently made of linen, silk, or gold thread. Pliny mentions that a particular Gallician flax was needed for making snares. Persian nets were made of silk embroidered with gold and silver, and it is recorded that Nero wore gold net.

Woodcuts of the Middle Ages sometimes show men and women wearing what appear to be hairnets. However, these were sometimes creations of the goldsmith and not soft knotting. Medieval woodcuts also show hunting scenes in which nets appear prominently.

Thirteenth- and fourteenth-century references to nets made for household or clothing use list them simply as nets or as knotted white threadwork (*album filum nodatum*). A cushion from St. Paul's Cathedral, London, dates from 1295, and Exeter Cathedral had network altar furnishings in 1327. The evolution of white linen network from this point onward was steady, reaching a high point of excellent production in the sixteenth and seventeenth centuries. Although hairnets of gold thread and pearls were made, useful, strong laces of white linen thread were the most common. Network provided a simple means of expressing bold Renaissance patterns as well as the handsome early geometric designs. The fact that great numbers of the laces survive is testimony to their sturdiness.

Decorated network was used to make many large articles such as coverlets, palls, altar frontals, and curtains. These articles were usually white or natural in color, although in the time of Catherine de Medici green was also used. Large projects were most often made by joining netted squares; frequently these netted squares were alternated with squares of openwork embroidery or with *reticella* (see the following chapter on "Needle Lace"). Catherine de Medici, whose bed was hung with decorated net, owned 381 unornamented and 538 decorated squares of *lacis* at the time of her death.

At an early date especially fine netting was made in Cyprus and Malta. Jewish women were renowned for their expertise. But not everyone who made netted lace was expert. In many households all the maids worked at it, filling the meshes of small squares with designs in cloth stitch, the earliest prevailing stitch for linen work and the one most resembling weaving. Workers also developed elaborate forms of tassel-making,

Network sampler. France, early 19th century. Darning, interlacing, and loop stitches. 38 x 6 inches. Courtesy: Art Institute of Chicago.

using knotting techniques. Tassels were used for everything from banners for church and battlefield processions to clothing adornment. The tassels were often works of art in themselves.

There has never been agreement on exactly what the netted laces should be called. The lace has only a few variations of technique and is simple to make, but the terminology is complex.

A general term for a mesh base in any lace is *réseau*, (also *rézel*, *rézeul*, *rézuil*, or *rézeau*). For example, networks decorated in silk and gold were called *rézeuil d'or*. Terms of this sort appear in inventories after 1483.

Before ornamentation, knotted network is called *lacis*. A pattern can be created within the netting process itself, but when the net is to be embroidered, it is usually made as a simple square-shaped or diamond-shaped mesh, all meshes the same size and shape. In making a patterned network, the sizes of the squares and diamonds can be varied by using gauges of different sizes, making more than one mesh in a mesh of the row above, and otherwise elaborating the netting technique. One lace made this way was called *mezzo mandolina*, in which the squares or diamonds were of different sizes.

Panel (detail). Numerous stitches worked in several colors. Striped design.

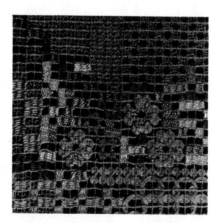

Square (detail). Numerous stitches worked in several colors. Random arrangement.

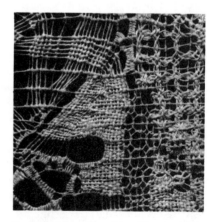

Panel (detail). Needle netting does not always have to have square or diamond-shaped meshes.

In the fourteenth century, decorated network was called by many names, among them *opus filatorium* and *opus araneum*. Later it was known as spider-work, *lacis, lavoro di maglia, modano ricamato, punto ricamato à maglia quadra, punto à maglia, ouvrages masches,* and *point conté*. In the nineteenth century, new names for netted lace were added: *filet brodé, filet brodé à reprises, filet guipure,* and *guipure d'art.* Each of the terms carries a special designation, either of specific technique or place of origin. For example, in Siena, *lacis* with darned patterns was called *lavoro di maglia. Modano* was the Tuscan term for lace with geometric designs on square network. *Modano ricamato* means embroidered network. *Punto ricamato à maglia quadra* was square-mesh netting combined with *point coupé* (see chapter on "Needle Lace"). In Spain square mesh is called *redicella;* diamond shaped mesh is called *red de pez.* Meshes in general are called *redes.* One should not confuse *redicella* networks with *reticella,* which is a specific type of Italian needle lace.

The term *darned netting* is heard frequently. The term is not always accurate, since darning is only one of the stitches used to decorate nets and is not the predominant one. Cloth stitch, which is also called *linen stitch, whole stitch,* and *weaving stitch* in various lace techniques, was the sole stitch used in decorating many of the early networks. It continued to be used, usually as the dominant stitch, in almost every type of decorated net lace that followed. In Sardinia and nearby islands, darning stitch did prevail over cloth stitch in designs that were a version of the satin and curl motif. In Spain the same stitches were prevalent; cloth stitch was called *punto de arpillera,* and darning stitch was *punto de zurcido.*

Guipure d'art was a nineteenth-century term for a lace-like technique in which machine net was used for the ground. Designs were worked freely on it, sometimes in high relief, unlike earlier decorations, which tended to be square-by-square readings from a drawing or woodcut, the embroidery perfectly flat. *Guipure d'art* was thought by many to be careless in workmanship and generally worthless, because the threads rode on the surface of the net, crossing several meshes without any tying stitch. Good netted laces, it was contended, must be reversible, and cotton, then coming into favor, was frowned upon by the purists, who would countenance only handspun linen thread.

This was the condition of the netted laces in the 1860s. In spite of admonitions, workmanship in general declined. Some effective new designs appeared in the early twentieth century, but an avalanche of bad designs turned taste against the form.

Tablecloth of Guipure d'art. China, 20th century cotton.

Panel, detail.

Tablecloth, detail.

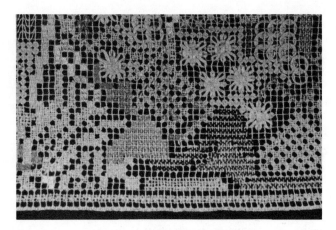

Square by Virginia Bath. Guipure d'art. Linen and cotton. 12½ x 11 inches.

Square, detail.

A few innovators saw the technique as a proper vehicle for their own more modern ideas, and their work looks surprisingly vigorous amid the reworkings of seventeenth century designs that were being turned out in such great numbers. About 1900 some unusual filet squares were designed by M. Méheut. Among the best of these are some naturalistic animal designs rendered entirely in cloth stitch. The drawing of the animals is simple, fine, and clear, despite translation to the squared format. Méheut's work also included botanical themes, among them languid sprays that were Oriental in feeling, cut off at the edges of the composition or "hung" from the top of it. Whistler often used this type of design. Méheut's designs were worked on a mesh that had rather large squares. He also used techniques associated with *guipure d'art*. In one such example he made a symmetrical arrangement of highly stylized animals worked in cloth and darning stitches. Around these motifs he left a row of unfilled meshes, emphasizing their contour. The rest of the background was worked entirely in *point d'esprit* except for secondary motifs in the upper corners. These were heavy whiplash designs and botanical motifs worked in darning stitch and woven wheels.

Eventually devitalized by lack of inspiration, *guipure d'art* disappeared into attics and second-hand shops, unloved and unwanted, but it should be revived. Its simplicity is its best virtue, and it is a technique with countless unexplored possibilities. Unfortunately, when members of the International Old Lacers were queried in 1973 about interest in reprinting directions for *guipure d'art*, there were only a few affirmative responses.

During World War I soldiers worked at making *lacis* decorations. During those years, working patterns on machine-made net was a popular diversion. One place where this white, hand-decorated netting can be seen as it was used in its last phase of popularity is at the Roosevelt home at Hyde Park, New York. There are many simply designed cushions throughout the house. They are particularly pleasing arranged against the large-flowered cotton slipcovers of heavily upholstered furniture. The crisp, white geometry of the lace is an ingratiating counterpoint to the curving, full-ripe patterns of the printed cloth.

Although the artists who today work with knotted netting are more interested in the knotting and the effects that can be derived from it than in surface decoration of the net, netted lace is by no means forgotten, as modern textile art proves. There are many more fine examples of contemporary network in the "Designs and Patterns" section of this chapter. Experiments with macramé and other related knotting techniques have also expanded the possibilities of network as a modern art form.

Patterns and Designs for Netted Lace

Decorated networks of medieval Spain, Italy, France, Portugal, Germany, and England featured geometric patterns containing triangles, squares, and lozenges. Religious subjects also appeared at an early date. The Egyptian *fundata* and pine cones were popular. Usually motifs were worked onto small squares or in bands.

One design popular in netted lace was the lotus. Very often it was used in conjunction with symmetrical, lateral stems and birds arranged at each side. At times the stems grew out of a vase. In Spain, this is called the *jarro* design. It is seen in many European laces and embroideries, all of which seem to relate to the Persian "tree of life" design. Another popular design was the "satin and curl" motif, used to decorate many early lace collars.

Lacis and Other Nets

Narrow bands of *lacis* appear in many portraits of the late fifteenth century. A self-portrait of Lavinia Fontana, for example, shows her wearing *lacis* decorated with designs in both cloth and darning stitches, a type of work associated with Sicily and the islands. Much decorated *lacis* of that time was worked entirely in cloth stitch on tiny meshes.

Darning stitch and loopstitch were sometimes used to decorate *mezzo mandolina*, a netting that was in itself decorative because of variations in the size of the meshes or in the spacing of the netted loops. In the Bargagli in Florence, there is a cover that com-

Cover of alternate squares of cutwork and lacis. Italy, 16th century. Courtesy: Victoria and Albert Museum, London.

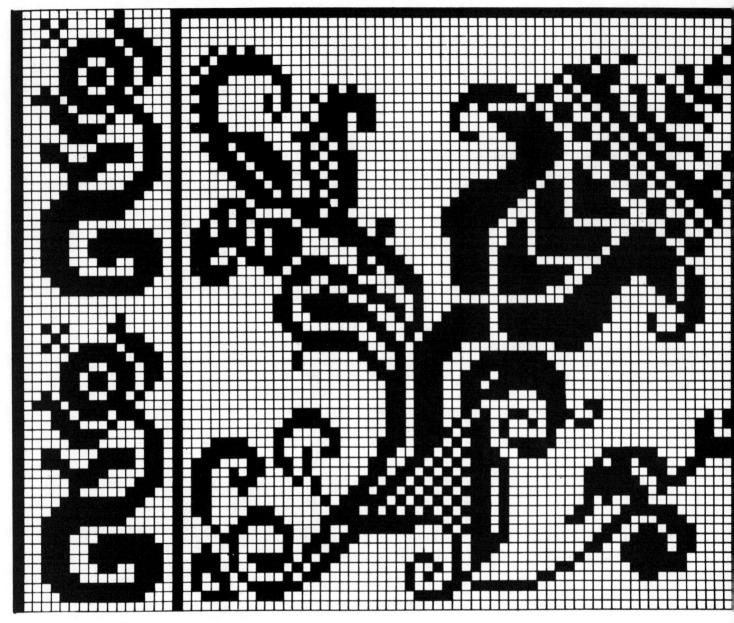

Pattern adapted from a square of network
in the cover on page 19.

Opposite page: Pattern adapted from
another square in the cover.

Satin and curl motif.

bines various types of network. It is a patchwork composed of large squares of *lacis* embroidered with figured designs, alternated with smaller squares tipped to lozenge position. These smaller squares have larger meshes than the others and are filled with designs reminiscent of the patterns of *reticella*. The leftover triangular spaces around the smaller squares are filled with triangles of *mezzo mandolina*. The combination is rich and unusual.

When it was used for bedhangings or tablecloths, *lacis* was frequently given a macramé fringe, but it could also have a Van Dyked, or pointed, edge.

Panel of machine-made net with cloth stitch. Design adapted by V. Bath from a network band in a private Spanish collection. Linen.

Pattern adapted from the network band.

Border of knotted netting with decorations in cloth, darning, and other stitches. Spain, late 16th-early 17th century. Courtesy: Museum of Fine Arts, Boston. Benjamin Pierce Cheney Donation.

A more detailed pattern adapted from
the network on the opposite page.

Pattern for the network on the opposite page.

Border, end of bridal pillow slip. Germany, 18th century. Knotted net with patterns in punto a rammendo and punto a tela. 27 x 15 inches. Courtesy: The Metropolitan Museum of Art. Rogers Fund, 1909.

Pattern adapted from the lace above.

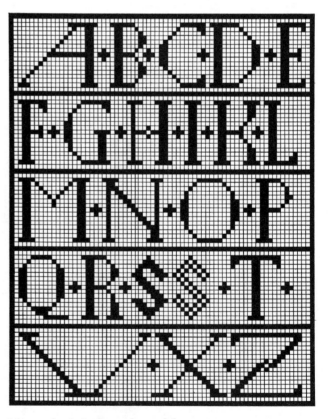

Network alphabet adapted from Zoppino's Essemplario, 1530.

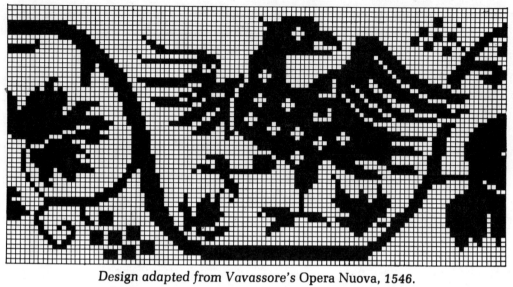

Design adapted from Vavassore's Opera Nuova, 1546.

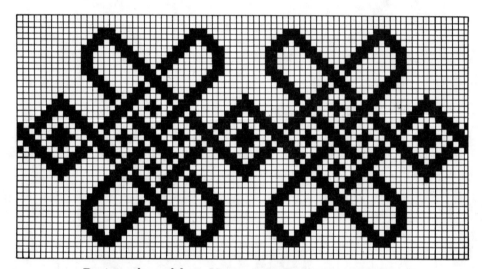

Design adapted from Vavassore's Opera Nuova, 1546.

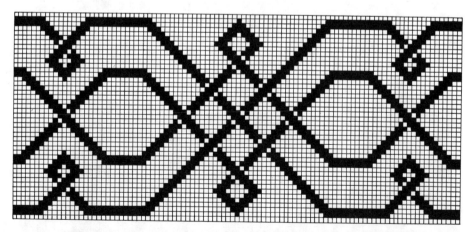

Design adapted from Vavassore's Opera Nuova, 1546.

Design derived from a 16th-century Spanish network in the Museu de les Arts Decoratives, Barcelona. These angels form the side borders of a horizontal panel. The standing angel is at the bottom and the floating angels are stacked above.

Design adapted from Matio Pagan's Opera Nova, 1546.

Opposite: Pattern adapted from a design by Giovanni Ostans, published in 1557.

Buratto

The same types of designs that were worked into *lacis* were worked in a technique called *buratto*. The word comes from the Italian *bura*, meaning "coarse linen." The meshes of the *buratto* ground are not knotted, but are woven. In the weaving, warp threads are manipulated in such a way that pairs twist around each other between each passage of the weft. The twists hold the wefts apart, and openings are formed. This type of weaving is called *leno* and is used for many purposes other than the making of lace grounds. For *buratto*, the threads used to make the ground usually are stiff, heavy linen.

All the designs of *lacis* also appear in *buratto*. There were biblical themes with all sorts of angels; the deadly sins were depicted. There were Occupations, Months, planets, astrological signs, Labors, and Seasons. There were confronting animals, winged lions, dragons, and unicorns. Hunting and fishing themes also prevailed: falconers, boars, stags, hounds, peacocks, boats, fish, and mermaids.

The patterns were worked in cloth and darning stitches. Sometimes rope, or stem, stitch was added. Colored threads, sometimes of silk, were used, especially in Sardinia, where *buratto* was popular. Russet and indigo were favored colors.

According to E. Lefébure, *quintin*, a fabric made in Brittany, was the same as *buratto*. The threads of the weave were of two thicknesses, so that the two threads used in one direction were about equal to one thread used in the other direction. In France *quintin* material was called *lacis*.

Insertion of buratto. Italy, 17th century. Linen and silk. 3 inches wide.

Macramé

The word *macramé* is derived from the Arabian *mahramah*, the root word of which is *harame*, meaning "to defend" or "to protect." The Arabic *migramah* means "ornamental fringe." Since among the early uses of netting was the making of nets that would be used to tie up valuables out of the way of curious animals, the origin of the word seems logical.

Knotted garments and other articles were made by the Pre-Columbians and Chinese as well as African, American Indian, and Eskimo cultures. Warriors of the Gilbert Islands wore knotted armor.

Knotting that definitely appears to be macramé appears in many paintings of the early sixteenth century. In Bronzino's portrait, painted about 1550, Eleanora da Toledo wears a gown trimmed with *mezzo mandolina* embroidered in *point de reprise* and has a band of golden Josephine knots in her hair. Paolo Veronese's *Feast in the House of Simon* and Sebastian Ricci's *Last Supper* show tablecloths that seem to be finished with macramé fringes. Leonardo mentioned the knotting of cords, using the French word *entrelacs*. Taglienti's 1530 pattern book for *groppi moreschi* and *arabeschi* had designs for Moorish fringes.

According to Elisa Ricci, the word macramé is used in Genoa and Liguria to signify a

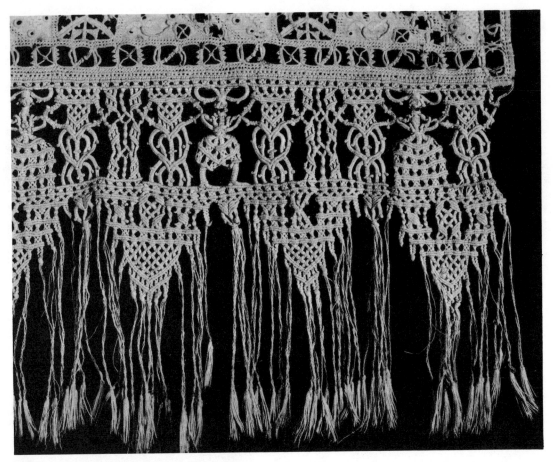

Border of macramé (detail). Italy, late 16th-early 17th century. Linen, beads. 20½ x 16½ inches. Courtesy: Art Institute of Chicago. Gift of The Antiquarian Society.

towel or the material from which a towel is made. Old macramé usually was made with the thread ends of an unhemmed piece of fabric and therefore was very dainty and small.

Long considered to be merely a sailor's craft and a Victorian pastime, macramé was actually a well-developed art in Europe in the seventeenth and eighteenth centuries. The Art Institute of Chicago owns a fine set of tiny, colored silk samples made in Germany. Museums also have samplers of macramé that also may be called *filet de carnasière*. The Paris Exhibition of 1867 contained very intricate examples.

In a nineteenth-century catalog, Mrs. Palliser stated that the schools and convents in the area around Genoa taught a "beautiful and ingenious work." In her opinion, the best macramé was made at Chiavari and in Genoa at the *Albergo de' Poveri*. Poor boys and girls were taught the art of macramé while very young. They worked on simple designs. In 1843 Baroness A. d'Asti sent an elaborate towel from Rome, which was picked apart and analyzed by a young girl, Marie Picchetti. This exercise enriched the macramé technique.

In the nineteenth century a patent was issued for a device that held threads in tension during the making of macramé. Usually work was done on a sand-packed pillow, perhaps nine by twelve inches. For accuracy the work was pinned in position as in making bobbin lace. A crochet hook or small knitting needle was used to assist in the making of small knots.

Contemporary Network Design

The inspiration for much contemporary design seems to come from Peruvian, African, or Indian art. Added interest in the new pieces is often achieved by dyeing, a technique practiced skillfully by the Peruvians in making their open-weave garments, rather than by embroidering.

Other artists seem inspired by the vastness of fishermen's nets. Made of hemp or oiled silk (the Chinese oiled nets to make them invisible), these intricate nets have patterns with fluid lines that are always appealing to the eye.

Roundel, detail. Virginia Bath. Raised network.

Handbag by Virginia Bath. Embroidery and hand-made knotted net with cloth stitch. Man-made suede, nylon and rayon cords, linen, wool, silk. 8½ x 7 inches.

Shaped headband by Virginia Bath. Needle-knotted net made of nylon cord. Suede and velveteen border. Beads, wool. Cloth stitch on net in linen; also with detached buttonhole stitch, couching, ivory stitch.

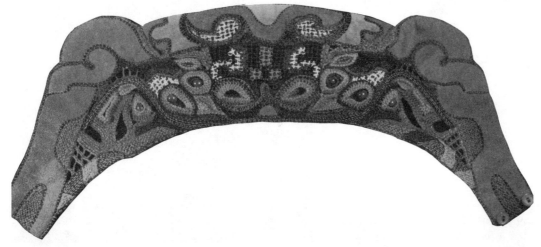

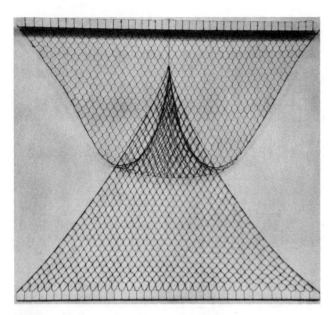

Filet relief work by Josef Pelisek. Prague, 1967. Flax. 80 x 60 cm. Courtesy: High School of Applied Arts, Textile Department. Head: Prof. A. Kybal.

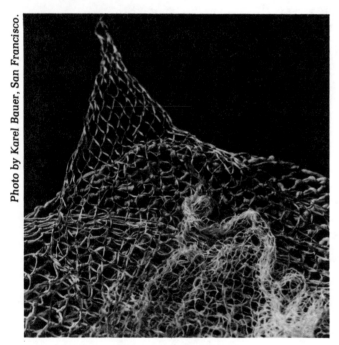

Photo by Karel Bauer, San Francisco.

"Surf," Lillian Elliot. Network. Cotton, synthetics. 4 layers, 3 x 3 feet. Courtesy: Artist.

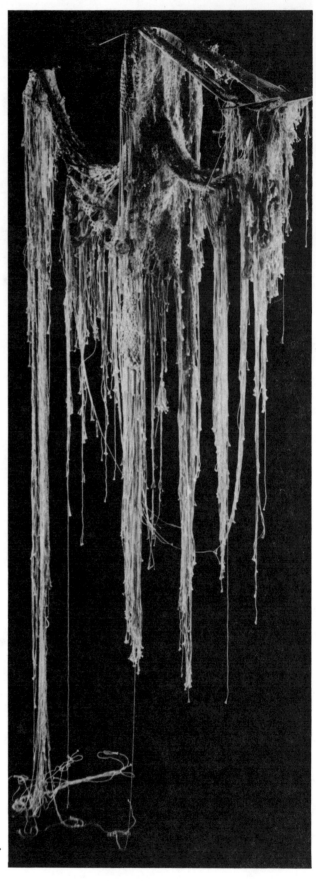

Hanging by Marie T. Kelly. Macramé. 8 x 6 x 4 feet. Courtesy: Artist.

"Black Comet Dream," Luba Krejci.
Knotted construction. Linen. Courtesy:
Art Institute of Chicago.

Techniques for Making Netted Lace

The techniques of network are comparatively simple, but the possibilities within the technique are limited only by the artist's imagination. Because network is based on squares, the same designs that are used for network can be used for thread-counted embroidery.

Making the Net

The procedure for netting long antedates Milour Mignerak's *Discours du Lacis*, (1605) in which he wrote, "Begin with a single stitch and increase on each side until the required size is obtained." Mignerak's illustration showed netting fastened to a cushion for work. In fine early network the making of the netting constituted the greatest part of the labor in the making of the lace, and connoisseurs of *lacis* have considered the fineness of the mesh the most important factor when choosing among examples. Purists prefer *lacis* with motifs in cloth stitch only. This stitch, when evenly made, shows the knots of the mesh as a dainty texture on the flat, clothlike portions of the lace. In none of the later laces does the net play so prominent a role as it does in the early networks decorated entirely in cloth stitch.

The most important tool in making netting is the netting needle or shuttle, which must be the correct size to produce mesh in the wanted scale. The shuttle should be designed to hold as much thread as possible. It may be of metal, bone, wood, or plastic. Unfortunately, although netting needles from Roman England and Coptic Egypt can be seen in museums, netting equipment is no longer readily available in shops.

The mesh stick, or gauge, holds loops at a constant size during the netting. Its size must correlate to the shuttle or needle, so that the loop it makes is large enough to allow a shuttle full of thread to pass through it. The gauge is a simple tool. Apart from size, the only other requirements are that it should be the same width and thickness throughout its length and that it should be smooth so that it will not snag threads as loops are made. A gauge may be round or flat.

The fishnet knot is used for mesh making and is found on very ancient textiles. In *Primary Structures of Fabrics*, Irene Emery pointed out that both sheetbend and fishnet knots may be called *filet knots*, but that only the fishnet knot is used for netting. Tightened into soft threads, the sheetbend looks very much like a fishnet knot. Some meshes may be made with other knots, and netting also may be made with a needle.

When a completed piece of netting is to be ornamented with embroidery, it can be held in tension by stretching it in a little wire frame, or, if the project is a large one, it can be put in an embroidery frame. It should be remembered that the larger the project the more difficult the problem with keeping tension. For some work, mounting the net on a base of paper and cloth may be a solution. Like netting needles and shuttles, small wire frames for netting are hard to find today, but one can be improvised. A piece of coathanger or similar wire bent to a square and welded would suffice. The wire should be wrapped with ribbon, tape, or felt, or it can be buttonholed. A flange of tape or ribbon can be sewn along the inner edge and mitred at the corners. The netting is attached by first tying it to the corners and then sewing it evenly along all sides.

Old pattern books show designs on squared grounds, so that the filling stitches can be counted as for thread-counted embroidery, but in the *Musées royaux du Cinquantenaire à Bruxelles*, there is an early network still on its backing that shows a strong black line

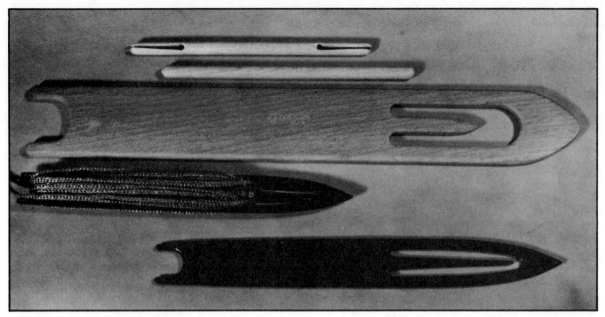

Shuttles for netting. The smallest shuttle is shown with a gauge.

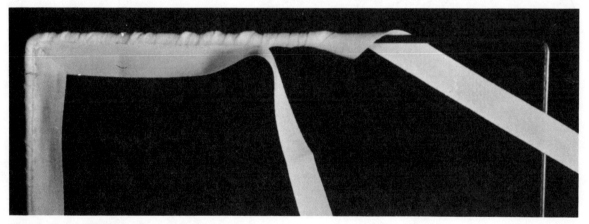

Frame for network. The wire frame is wrapped with twill tape, and a tape flange is sewn onto it.

as a guide, indicating that this type of work was done sometimes with relatively casual foredesign.

It is possible to buy machine-made nets of good quality for use in making decorated netting. They are not widely available, but they can be ordered by mail. On these prepared nets, striped effects can be made easily. Stitches can be tried in a sampler of this sort and the finished cloth used for a cushion cover, carryall, or similar project. Another way to try stitches is to spot them at random, giving the shapes a different contour on each side. As each new spot is juxtaposed, the effect of the pairing can be noted for future reference. Making one such sampler will teach the worker much about this type of lacework.

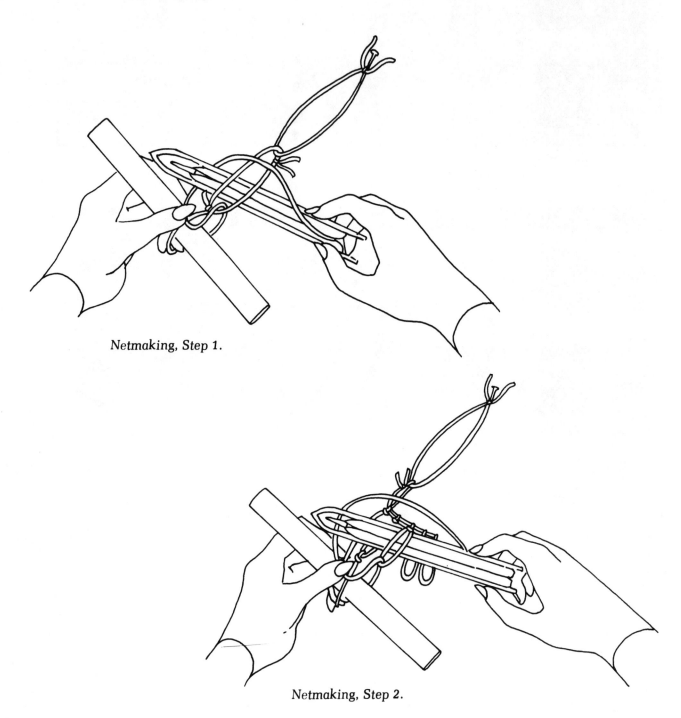

Netmaking, Step 1.

Netmaking, Step 2.

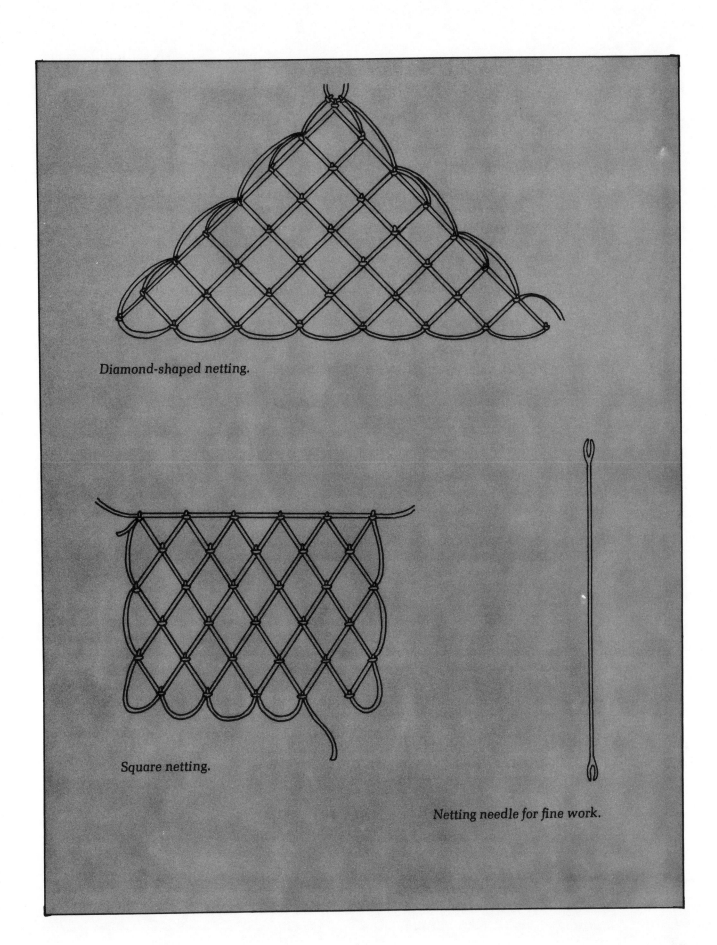

Diamond-shaped netting.

Square netting.

Netting needle for fine work.

Stitches for Ornamenting Nets

The most common stitches for network are cloth stitch (*point de toile*), darning stitch (*point de reprise*), and loop-stitch (*point d'esprit*). Most of the other stitches used were variations of these stitches or of the buttonhole stitch. On circular knotted pieces, accents of needleweaving (darning) were called *tress stitch*.

The best threads for *lacis* or *buratto* decoration are linen with a twist that cannot be detected easily. It is customary to work cloth stitch and many other stitches from right to left. Work all threads within a given area in one direction before you work in the crosswise direction. Tie the threads into a corner with a square, or reef, knot and snip short. When threads must be joined, use a weaver's knot (sheetbend). Work this knot into the embroidery as inconspicuously as possible, and, after embroidery in the area is complete, snip the ends.

When you turn the working thread on a single bar, and if you are using only two threads in each direction within the mesh, give threads an extra turn around the bar to help keep good spacing. When you turn a corner, weave the working thread in and out of all threads at the juncture, making a looped turn as you weave the thread around the corner. Traditional nets have from four to twelve threads per inch. The delicacy and technical proficiency exhibited in the making of the ground determine to a great extent the costliness of the lace.

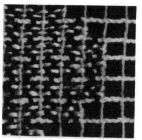

Cloth stitch.

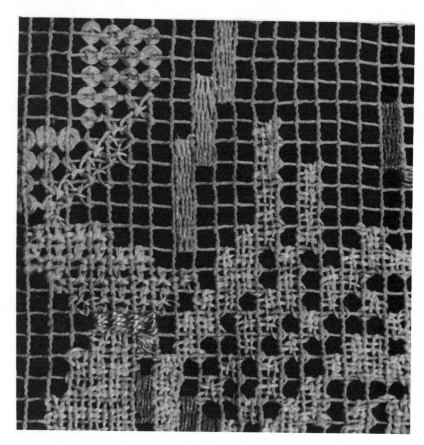

Stitches for network.

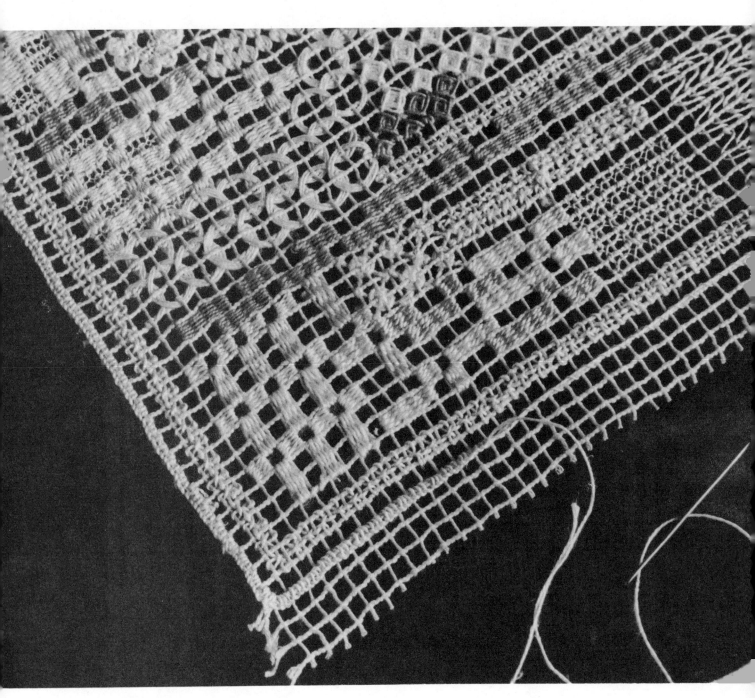

Edge finish for network. A thread is couched onto the net where the edge of the shape will be. This thread and the one to which it is couched are buttonholed. Excess netting is cut off.

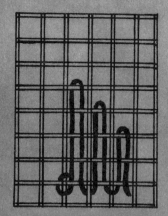

Cloth stitch, Step 1.

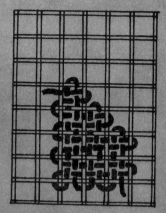

Cloth stitch, Step 2.

Fishnet knot.

Reef knot.

Tenerife knot.

Weaver's knot.

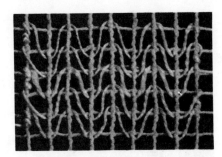

To work the wave stitch, use a single thread. Work the thread under the crossings, alternating between two rows of horizontal threads.

Make decorative fillings by preparing a foundation of diagonal threads and then working stitches into them. The most commonly used stitch is the darning stitch. Nubby effects can also be produced. Use the buttonhole stitch, alternating stitches from side to side on the foundation stitches. Feather stitch can also be used.

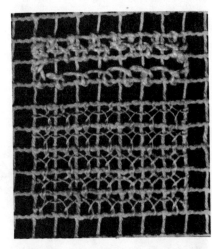

Work this stitch from left to right. Attach the working thread to the center of the left vertical thread of the space to be filled in the top row. Make a loop over the top threads of each square in the top horizontal row of open squares. Your working thread should lie on top of the net where it passes vertical threads of the mesh. When you complete the row, loop the working thread around the middle of the first vertical thread on the right side of the opening in preparation for the second row of loops. In making the second row, as you approach vertical threads of the mesh, pass the working thread under them and above the thread forming the first row of loops. The second row of loops completes the filling of the first (top) row of open meshes. As the second row of horizontal squares is worked, the procedure is the same, except that loops are always linked into the loops of the row above. The interlocking stitch can also be worked diagonally. When it is worked this way, it resembles the embroidery stitch of the same name.

In working the stitch diagonally, make loops around the crossings of threads rather than in the middle of them. It is necessary to follow the over-one-under-one procedure carefully in working around the threads of the crossing. When the threads pass to the other side of the square, however, you may not always be able to follow this order, because the weaving pattern may call for over-two so that a later thread can be worked into the under position between them. If you work them correctly, the threads will interweave perfectly. Worked into alternate rows, this stitch will produce a pleasant open texture.

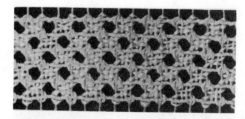

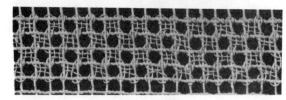

Interlocking lace stitch worked diagonally.

Backstitch Lozenges

To make these stitches, attach the working thread to a crossing, then work continuously around and around the crossing, making a back stitch around each thread of the mesh as you proceed. This stitch is effective both in front and in back.

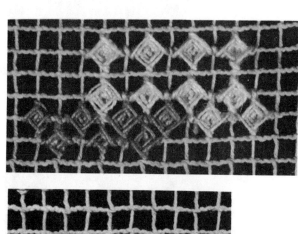

These stitches require extra foundation threads. Attach a thread at the crossing of the four squares within which the center of the wheel is to come. Pass the attached thread diagonally to the opposite corner of one square, around it, and back to the center, with two or more twists around the original pass as the thread returns. In the same way, make three more passes to complete the star into which the wheel will be worked. To make the wheels, weave the working thread in and out of the eight points of the star as many times as necessary to give the desired effect. Of course, the prepared foundation is itself decorative and can be used with no further filling.

Woven Wheels

These stitches are worked into the same type of foundation as woven wheels. Instead of weaving the working thread into the star-spokes, work it in back stitch. This wheel is attractive on both sides.

Backstitch Wheels

Make this stitch by weaving the working thread around each crossing of the mesh as many times as necessary for the desired effect.

Filling Stitch with Small Circles

Filling Stitch with Large Circles

Begin by knotting the working thread to a crossing. Then pass it upward diagonally to the right and under the first crossing to the right in the row above. Bring the thread diagonally downward (still to the right) to a point opposite the starting point and under that crossing, then down and to the left and under a crossing in the row below that is one crossing to the right of the starting point. Then move the working thread up and to the left to the starting point. Work around the circle again as many times as necessary for the desired effect. The circle ends at the point where the next circle begins. To begin the second circle, wind the working thread once around the ground thread. Continue as you did on the first circle. To give the best effect, the circles should overlap generously, but they should not entirely fill the mesh. Because of their stiffness, linen threads will produce circles; softer threads will make lozenges when the same procedure is followed.

Laid Stars

These stars are usually worked over sixteen squares. Starting from the center, carry the working thread between opposite corners, either vertically and horizontally first, then diagonally, or diagonally first and then in the vertical-horizontal directions. The number of passes made in each direction is a matter of preference. When you have made the desired passes, return the working thread to the center, twist it once around the center crossing, and then weave it over and under loops several times around before you fasten it on the back in the center.

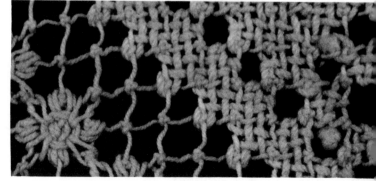

Laid stars with cloth stitch. Detail from early 20th century guipure d'art.

Like laid stars, these stitches are usually worked over sixteen squares. Starting at the center, carry the working thread diagonally from one corner to the other across the sixteen-square block. Then pass it diagonally in the other direction. Carry the working thread from the center to one outer corner, and darn between the threads of one of the loops just made, keeping the first and last stitches tighter than the rest. Darn the other three loops in a similar fashion. For a leaf, divide the threads of the loop into three sections and weave in and out of three groups of threads instead of two. Raised stems and leaves can be made with this procedure, as well as many other configurations. Darned leaves look very much like the matting stitch or darned leaves of bobbin and needle lace and in some later netted laces are intended to imitate them.

Darned Crosses and Leaves

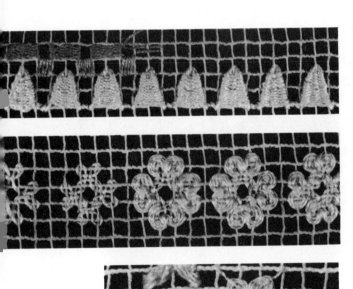

These patterns may be arranged to form larger motifs. They may be worked with darning stitch, back stitch, or buttonhole stitch. The eight-petaled flower pictured here was made by darning three-quarter circles around two corners of each of four squares of *toile* stitch, the four squares arranged around one open mesh. Semicircular corners and triangles can be worked in various arrangements to form other motifs.

Darned Semicircles and Triangles

*Darned
Squares
with
Inter-
locking
Stitch*

These two stitches can be worked in alternate groups of four meshes to form interesting patterns. Other patterns can be worked out using rectangles of darning or working other stitches between the darned blocks. Wheels and cross stitches are sometimes used.

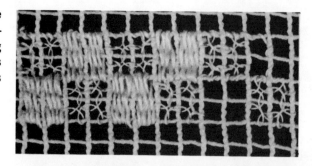

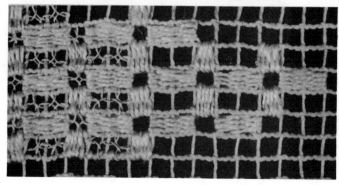

*Crossed
Inter-
locking
Stitch*

This variation is first worked in interlocking stitch; then diagonal threads are worked in to give a denser filling. Work the diagonal threads under the crossings of the ground mesh and second thread of the filling in one direction and over the crossings in the other direction. Be sure the other threads are carefully woven so that the over-one-under-one sequence of weaving is maintained.

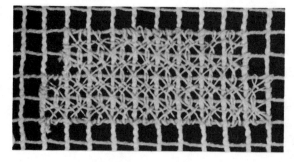

Macramé Techniques

The primary difficulty in macramé making is the tendency of the knot-bearer, the thread or threads upon which all the other knotted threads are hung, to loosen and sag, making it impossible to keep proper tension in the work. To keep the tension correct, needleworkers of the past stretched the knot-bearing threads on a hard, flat pillow or, in the nineteenth century, on a special frame. While macramé can be made with nothing more than a stable anchoring position for the knot-bearers, it is easier and results will be more satisfactory if a pillow or substitute is used. A piece of fiberboard covered with colored fabric to contrast with the macramé and to keep the fibers from shedding is a satisfactory base for macramé. The board or cushion can be held in position on a table with clamps, if desired.

Long, strong pins are needed to pin threads in position for accurate spacing. Long, pointed thumb tacks can be used with fiberboard. Scissors and a crochet hook should also be available.

All sorts of threads are used for macramé. Most macramé threads are smooth, allowing the configuration of the knots to show to advantage without being confused by the plies of the thread. Usually the threads have a rather hard finish. Nylon line makes precise knots, but many other synthetics do not hold knots well. The work is easier if the material you choose adapts well to the knotting.

Macramé can also be made on the ravelled edges of a piece of cloth or with the threads left at the end of a piece of handweaving when it is taken off the loom.

To mount threads on the knot-bearer, stretch the knot-bearer, which is usually a double thread, between two points. Keep it taut and fasten securely. Cut the work threads in double lengths. Fold each thread to make a loop with even ends. To make the simplest mounting, bring the loop of the doubled working thread above and behind the knot-bearer. Slip the ends of the working threads through the loop from behind. Tighten the loop into position by pulling on the ends of the threads. There are numerous other methods of hanging on the threads; most of them involve procedures also used in the making of the macramé patterns.

One mounting combines the flat knot and picot knot. Hang two doubled threads onto the work together. Pin the threads up as two picots, one slightly above the other. Both should be above the knot-bearer at about the height of two flat knots. Make a flat knot with the threads above the knot-bearer. Then join the threads to the knot-bearer with buttonhole knots to form a horizontal bar. Or, you may use the same procedure but make two flat knots above the knot-bearer instead of just one. *Double chain* mountings can be made with two loops to the right and two loops to the left. A simpler mounting can be made with one right and one left loop. *Multiple picots* can also be arranged as headings. Pin the loop of each thread in the multiple picot slightly above the last, and attach the threads to the knot-bearer with buttonhole knots.

Mountings

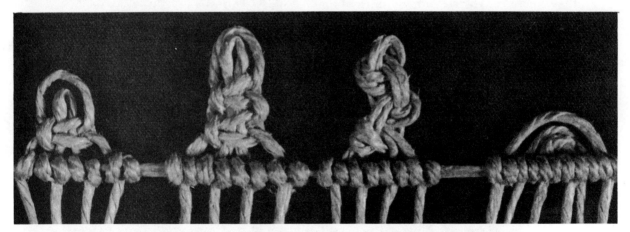

Fan or Bow Knot

For a bow knot, make two loops side by side, pinning evenly. Join the two doubled threads in a flat knot. Join the thread ends of the flat knot to the knot-bearer with buttonhole knots. To make a fan, hang three loops close together, the center loop slightly higher than the end loops. Join the six thread ends in a collecting knot and then join them to the knot-bearer with buttonhole knots.

Button-hole Knot Scallops

These knots may be used to decorate mountings. Hang a doubled thread upwards on the knot-bearer. Make loops around the right-hand thread with the left-hand thread until there are a sufficient number to make a graceful arch. Then make two more buttonhole knots to join the thread to the knot-bearer again. The hanging ends are now your working threads. Other hanging threads can be hung onto the knot-bearer to fill it with the required number of hangers in proper spacing.

Braid made with half flat knots.

Flat Knot

The flat know is also called the *square* or *reef* knot. The steps of making the knot are shown in these pictures. The second and third of the four threads used to make the knot remain as hangers, while the first and fourth threads are active. Note that in the first half of the knot, the left thread is on top of the hangers and the right thread is behind them. In the second half of the knot, the right thread is in front and the left thread behind. There are numerous variations of this knot. The flat knot can be repeated on the same four threads so that the knots make a braid. Another flat knot braid is made by repeating the first half of the flat knot only. This braid twists naturally.

Triple knots are often used in series, as in this picture. The triple knot is the same as a flat knot, except that the first half of the knot is repeated.

Triple Knot

A small collecting knot is made when a loop is made around more than one thread in the same manner as is used to make a buttonhole knot. A large collecting knot involves six threads. Make a flat knot with the center four threads. Then leave the center four threads and make a flat knot around them with the first and sixth threads. Finally, make a flat knot with the center four threads.

Collecting Knots

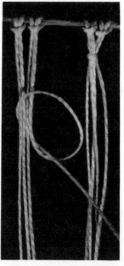

Crossed Knots

To make a single crossed knot, make a flat knot with four threads. Then firmly take the left thread to the right side and the right thread to the left side; in effect, turning the knot over. Make the next knot. This picture shows a series of single crossed knots. Double crossed knots are made in the same manner as single crossed knots, except that the flat knot is followed by one half of an additional knot before the knot is turned over.

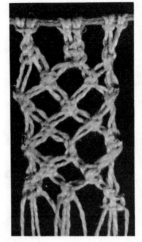

Double crossed knots.

Single crossed knot.

Picots with Flat Knots

Make two flat knots with the same four threads but keep them at a little distance from each other. Then push the two knots together, making two lateral loops. Another picoted effect can be made by making a flat knot or one and one-half flat knots. Then, on the outer threads of the four threads you used for the flat knots, make knots close to the flat knot. Under these knots make another flat knot, pushing it up close to the other knots.

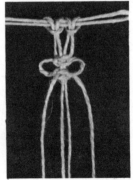

50

Buttonhole knots or half hitches are made with two threads. Making the knots is like making two buttonhole stitches, using the fingers instead of a needle. Either the right or left thread can be the knot-bearer. The knot-bearer can change with each loop, producing a single chain.

Buttonhole knot, single chain, double chain.

To make a single chain, first loop the left thread around the right thread. Then reverse the procedure and loop the right thread around the left. In actual work, the loops are drawn up tightly as they are in the double chain. This chain is made in the same way as the single chain, using four threads instead of two. The pairs are handled as single threads.

Bars of Knots

The buttonhole knot is used to make horizontal or diagonal bars composed of a series of closely set buttonhole knots. Extra threads may be introduced to carry the knots in horizontal bars, but it is more usual to use the hanging thread on the extreme left or right of a series to be the knot-bearer in a diagonal bar. **In the photo at the right,** two adjacent sets of threads have diagonal bars. There will be three bars on each side. As each bar was begun, the outer thread was used as the knot-bearer. Each thread was looped around it twice. After the third bars on each side were made, the two sets of bars were joined with a flat knot.

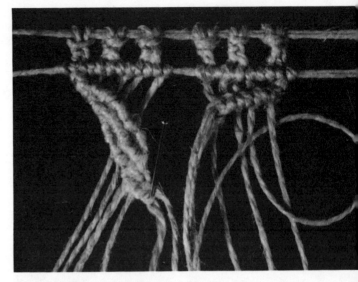

Bars on adjacent sets of threads

Sets of bars joined with a flat knot.

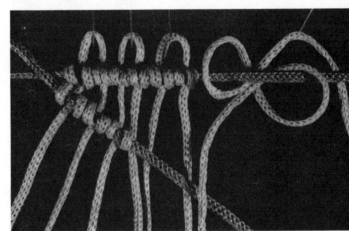

Bars with buttonhole knots.

Plaited Knots

To make a plaited bar or row of knots, begin by looping the second thread from the right around the right-hand thread. Then cross the third thread from the right over the second thread from the right. Using a crochet hook inserted above the loop, draw the third thread behind and around the second thread to form another loop. The interlocked loops should look like rows of knitting.

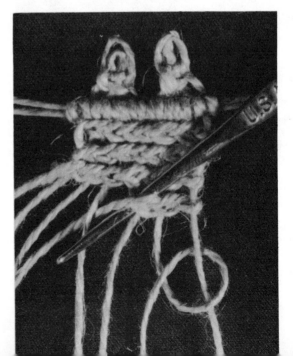

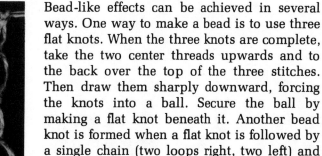

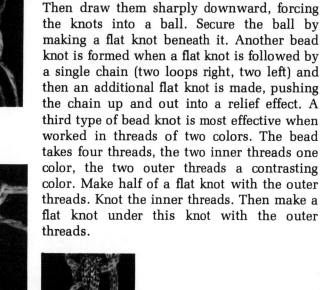

Bead-like effects can be achieved in several ways. One way to make a bead is to use three flat knots. When the three knots are complete, take the two center threads upwards and to the back over the top of the three stitches. Then draw them sharply downward, forcing the knots into a ball. Secure the ball by making a flat knot beneath it. Another bead knot is formed when a flat knot is followed by a single chain (two loops right, two left) and then an additional flat knot is made, pushing the chain up and out into a relief effect. A third type of bead knot is most effective when worked in threads of two colors. The bead takes four threads, the two inner threads one color, the two outer threads a contrasting color. Make half of a flat knot with the outer threads. Knot the inner threads. Then make a flat knot under this knot with the outer threads.

Bead
Knots

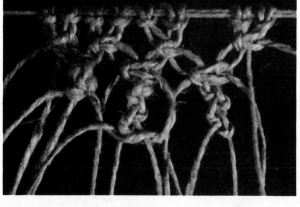

Bead knots with flat knots.

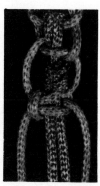

Bead knots with flat knots and single chain.

The Josephine knot, or Double Carrick Bend, is used in macramé in both the open and closed forms. This picture of the open form shows the course of the two threads as they interweave.

Josephine
Knot

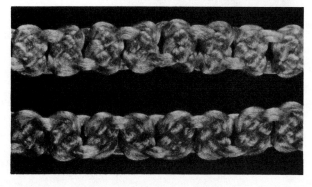

Josephine knots with flat knots in two colors.

Needle Lace

It is generally conceded that the greatest laces were made in needle lace technique, an essentially simple process that nevertheless requires precision, ingenuity, delicacy of touch, and an understanding of how to design in transparency. The evolution of needle lace was from simple geometric designs, to heavily scrolled, highly stylized formal designs, and then to light designs worked against a mesh ground. Lacemakers developed an enormous reservoir of techniques, which the modern textile artist can adapt and expand. Needle lace offers the lacemaker almost infinite design possibilities.

Tablecloth (detail). Whitework embroidery. France, 19th century. Courtesy: Art Institute of Chicago.

Sampler. Needlepoint lace. England, dated 1649. Courtesy: Victoria and Albert Museum, London.

Runner (detail). Reticella. Purchased at a convent in Quebec City.

Sampler. Embroidery with reticella and punto in aria. England, mid-17th century. Signed: An Bourne in reticella. Ex. Coll: Sir William Lawrence. 36 x 6¾ inches. Courtesy: Art Institute of Chicago. Gift: Mrs. Chauncey B. Borland.

Needle lace seems to have been developed a little earlier than bobbin lace. Italy claims to have invented it, and most of the good, early needle laces that exist seem to be Italian, but the claim is not unchallenged. In the Low Countries, an idea prevailed that needle lace was of oriental origin and came north with homecoming Crusaders. Byzantines and Greeks, as well as Italians, practiced needle lacemaking at an early date. The art could have been introduced into Venice by way of Ragusa, the principal port of the Republic of Venice, in the fifteenth or sixteenth century. Ragusa, close to northwestern Greece, was the seaport through which the gold-worked cloths of Cyprus entered Venice.

Needle lace has its origin in embroidery. By the latter half of the fifteenth century undergarments were often decorated with white embroidery. However, unless it is particularly excellent in design and technical quality, entirely white embroidery is apt to be unexciting, since its effectiveness depends entirely upon relief work. Embroiderers soon developed cutwork and drawnwork as means of adding variety. A modest number of tiny eyelets and pulled openings can be found in some early pieces. To make these openings, the worker simply pushed the threads of the ground apart and embroidered around the openings to keep them from closing again.

Next, embroiderers developed a simple form of drawnwork in which threads were drawn out of the ground in one direction only and the remaining threads were worked in weaving, darning, buttonhole, or loop stitches. Decorative patterns were usually worked in with the threads that had been withdrawn from the ground, but occasionally a heavier thread was used. This simple drawnwork was called *punto tirato, deshilado, de tramma paralela,* and *fil tiré.* Drawnwork was used to trim ecclesiastical linens, hangings, towels, table runners, bed linens, and pillows as well as clothing. Often it was combined with network and cutwork.

To make cutwork, the embroiderer prepared certain areas of the ground for the embroidery by cutting out all but a few threads, leaving groups of two or four threads at regular intervals so that stitches could be worked over them and between them. The worker left both vertical and horizontal threads. The cut edges were finished with buttonhole stitch.

In another type of cutwork, the pattern motifs were left intact in the ground linen, but threads were removed from the background. The remaining threads were overcast or embroidered in such a way as to make the motifs seem to stand out against a background mesh. From these processes, needle lace emerged.

By the fifteenth century, Venice was a flourishing center of needle lacemaking, attracting skilled needleworkers from as far away as China, Japan, and Persia. Of the 140 manuals for needlework and lace published in France, Germany, and Italy between 1525 and 1600, 100 were Venetian.

The state of lacemaking and embroidery in Venice is clearly documented by official records. Textile laws were passed at frequent intervals. In 1476, the Venetian senate

Runner (detail). Virginia Bath. Hardanger. Cotton.

decreed that no bed in the city or province could be decorated with *punto in aria*, either of flax or gold. By 1535 *reticella* and ivory stitch *(punto avorio)* could be used for seam joints, but they could not be wider than the breadth of two fingers. During this same period, young Venetian men were not allowed to wear lace until their twenty-fifth birthdays. Laces were not incidental trimmings but prized possessions, to be itemized in any listing of one's assets. At times they were used to pay debts.

Before cutwork evolved into lace, a variety of related techniques were invented, and these were later used along with early lace, many times in large assemblages of units worked in alternating techniques. Spanish needleworkers used a technique called *bocadillo*, the simplest of cutwork embroideries. *Bocadillo* was made by snipping little straight or curved slits in a pattern in a linen ground. The slits were turned under as for a hem and overcast along their edges. The resulting shapes were crescent- or almond-shaped. Series of these small shapes were arranged to form stars, lozenges, and Arabic octagons. If the openings were so large that they threatened the stability of the fabric, threads were thrown across the opening and it was overcast or buttonholed. *Bocadillo* was used widely in patchworks, alternating squares of the cutwork with squares of *lacis* or *reticella*, the earliest of the needle laces.

Cutwork retained its popularity even after lace began to be made, partly because lace was very expensive and whitework could be substituted for it. For intricate, lacelike cutwork, a French linen called cambric was used. Using this fabric, the worker could **simply push the threads into little groups to make the smaller openings.**

Early geometric needle laces were made using techniques similar to those used in folk embroidery. The two most obvious examples are *hardanger* and *hedebo*, which are still made in Scandanavian countries. *Hardanger* work may be done on a specially woven cloth in which threads are paired, so that counting them for withdrawal and cutting or for embroidery is easy. Weaving, darning, back, satin, buttonhole, and other stitches are used, as are picots, wheels, woven leaves, and loopstitch filling. A small detail showing **a simple arrangement appears in the *hardanger* border on page 57. The border is made of satin stitch and darned and picoted bars. *Hedebo* is a type of Danish linen work that** uses a special buttonhole stitch. Its fillings are most often worked into round or almond-shaped openings. One difference between the two lacelike embroideries lies in the fact that in *hardanger* the lacy fillings are worked into openings that are usually drawn, rather than cut, out. In *hedebo* the openings are more often cut, so the work has more curving and circular motifs.

Traditional Ukranian needleworks, *myreschka* and *prutik*, are both drawnwork. *Myreschka* is rendered in darning stitch, while *prutik* is done in darning and overcasting, a great deal like rows of fancy hemstitching. Spanish and Mexican drawnwork borders are more dramatic and include woven wheels. Greek and Italian drawnworks resemble *reticella* or Greek lace.

Although we do not know the exact date of the first lace, details that look like needle lace first appear in paintings done in the mid-fifteenth century. These first needle laces were used for small edgings and seam joints. From a decree of the Metropolitan of Siena, we know that *reticella* was in use by 1482. In Venice sumptuary laws concerning lace were enacted in 1530, when, in addition to prohibitions against embroidery, there appeared a restriction against linens worked *de aco a ago* (with thread and needle). Presumably this referred to something other than already-mentioned types of embroidery and indicates thread (linen) lace. A 1535 edict that allowed thread trimmings of not more than two fingers' breadth probably refers to lace trimmings made with ivory stitch *(punto avorio)*, or to *reticella*.

Punto tagliato, a cutwork that had a background grid made by withdrawing threads, was described in *Ornamenti*, a 1542 pattern book by Mathio Pagan. We may assume that *reticella* already had been developed, although, as far as we know, the actual term *reticella* was not used until 1591. For a time making *reticella* seems to have been an al-

"Judgment of Solomon." Panel in needlepoint lace with relief work in detached buttonhole and other stitches. England, second half of 17th century. Linen, seed pearls, beads. Courtesy: Victoria and Albert Museum.

Casket worked in high relief embroidery (stumpwork). Made by Rebecca Stonier Plaisted. England, 1668. Height: 15½ inches. Scenes from the Old Testament in silk, silk chenille, metal and seed pearls. Initial R. S. and I. P. Dated. Courtesy: Art Institute of Chicago. Gift: Mrs. Chauncey Borland and Mrs. Edwin A. Siepp.

most exclusively Venetian venture, but by the end of the sixteenth century the craft had spread throughout Italy.

Reticella evolved gradually into *punto in aria* (point in the air). As openings for the lacy fillings in cutwork embroideries increased in size, it became necessary to devise a means for maintaining the stability of the ground fabric while the work was in progress. To keep the material from loosing its shape, the worker mounted it on a parchment backing, using basting stitches. Eventually all that was left of the ground fabric after preparation for the embroidery was a gridwork of a few horizontal and a few vertical threads. It was obvious that a foundation for embroidery could just as easily be made by simply laying threads on the foundation at right angles and couching them into position. Of course, the basted threads did not have to be bound by the horizontal-vertical relationship of the warps and wefts of a woven ground, and cursive designs were possible.

The term *punto in aria* was in use by 1528, when a stitch by that name was first mentioned in a pattern book by Tagliente. From later pattern books published in Venice in the early seventeenth century, we know that the technique was by then being used by Flemish as well as Italian lacemakers.

English needle laces of the sixteenth and early seventeenth centuries were entirely different from the laces being made on the Continent. It is impossible to see the English laces without immediately thinking of the so-called stumpwork embroideries, with which they were contemporary and with which they have everything in common except for color and the presence of a background fabric. The designs for the laces are heavy and naturalistic, and the subjects are similar to those used in stumpwork.

In Italy *punto in aria* was followed by *punto tagliato à fogliami, gros point de Venise,* rose point, and many other scrolled patterns of the Renaissance. These laces carried design to an almost opposite extreme from the flat, geometric, horizontally and vertically oriented patterns of *punto in aria*. Large-leafed foliated scrolls in undulating, space-filling patterns appeared in many pattern books in the middle of the sixteenth century. One has only to recall the marble portrait busts of the seventeenth century, which so often show their sitters wearing *punto tagliato á fogliami,* to realize the accuracy of the description of that lace as like relief carving in ivory. Most of the gros laces were heavily ornamented with thick cordonnets in high relief. To make the sculptural cordonnet, the worker bundled together a dozen or more threads and made close buttonhole stitches along the contours of the lace motifs.

Border (unfinished, on foundation). Raised needlepoint guipure. Italy, 19th century. Courtesy: Museum of Fine Arts, Boston. Gift: J. W. Paige.

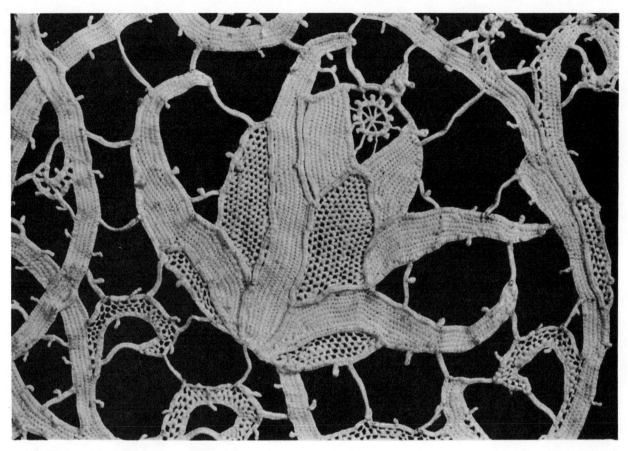

Fragment of needlepoint lace with close stitch and spaced buttonhole stitch motifs, guipure bars. Italy, 17th century.

In time, the extremely popular Venetian laces were rivaled by the needlepoint laces of France. Colbert's action to stop the importation of Venetian lace by establishing a French industry was at least in part responsible for the decline of Italy as the Continental fashion center for lace. Colbert brought lacemakers from both Italy and Flanders to assist in the establishment of lacemaking centers in various French towns. Workers from Venice were sent to shops at Alençon, Argentan, Arras, Aurillac, Le Quesnoy, Loudon, Reims, and Sedan. Thirty Italian experts went to these towns, while about two hundred Flemish workers went to other French shops. By January, 1673, Colbert wrote, French relief laces had become the equal of Italian. This had been accomplished less than seven years after the October 12, 1666 restriction against the use or sale of imported laces.

The firm established by Colbert in 1665 had a ten-year monopoly on French lacemaking, given to Pluymers, Talon, and de Beaufort. After this monopoly ended, new patterns began to be introduced. Madame Despierres states that during the years of the de Beaufort privilege all laces produced in France were called *point de France*, regardless of whether they were needle or bobbin lace. Today only needle laces of that period are called *French point*.

By the third quarter of the seventeenth century, the French were fashion-setters in lacemaking. The French lace industry grew enormous, developing a wide variety of patterns and techniques.

French laces were usually named for the town of their origin, a fact that sometimes only adds to the difficulty in identifying them. The laces made at the neighboring towns of Alençon and Argentan, for example were, in many cases made by the same workers, using the same patterns and materials. In the eighteenth century the workers of Argentan abandoned the festooned mesh, which required that each loop be knotted with a tiny buttonhole stich, for the *bride tortillée,* in which mesh threads were twisted rather than buttonholed. This labor-saving device was soon taken up by the workers of Alençon. This was only one of many instances in which changes in lacemaking spread from town to town.

The needle lace industry effectively ended with the French Revolution, in spite of efforts made by Napoleon to revive it. Bobbin lace, which had by this time overcome some of its early technical limitations, came into widespread use. The softness of bobbin lace made it more adaptable to the lighter fashions then in vogue.

Needle lace made entirely by hand gradually declined during the nineteenth century, and, with few exceptions of note, had disappeared by the 1930s. Laces made with tapes were produced much more rapidly and were boldly effective, making a substitute that contented all but truly discerning eyes. With changes in fashion, lace was less and less in demand.

The possibilities of needle lace have remained largely unexplored for the past few decades, perhaps because embroidery and needlework have been left to the hobbyists. Only a few designers have experimented in this field. Needle lacemaking also suffers from the myth that the dullest and least endowed of humans can embroider; anyone with sharper wits is supposed to do something more worthwhile. One has only to look closely at the so-called peasant embroideries in any museum to see that this idea is ridiculous. One superb design after another is found. The colors are good, and textures are full and rich. A tremendous amount of creativity was channeled into this work, which was done with taste and intelligence as well as patience and care.

Lappet of point plat de réseau. *Italy, 18th century. Courtesy: Victoria and Albert Museum, London.*

Panel. Raised needlepoint, Raphaellesca type. c. 1880. Linen, app. 3 x 5 feet. An unusual, late, very large panel. Courtesy: Museum of Art, Carnegie Institute, Pittsburgh, Pa.

Patterns and Designs for Needle Lace

Needle lace patterns usually reflected current design trends, and they ranged from elaborate *tours de force* to ingenious, simple maneuvers that coaxed clever patterns out of fast-moving techniques.

In very early drawnwork the designs were of necessity geometric: rectangles, lozenges, and stars. Where there was Arabian influence, the octagon appeared. In Spain, even after Renaissance patterns held sway, there was a tendency to retain early geometric forms. Figurative patterns also appeared in early drawnwork. The Alb of St. Francis, in the keeping of Saint Clare's Convent, Assisi, is of *tela tirata* (drawnwork). It has animal designs as well as the Coptic *gammadion* (sign of the cross) and about two dozen different motifs based on polygons.

The earliest cutworks and *reticellas* also had relatively simple geometric designs. At first they were narrow edgings with scallops or points. Diagonal crossbars worked into their basic grids produced triangles. From these triangles were coaxed star and medallion patterns. Then, as the borders became wider, patterns were elaborated and eventually became birds, animals, *putti*, flowers, and a whole range of Renaissance motifs. Floral motifs were the most popular by far of the naturalistic designs.

The timetable read something like this: Triangular shapes and points in the fifteenth and sixteenth centuries; simple geometric shapes, called Gothic, until about the midsixteenth century; elaboration of design, after the bar ground and filling stitches were introduced in the latter half of the century. Points (zigzags) were superceded by scallops. Then followed the conventionalized floral designs of the Renaissance, which were well suited to the groundless lace.

In fact, once *punto in aria* had been developed, there were few technical limitations that had to be taken into account in designing needle lace. A thread could travel about the same route as a pencil line, shapes that it made could be filled solidly or with texture, and anywhere the subject matter was sparse or spread apart, all that had to be done was to pencil onto the pattern little bridges or bars at points where they would not

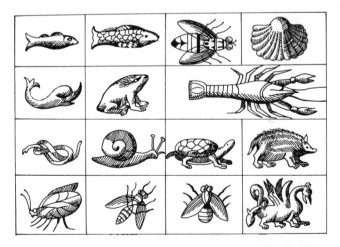

Design adapted from a page in the Essemplario *of Zoppino, 1530.*

interfere with the design and where they would, in their combination, keep the parts of the lace together firmly. In needle lace there is little difficulty in starting and stopping the threads. One can work as fancy dictates, changing areas, cutting out parts that don't satisfy or otherwise altering the original concept without creating monumental technical problems.

On the pages that follow are some examples of several specific types of needle lace. From some of these lovely historical patterns, I have adapted designs for the modern needleworker to follow, using the material in the section on "Techniques of Needle Lace." Working one of these patterns will help you develop a feel for needle lace; once work is in progress, you will undoubtedly begin to experiment.

Reticella and Related Laces

The distinguishing feature of *reticella* and related laces is that their groundwork forms a strict vertical-horizontal grid. The patterns are therefore predominantly geometric, based on grids of squares.

There are two methods of preparing the groundwork for *reticella*. One is to cut out or draw out threads from a linen ground and work the lace into the openings. This is the method that was used for early cutwork (*punto tagliato*) and drawnwork, as well as for *punto reale*.

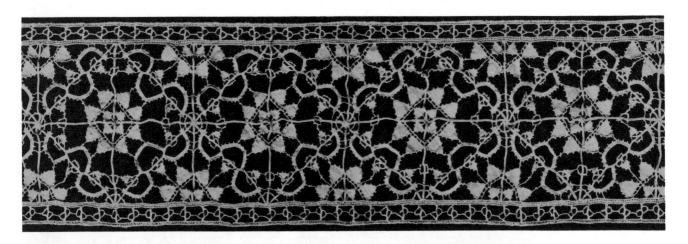

Borders of reticella. *Italy, late 16th-early 17th century. Courtesy: Victoria and Albert Museum, London.*

In a museum in Palermo there is an unfinished piece of antique lace. In one part of the lace a series of threads has been withdrawn in one direction. On the remaining threads, work has begun on some patterns, using needleweaving. Other areas have threads withdrawn in both directions and the order of work shows clearly. Before the threads were cut out, the edges that would have been left raw were secured with embroidery. Paired diagonal threads, forming Xs, were laid across these areas after they were opened. The threads were needlewoven. The first fillings to be put in were corner devices. After these were made, triangles of buttonhole stitch were added. Picoted ornamental details came last.

A second method for preparing the groundwork developed when lacemakers began to remove so many of the ground threads that only the frailest of scaffolding remained. This fragile ground fabric needed the support of another cloth to keep it from pulling out of shape or falling apart completely. To meet the need, lacemakers devised a linen and parchment base for their work. The base consisted of two or three layers. The top layer was parchment, which could withstand much use. It was smooth so that a needle would not catch in its surface. The lace design was drawn on the parchment in ink. One or two layers of linen were basted under the parchment. Although these helped to make the base for the work even more stable, the main reason they were used was to form protection for the lace when it was cut off the parchment after work was completed. The decorative buttonhole stitches of the lace, which often were worked with threads withdrawn from the ground, were not allowed to pierce the parchment. Only the ground fabric, or the threads basted onto the parchment in imitation of the ground fabric, were sewn onto the parchment and linen base. All other stitches were attached to these threads.

Pattern for reticella *adapted from the lace on the opposite page.*

Patterns adapted from Matio Pagan's Opera Nova, 1546.

When the lace was finished, the basting stitches were cut between the two layers of linen with a razor blade or knife. The decorative buttonholing remained undisturbed, and the crossbars and other stitches that had been added to the frail ground or foundation threads created a lace that was quite substantial. This method was used to make such laces as *punto di cartella* and *punto di cordella*. In *punto di cartella* or *punto di cordella* heavy threads or cords were basted onto a parchment base as the first step in the lacemaking, and then designs were worked on them and between them with buttonhole stitch, detached buttonhole stitch, matting stitch and others.

Because there is more bulk on one side of a buttonhole stitch than on another, the outlining threads sometimes curved, usually adhering, of course, to a generally geometric design. Lacemakers took advantage of this feature of the stitch to make circles, semicircles, S-curves, and other motifs to their *reticella* patterns.

Related laces include Venetian *guipure*, (lace made with a bar ground) Roman lace, and Greek point. Greek point was made in the Ionian islands and in Venice from the fifteenth century, reaching its greatest prominence in the sixteenth century. Greek point is very open and symmetrical in pattern. The main difference between Greek point and Italian laces of the same type lies in the fact that the Italian points are made more finely than the Greek.

For large covers and hangings, *reticella* was often combined with embroidered linen. A usual arrangement alternated squares of cutwork linen with squares of needlepoint lace. Bobbin lace or *punto in aria* were frequently used as edgings. Gold thread sometimes was combined with the white threads of *reticella* for rich effects.

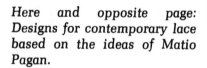

Here and opposite page: Designs for contemporary lace based on the ideas of Matio Pagan.

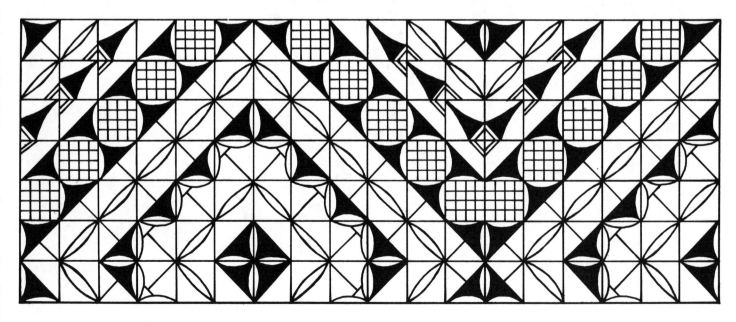

Here and opposite: Designs derived from Matio Pagan's Honesto Essempio, 1550.

A design for contemporary lace based on Matio Pagan.

68

Punto in Aria

Punto in aria took the fashion world by storm when laces began to be used for secular purposes during the Renaissance.

The gridwork background that had been a feature of *reticella* gradually began to disappear. *Punto in aria* means "point in the air," a way of expressing the idea that stitching could be made without its being permanently attached to a ground fabric. Unlike in *reticella,* in which threads were arranged to imitate warps and wefts, in *punto in aria* the ground threads curved and doubled in any direction the designer chose. The outline threads were basted onto the parchment pattern, usually in pairs. These threads, called *fils de trace,* followed the contours of the motifs and were couched into position through pricked holes in the parchment. Only the *fils de trace* were sewn onto the parchment. All other stitches were attached only to *fils de trace* or into one another.

As the foundation grid disappeared, it became necessary to devise a means of holding together parts of a design. Where motifs touched, there was no problem, but for clarity of design they often did not touch, and joinings were necessary. Little buttonholed bars, also called *brides* or *legs,* were arranged throughout the background area. These were decorated with little picots, rosettes, or crowns (*couronnes*). An example of unfinished *punto in aria* shows that, in at least this one piece, the motifs were finished before the ground was put in.

The designs most frequently seen in *punto in aria* include human figures, animals, boats, birds, urns, jewels, candlesticks, coral, seaweed, radiances *in nomine Jesu,* Lambs of God (Ecce Agnus Dei), scenes from the Bible, doubleheaded eagles, arms (for example, Borghese eagles and dragons), and, of course, scrolls and flowers. All these are typical designs, but occasionally an unusual lace shows a particularly original effect. For example, in one piece there is a ground pattern of overlapping rings, much in the manner of double wedding ring pattern. In another, very openly worked flowers and leaves are set against a crackle background of such insistent pattern that the overall affect is quite indefinite. Occasionally a piece of *punto in aria* includes motifs cut from linen (or worked in cloth stitch) with a picoted gold cord couched around the edges.

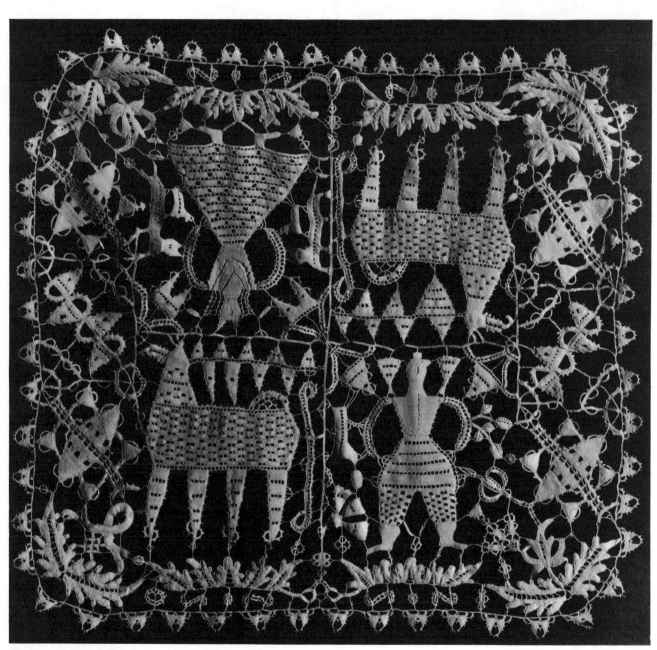

Chalice cover of Punto in aria. *Italy, late 16th century. Linen. 17 x 15 inches. Courtesy: Art Institute of Chicago. Gift: Honoré Palmer.*

Pattern derived from the lace on opposite page.

Border of Punto in aria. Italy, late 16th-early 17th century. Courtesy: The Metropolitan Museum of Art. Gift: Mrs. Edward S. Harkness, 1930.

72

Patterns adapted from the lace on page 70.

Here and opposite: Designs for points adapted from Vecellio's Corona, 1600.

Punto Tagliato à Fogliami, Gros Point, and Other Relief Laces

Unlike *punto in aria,* which was flat and either geometric or highly stylized, *punto tagliato à fogliami* and *gros point* were restlessly asymmetrical and sculptural. In these relief laces, the edges of the motifs were raised to varying degrees. Some were so dramatically high that they cast strong shadows. In addition, the lace had many types of picot ornaments, some of them elaborate and gemlike. The thread used for this lace was so smooth and the stitches were made so closely and evenly that a well-worked *cordonnet* seemed more like a carving than a sewing.

Gros point, also called *gros point de Venise, Venise à gros relief,* and *punto a relievo,* rose to prominence in the middle of the seventeenth century. *Gros point* looked especially effective when used for men's neckwear, for the *col rabat,* the cravat, or the large circular collar called the *camail* that was worn by Venetian noblemen. *Gros point* was also an effective church lace. Its boldly sculptural design could be seen at a distance, and it was a sturdy lace. On an alb, *gros point* designs with edgings of sharp points were dramatic but dignified.

Point de Venise rosaline is a seventeenth-century Venetian needle lace worked on a ground of picoted bars. At the juncture of the bars there are three pearls or picots. The motifs of the lace are serpentine, and they have cordonnets decorated with wheels and

Flounce of rose point. Italy, 17th century. Courtesy: Museum of Fine Arts, Boston. Gift of Mrs. Winthrop Sargent.

spirals, and especially with crowns and flying flowers (*fleurs volantes*). In the most flamboyant of these laces, the relief was worked to as much as a full half inch in height. The objective was to create the effect of a blooming rose bush. Like some of the other relief laces, this lace is characterized by its *entoilage* (clothwork) into which open, geometric patterns have been worked.

Point de Venise à rose and *point de France* are similar. Their designs are smaller than the patterns of *gros point*. One difference lies in the characteristic restraint that embues most French design. In some French examples, the grounds are more closely worked, and there is sometimes a difference in the buttonhole stitches used.

Spanish lacemakers made relief laces similar to those made in Venice, called *Spanish point* or *scolpito in rilievo*. The Spanish designs were in the Louis XIV style.

Mezzo punto, also called *Venise au lacet* and *point de canaille*, is a mixed Venetian guipure that has raised work in the manner of Venetian guipure, but that was made with bobbined tape. The tape was sewn to the pattern, and fillings were needle-made, sometimes with silk thread. Connecting bars were distributed in random fashion and picots were used generously. The same thick bundle of threads that was buttonholed to make the cordonnet of *gros point* was used in making *mezzo punto*, which was said to have originated in Naples in the seventeenth century.

Cuffs of gros point. Italy (Venice), 17th century. Heavy cordonnets, pinhole modes. 23½ x 8 inches. Courtesy: The Metropolitan Museum of Art. Gift of Mrs. Edward S. Harkness, 1930.

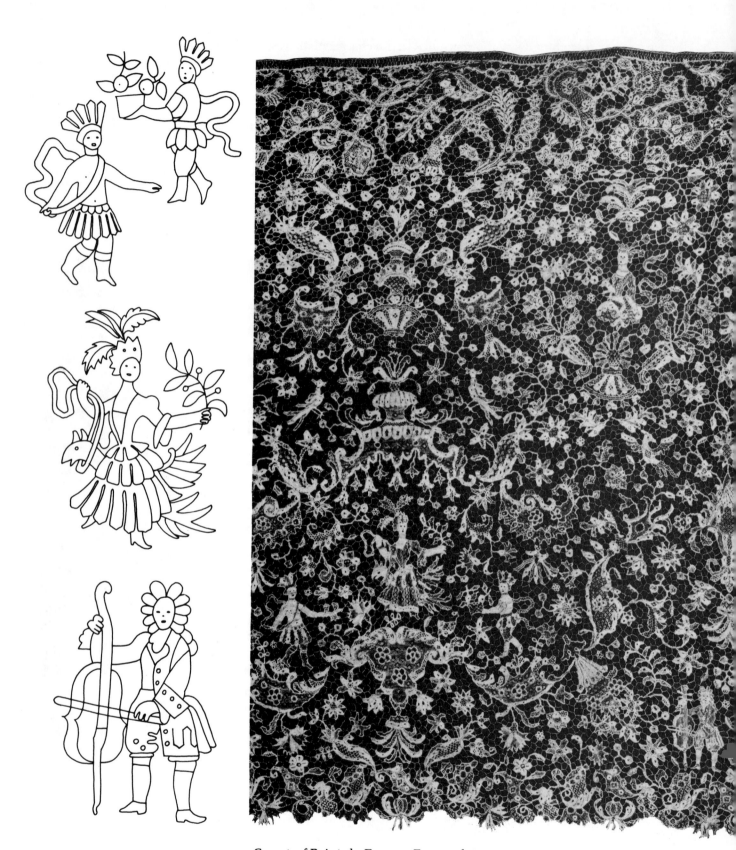

Cravat of Point de France. France, late
17th century. Courtesy: Victoria and
Albert Museum, London.

Design adapted from Vavassore's Opera Nuova, 1546.

Flounce (detail). **Pious Pelican, mezzo** *punto. Italy, early 17th century. 83 x 72 inches. Courtesy: Art Institute of Chicago. Gift: Mrs. Charles Schweppe, through The Antiquarian Society.*

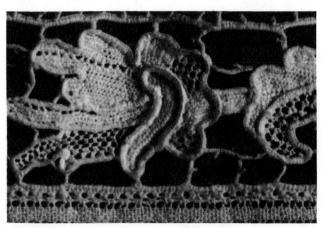

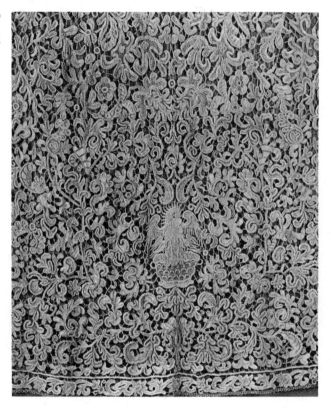

Edging of needlepoint guipure. Italy, 17th century. Linen. Width: 1⅛ inches.

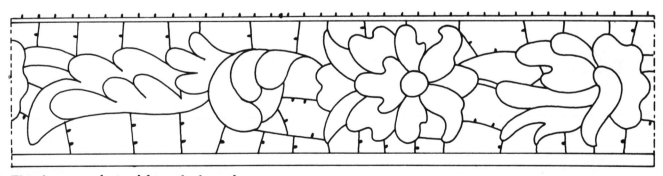

Floral pattern derived from the lace above.

Point Plat de Venise and Other Flat Italian Needle Laces

Point plat de Venise is worked flat, and its designs have no raised outlines. To make the ground of *point plat de Venise à réseau*, the mesh-grounded version of the lace, the worker threw a thread across a span and made looped stitches on it, giving each an extra twist. The needle worked towards the lacemaker.

The flowers and ornaments of this lace, only a little of which still exists, are simple and stylized. They are outlined with a row of small square meshes of the same type as are used in making the ground. In appearance the lace is much like Alençon.

Seventeenth-century *coralline* lace has an all-over, branching pattern that looks like coral. A legend attached to *coralline* states that a young sailor brought home a gift of a coral from the South Seas for his sweetheart. The girl imitated it, making a *guipure* lace, which became very popular. The coral patterns of the lace are more natural in appearance than is usual for most of the botanical subjects used in Italian laces. The *coralline* ground is *brides picotées*. The toile is open in parts.

Old Burano point is similar to *point plat de Venise à réseau*, but it is not as fine. The mesh of Burano is square and it has a horsehair cordonnet that is not buttonholed. The origin of old Burano point is uncertain. In the eighteenth century, it consisted of a border and flowers coarsely outlined on a mesh ground that was worked in rows, top to bottom, on a cushion. Flowers were made in the manner of *punto in aria*, with some portions needlewoven in *punto à cordella* or darning stitch. In the middle of the nineteenth century, workers used uneven threads, producing a mottled *réseau*. Other laces made at Burano were *Alençon*, Brussels, *rose point de Venise*, *punto tagliato à fogliami*, and *point d' Angleterre*.

Flat Italian peasant laces are well-designed and strong in pattern. In the eighteenth century, the peasants of Lombardy wore fine point lace, which they could purchase at reasonable cost. Rural laces derived their patterns from fine church and other laces, or sometimes they were original. Italian women made patterns by cutting silhouettes in paper and folding the paper down the center to form symmetrical designs.

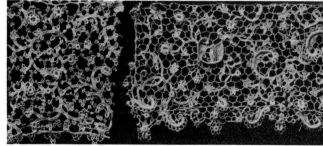

Fragments of needle lace. Above right: point plat de Venise à reseau. *Italy, 17th century. Below right: rose point, Italy, 17th century. Above: Burano. Italy, 19th century. Courtesy: The Metropolitan Museum of Art. Gift of Mrs. Nuttall, 1908.*

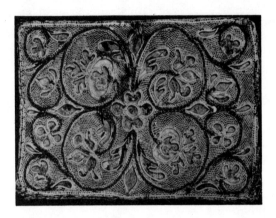

Cover of needle lace. Spain, 17th-18th century. The stiff cover was made of a sheet of mica, lined with brocaded fabric. The lace on the outer surface was made with wired outlines. The main motifs are left in reserve to show the mica. The netting was worked in double Brussels stitch. Silver-covered silk cord, couched in place, was used for scrolls. A few spangles were added. Courtesy: The Art Institute of Chicago.

Hollie Point

The lace called *hollie point* (or sometimes, *holy point*), was made by the same technique used to make the flat, geometrically designed fillings in some of the more solid Venetian laces. This technique could be adapted well to inscriptions; thus, it was well suited for use by the church.

This restrained, dignified lace seems to be an exclusively English and American product, although it is so similar to the flower fillings of laces made on the continent. A typical hollie point sampler of the time of Queen Anne was about eight or nine inches square. It had alternating bands of embroidered and hollie point ornaments and narrow stripes of embroidery in satin and other stitches, usually threadcounted. The wider bands had squares or circles cut out of the ground fabric and filled with *reticella*, hollie point, or both. In some examples hollie point was worked over drawn threads.

Hollie point designs were usually simple and geometric. Lozenges, chevrons, diapers, letters, and numbers were used. Crowns, *fleurs de lys*, and acorns were also common, as were roses, lilies, and strawberries, much like those used in embroidery. Sometimes the designs also contained rabbits, cocks, and squirrels. Hollie point flourished between 1680 and 1780. In its final period only geometric bands were attempted. Buttonholed loops sometimes were used along the edges of the pieces.

Most of the linens that were decorated with hollie point were used and worn out in the seventeenth and early eighteenth centuries, so that not many of the functional pieces that were made remain intact, although a good many hollie point samplers do exist. Baby clothes were decorated with hollie point, and probably because these were used little, quite a few also survive. Hollie point was a popular adornment for baby caps.

Sampler of hollie point and reticella. Signed: Sarah Uesley, dated 1739. England. Courtesy: Museum of Fine Arts, Boston. Gift of Philip Leham in memory of his wife Carrie L. Leham.

Alençon

Alençon is the name given to needle laces that were made in the French town of Alençon in Normandy. One distinguishing feature of Alençon laces, at least those made before the nineteenth century, was that they were not naturalistic in design, unlike the needle laces of Brussels with which they were contemporary.

Alençon had an important cottage industry for lacemaking long before Colbert established a lace manufactory there in 1661; in fact, Catherine di Medici, who was given the Duchy of Alençon by Charles IX, may have introduced cutwork *(point coupé)* to the area.

It was Colbert's venture, however, that made Alençon a lace that was coveted worldwide. Colbert's goal was to stimulate the local product so that it could compete with foreign imports, which were preferred at the time, their purchase draining funds out of the country at an alarming rate. *Point de France*, as the new lace was called, was comparatively inexpensive, and Colbert saw to it that it was worn at court. The lace, a copy Venetian point lace, was very lovely and soon became popular on its own merit. It was exported to Poland, Russia, England, and even to Venice.

In the early years there was little difference between the laces made at Alençon and Italian and Spanish needle laces. All were made almost exclusively with buttonhole stitch, and all had bar grounds. The bars were ornamented in various ways. Two of the most popular treatments were picots and flying flowers. Flying flowers, which appeared about 1677, were attached to the lace with only a stitch or two, hence their name. Groundless designs were developed during the third quarter of the seventeenth century. The forms of the patterns touched each other, forming a natural bridge. Like previous laces, seventeenth-century laces had scrolls and sprays accented heavily with corded contours, giving the lace a carved look.

From 1665 until about 1720, Alençon was called *point de France*; thereafter it was known as *Alençon*. Needlepoint laces, with or without barred grounds, were replaced after the deaths of Louis XIV and Colbert with laces having mesh grounds. Scrolls and flowers were opened to admit decorative filling designs *(modes, jours)*, but the basic design of Alençon lace continued to be large and bold. Sometimes the groundwork was composed of a series of designs of varying degrees of elaboration and fineness. The restless undulations of the scrolling motifs were slowed a bit, and the motifs were slimmed. Areas of flat, geometric design were used, along with the acanthus-derived patterns of long standing, which gave some of the laces a vaguely oriental flavor.

The *candelabre* pattern was first used in Alençon in the third quarter of the seventeenth century as France became the fashion pace-setter of Europe. With its delicate threadwork and small, spaced patterns, the new lace was fine for gathering into ruffles.

When the vogue for formal, stylized Bizarre silk patterns arrived, Alençon laces took on some of the devices of that type of composition. Designs called Bizarre often featured a certain ambiguity between background and motif, which was well suited to lace. Backgrounds became as texturally interesting as foregrounds. Snowflake and *oeil de perdrix* fillings and grounds were much used.

In the years before the French Revolution, Alençon patterns featured border designs on large areas of mesh, which were powdered with small dots or sprigs. In this period the stiff and formal needle laces lost their eminence and soft bobbin laces came to the fore.

The industry at **Alençon** was virtually wiped out by the French Revolution. Napoleon I loved lace and tried to revive the business with his patronage, but that renewal was short-lived. Napoleon III's efforts at revival were successful to a modest degree, but really great laces were made only infrequently. After the introduction of machine-made grounds for lace, the Alençon industry once again began to grow.

Despite the fact that it was the finest of nineteenth-century handmade laces, Alençon gradually lost its position as the premier lace and was replaced by the *blondes*. When revivals were attempted later they were made difficult by the fact that new patterns had to be attempted by unexperienced workers. The personnel of the manufactories had scattered or gone on to the making of other laces, and veteran workers showed little interest in the new patterns for Alençon.

Although the Alençon lace industry was quite large in the nineteenth century, it is for the earlier patterns, worked in fine needle lace, that Alençon is noted.

The lace was made in parts on parchment, with twelve divisions of the labor. Each woman worked at only her one specialty. For a large piece of work, twenty-two lacemakers might be required. Designs were printed from copperplates onto parchment (called *vilain*, from "*vellum*") with the order of work numbered on the pattern. Originally, patterns were made of natural-colored parchment, but after 1769 green was used. The parchments were pricked and sewn to stout layers of linen. A double flax thread (*fil de trace*) was couched along the pattern outlines, a stitch at each pricking point. Then the *brides* or *réseau* were worked by the *réseleuse*. Solid areas of the design were worked with buttonhole stitch over a laid thread, working from left to right. The making of the *modes* and *jours* followed.

Alençon was a heavy, solid lace, considered a winter lace. Because the techniques used to make it were so complicated, the pieces were seldom very large. Smoothness and regularity of technique and the delicacy with which the parts are assembled are paramount considerations in judging Alençon laces. Eighteenth-century Alençon had a delicate, square-meshed *réseau*, with all loops made in the same direction and over extra horizontal lines of thread. Buttonholed motifs were edged with a gimp of horsehair, which, unfortunately, had a tendency to thicken in water. When the lace was finished, it was removed from the parchment and linen by slicing with a razor between the layers of cloth.

Border of point d'Alençon. *France, early 18th century. 3⅛ inches wide. Buttonholed hexagonal mesh, outlining cordonnets, various fillings. Courtesy: The Metropolitan Museum of Art. Gift of Ann Payne Blumenthal, 1936.*

84

Argentan

Argentan is ten miles away from Alençon, and, according to Madame Despierres, laces made there are said to date as early as 1377. The bureau of lace manufacture there, as at Alençon, dates from 1665, and the business was under royal edict from 1708. Laces of the two towns are similar because workers moved freely between the towns.

Manufacture at Argentan declined in the beginning of the eighteenth century, as it did in Alençon. In the early nineteenth century revival attempts were fruitless, and *Argentan* virtually ended in 1810.

The lace of Argentan differs from that of Alençon in its buttonholed hexagonal ground and, sometimes, in its bolder flowers and relief. Argentan lace is very complicated and strong. As in Venetian work, both the *toile* and the bars of the groundwork are closely worked. The bars are about one-tenth of an inch long. According to Mrs. Palliser, the bars have seven or eight buttonhole stitches each; according to Alan Cole's count, they have nine or ten. Many of the laces have picots.

Like Alençon, Argentan began, in the seventeenth century, to make Venetian-type laces with *bride* grounds. To make the *bride* grounds for Argentan, the worker pricked the upper angle of each hexagon. The hexagon was formed by passing needle and thread around the pins, then working buttonhole stitches over each bar, the work always running in the same direction. This ground was called the *grand bride* and was always popular in France, although elsewhere it was considered coarse. The *bride tortillée* ground, which was twisted rather than buttonholed, was probably an effort to produce a less costly lace. The *bride picotée* ground, also called *bride épingle* because of the pins required to make the picots, was discontinued in 1869. The *bride bouclée*, made with loops instead of picots, also ceased. In the nineteenth century the *grand bride* grounds of some Argentan laces were replaced with bobbin net, which was introduced in England in 1810 and in France in 1818.

Design for a needle lace or mixed lace adapted from an 18th-century needle lace (See Carlier de Lantsheere, Tesor de l'art Dentellier.)

Argentella

Argentella, thought to be an Italianate form of Argentan originating in Venice or Genoa, is a variant of *point d'Argentan* of greater than usual delicacy. Characteristic of this lace is the buttonholed hexagonal barred ground with solid hexes introduced into some of the meshes. *Argentella* is like *point de France*, but it does not have a heavy cordonnet. Instead it has one festooned (buttonholed) line; it also has a great deal of ornamental stitching. Manufacture of *Argentella* ended in the middle of the eighteenth century.

Right: Lappet of point de Sedan. *France, 18th century. Courtesy: Art Institute of Chicago.*

Left: Lappet of point d'Argentella. *Italy, 18th century. Courtesy: Art Institute of Chicago.*

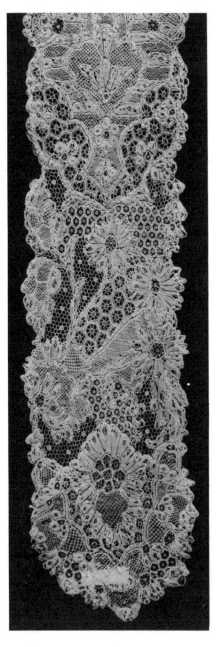

Point de Sedan

Point de Sedan is the most exciting lace of the Ardennes region. In the seventeenth century, this fine white lace was made at Sedan, Donchery, Charleville, Mezieres, Troyes, and Sens. Most of the lace was sold in Paris, but it also found its way to Poland, England, Holland, and Germany. *Point de Sedan* resembles late Venetian *réseau*-grounded needlepoint lace, but, like the lace of Alençon, it has a single thread rather than a cordonnet at the contours of motifs. *Point de Sedan* is sometimes said to be a variant of Alençon, and it has also been identified with the laces of Brabant and Liege.

Point de Sedan designs have some distinguishing features. Their bold, usually scrolling patterns are large in scale. The lace has no heavily corded edges; instead, raised areas of the lace are made at little focal points, sometimes in the center of a shape. In keeping with the vigor of this lace, some of the meshes are large and picoted (*grande maille picotée*).

Point de Gaze, Point de Bruxelles, and Rose Point

Point de gaze is a Flemish lace that takes its name from the fact that the mesh of its ground is usually filmy. This mesh is constructed of a single thread, and each loop consists of a single buttonhole stitch. The other parts of *point de gaze* are constructed in the manner of other needle laces, but they are very fine. The lace's cordonnets are made up of a half-dozen closely buttonholed threads. The cloth parts of the lace were buttonholed in one direction only and over a laid thread.

Brussels needlepoint *guipure* is made in the same way as *point de gaze*, except that the design is so arranged that little background treatment is required; a few bars are used whenever needed. The rose point version of Brussels needlepoint lace, which began to be made around the middle of the nineteenth century, is accented with buttonholed rose petals applied over the lace so that the roses in the pattern have an effect of slight relief. The designs of all these laces are rich, sometimes over-rich, and are embellished with borders, swags, and classical elements that combine to make an extravagant display of texture. The finest of these laces also are virtuoso displays of stitchmaking, carefully controlled to create a moderated range of values rivaling the shadings of naturalistic paintings.

Late in the nineteenth century *point de Venise* types of lace were made, usually by a single lacemaker who worked flowers and grounds simultaneously. Like their flat Venetian counterparts, these *point a l'aiguille gazée* laces had clear grounds, rich fillings, and buttonholed solid areas that were not bordered with a heavy cordonnet, but with a thread only.

Point de gaze and *point de Bruxelles* were manufactured widely after 1830. Both cotton and linen threads were used to make dresses, shawls, parasols, flounces, handkerchiefs, and fans.

Gown (detail). Rose point variation. Belgium, 19th century. Detail shows extra rose petals applied to flowers. Mixed bobbin and needle lace. Machine net ground.

Veil of point de gaze. Made for the Russian Imperial Family. Belgium, about 1810. Linen. 72 x 72 inches. Courtesy: Art Institute of Chicago. Gift: The Antiquarian Society.

Wool Laces

In addition to linen, silk, and cotton, wool was used to make lace. Shetland point was made in England; *trina de lana* was made in Italy. Woolen lace was used for baby shawls, quilts, scarves, and other articles to be used for warmth. To make wool laces, traditional patterns were enlarged; filling stitches were about the same. Instead of cordonnets, rows of chain stitch embroidery were worked around the edges of the solid parts of the lace. Twisted bars were used instead of buttonholed bars, and the bars were picoted frequently. Wheels were used to stabilize the bars as well as to decorate the lace. Yak lace was made in Northampton and Buckinghamshire in the manner of Maltese *guipures*.

Punto Avorio

In the Italian Alps a kind of heavy lace using a double buttonhole stitch is made. This lace is known as *punto avorio*, or ivory point. It has other names as well, and the same lace may be called *Saracen point (punto Saraceno), Alpine point (punto Alpino),* or *little point (pizze ponsetto)*. The bulkiness of the stitch and the thread used for it make it necessary to use simpler designs than those from which *reticella* are made. Color often figures in the work. Tan and brown linen threads are used, as well as red, yellow, blue, and green silk. The designs are usually little triangles, crosses, rosettes, or stairsteps. *Punto avorio* is an extremely durable lace.

Fragment of punto avorio. Italy, 17th century. Linen, 1¾ x 2 inches. Ex. coll.: Ida Schiff, Florence. Courtesy: The Metropolitan Museum of Art. Rogers Fund, 1920.

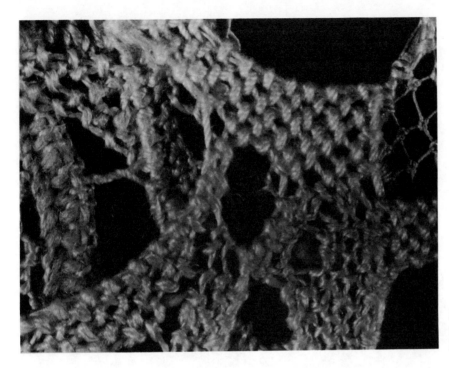

Detail showing punto avorio *in a contemporary lace construction. V. Bath.*

Sols and Ruedas

Round motifs and woven patterns with rays emanating from the center are combined to make a distinctive type of lace that is especially fine in examples made in Latin countries. The patterns of these laces are called *sols* (suns) or *ruedas* (wheels). In Paraguay they are called *nanduti* (webs), and a similar type of work done in the Canary Islands is called *Tenerife* after the place where it is made.

In early Castillian and Catalán work, the wheel pattern was usually set in a square. The circle was a combination of concentric rings and rays. The sun pattern was similar, but it had a prominent circle worked close to the center with radials emanating from this circle. In some very different examples the needlewoven circle contains a symmetrical doubleheaded eagle or palm rather than a wheel or sun.

The origin of this type of lace is not known. While early examples of collars, handkerchiefs, and other items of apparel still exist, most objects of this lace were made for church use. In Cataluña both *ruedas* and *sols* were made; in Salamanca only the sun center was used (*sols salmantinos*). In the Canary Islands, where much drawnwork was made, Tenerife lace was made on a frame with white and colored threads. The technique used to interweave the designs into the basic star-ground of stretched threads is similar to that used in drawnwork embroidery. At Tenerife, the sun and wheel patterns were made independent of a linen ground and assembled after making.

According to Florence May, a woman who went to the New World with the conquistadores took the technique there. The lace is worked in Bolivia, Brazil, Paraguay, and Mexico. Small rosettes are made on a circular cushion that has fifty-two pins around the edge. The rosettes are made one on top of the other, with paper discs separating them. Later they are taken off the cushion and joined in a pattern.

In Paraguay, *nanduti* is made on muslin stretched in a frame. Cotton, silk, or linen thread is used to make small, juxtaposed circles and squares. This technique was brought to Paraguay by the Jesuits or the Portuguese settlers. In Paraguay each pattern has its own name. Very large hangings were created. It was also a custom to tie a band of *nanduti* around a candlebearing black cross as a tribute to a deceased friend.

Spanish network, Cataluña, 19th century. Courtesy: Metropolitan Museum of Art, Gift of Mrs. Nuttal, 1908.

Panel of needlewoven network. Spain, early 17th century. Courtesy: The Metropolitan Museum of Art. Rogers Fund, 1906.

All threads having been removed from the corner of the drawnwork stripe on this handkerchief, a motif was worked onto a wheel of threads added to the linen. China, 20th century.

Rosettes and the pillow for making them. The pillow is improvised of layers of felt sewn together and glued into a lid.

Making a rosette. The center motif, common in Tenerife work, is made by weaving over and under groups of threads, advancing the starting point for the weaving by one or more stitches in each row. Petals are made with the needle, using plain weave.

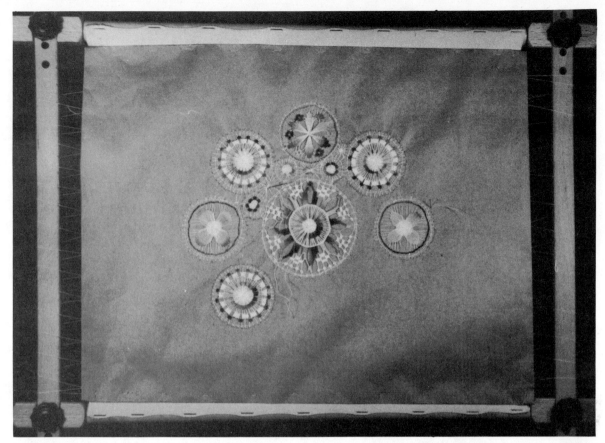

Making Tenerife-type lace on a frame. Paper has been added to the ground cloth to keep the needle from picking up threads of the ground. The design is drawn lightly on the paper. Radiating threads are arranged by looping the thread of the spokes into a row of running stitches around the circumference of the circle.

Doily of needlewoven network. Argentina, 20th century. Linen and cotton in three colors.

Arab Lace and Bebilla

Arab laces and *bebilla* laces *(oyah)* are needle laces made with knots. Made in Armenia, Cyprus, and Palestine, the laces have designs that are much like hollie point.

Bebilla has been claimed by Armenian, Greek, and Turkish lacemakers as an art native to their own countries. It is related to ancient rugmaking, which existed in Syria for at least six centuries before the birth of Christ. Although it has a different name in each country in which it is worked, the same knot is used in all the laces. It is similar to a fisherman's knot. It is worked from left to right with needle and thread, the needle pointing away from the worker.

Wire may be introduced into the little *bebilla* motifs, which are usually silk. The most frequently made motifs were flowers, but witty little fish and animals also were constructed.

Bebilla was worked in both white and colors and in both heavy and fine threads. In time the old technique was translated into crochet.

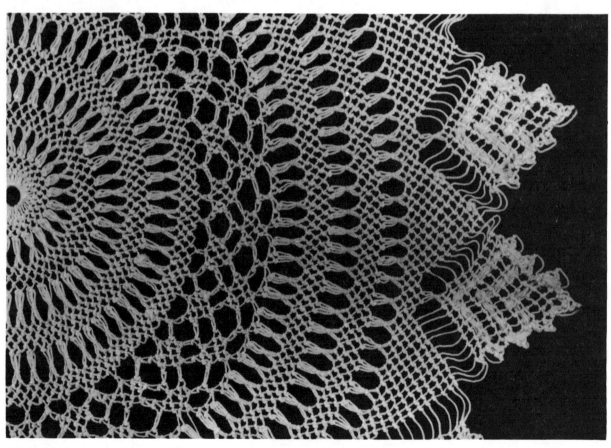

Doily of Armenian lace. 20th century.

Collar of bebilla. Cyprus, c. 1886.
Exhibited at the Colonial and Indian
Exhibition, 1886. Silk. Courtesy: Victo-
ria and Albert Museum, London.

Contemporary Needle Lace Design

Today's textile artists are rediscovering needle lace. As the following pages show, few kinds of lace offer more possibilities for the modern craftsman. There is an almost infinite variety of stitches possible. Needle lace can be used to express almost any contemporary design, whether the design is tentative and ambiguous or clearcut and hard-edged. The technique can accommodate any thread that can be found in a yarn shop—even fishline, cords, ropes, plastic tapes, and natural materials such as reeds and grasses offer no difficulty.

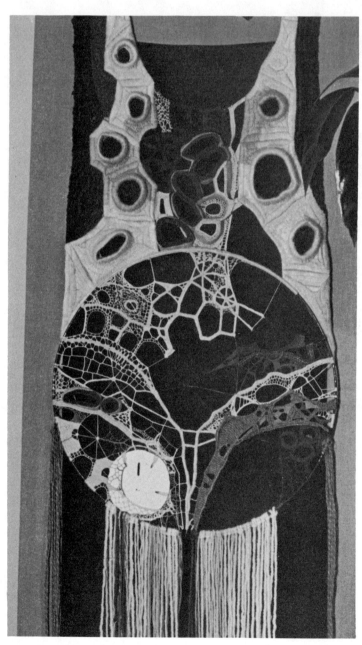

"Sand Dollar," wall hanging by Virginia Bath. Embroidery and needle lace. 5 feet, 6 inches by 1 foot, 3 inches. Linen, wool, synthetics, shell.

"Sand Dollar," (detail). Needle lace
technique expanded to very large
scale; relief embroidery included.

"Fibrous Raiment," Debra E. Rapo-
port. 1971. Weaving, netting, macramé. Wool, rope, feathers, plastic,
video tape. Courtesy: Artist.

Photo by Demetre Lagios

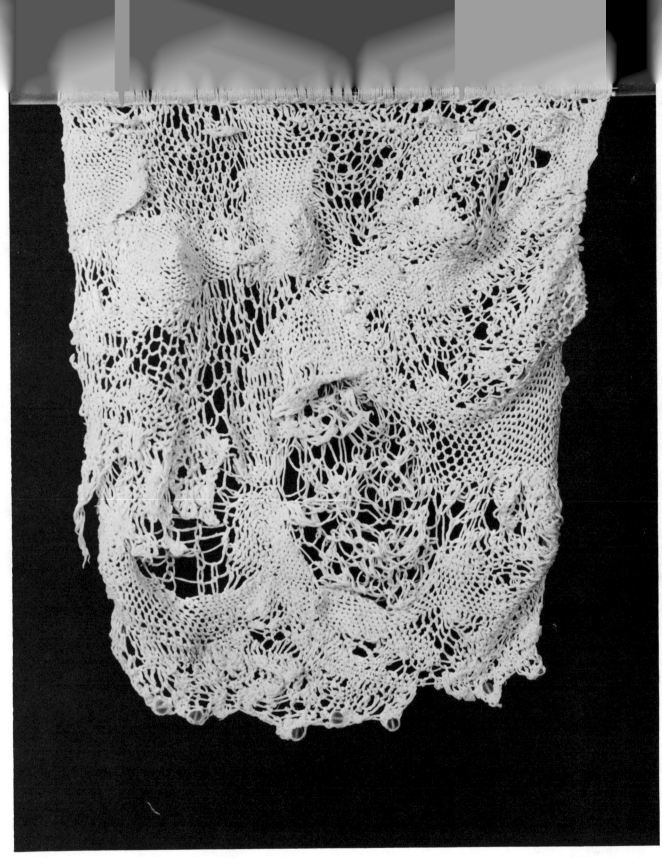

Punto in aria, Joanne Brandford.
Needle lace. Linen. 22 x 22 inches.
Courtesy: Artist.

"Craters," Virginia Bath. 1970. Needle
lace construction. Linen, cotton, wood,
metal. 12 x 12 inches.

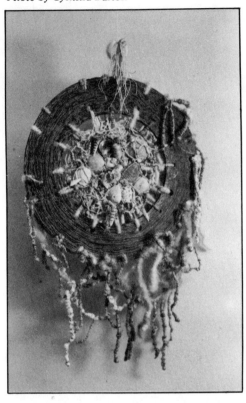

"Sea Web," Barbara Aubin. Mixed construction. Fiber, shells, found objects. Diameter: 10 inches. Courtesy: Artist.

"To Soar," Virginia Bath. 1971. Embroidery and relief needle lace with patchwork. Wool, linen, silk, feathers. 26 x 36 inches.

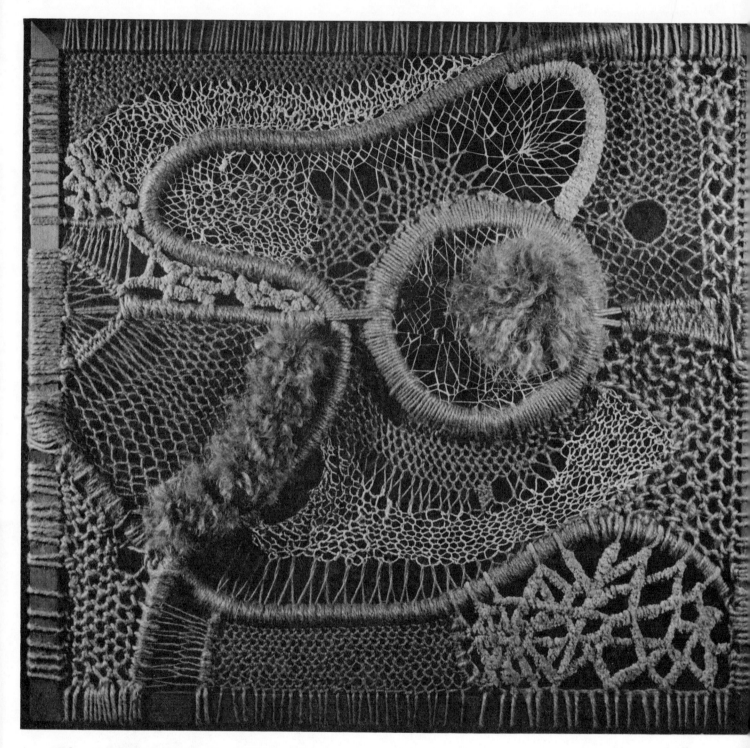

"Fiber Screen 1," Evelyn Svec Ward.
1972. Netting knitting, wrapping.
Sisal, ixtle, cotton, cotton chenille. 36
x 40 inches. Courtesy: Artist.

"Mexicana Rose," Evelyn Svec Ward. Embroidery with appliqué and needle netting. Burlap, net, felt; cotton, synthetic, metallic threads, Mexican maguey, on wool. Courtesy: Artist.

"Winter Window," Evelyn Svec Ward. Embroidery, knotting knitting. Lucite frame. Burlap, wool, synthetic, linen, cotton, and cotton chenille threads. 13½ x 23½ inches. Courtesy: Artist.

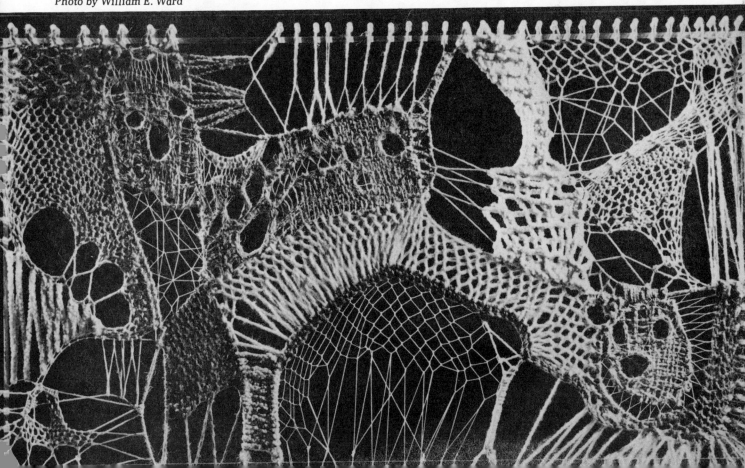

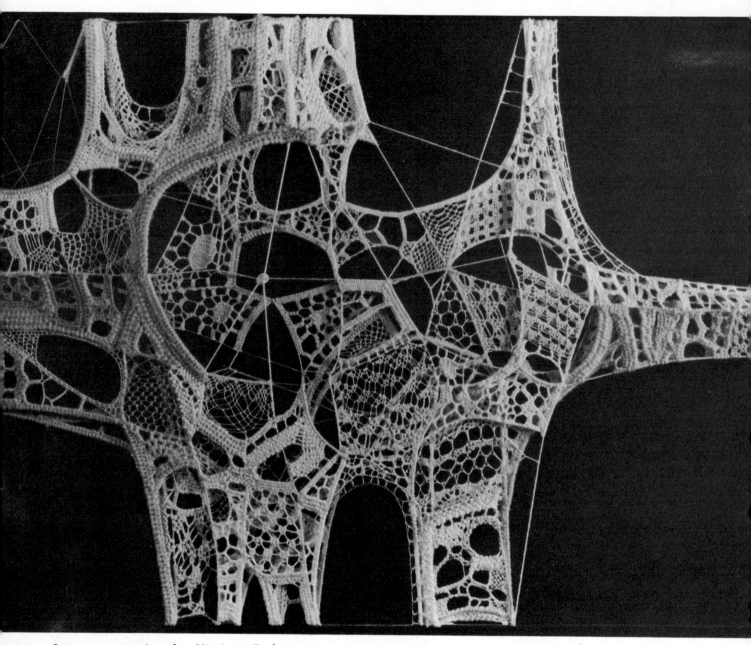

Lace construction by Virginia Bath.
Linen, wool, and silk on plexiglas.

"Semena," Otto Thieme. Needle lace
on plexiglas. Cotton, linen, rattail,
beads. 8 x 14 inches. Courtesy: Artist.

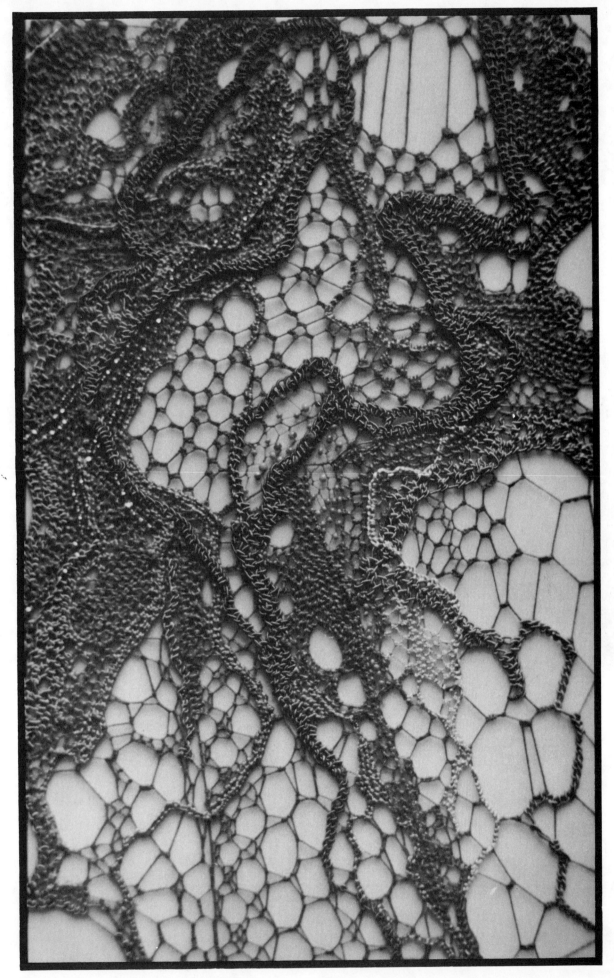

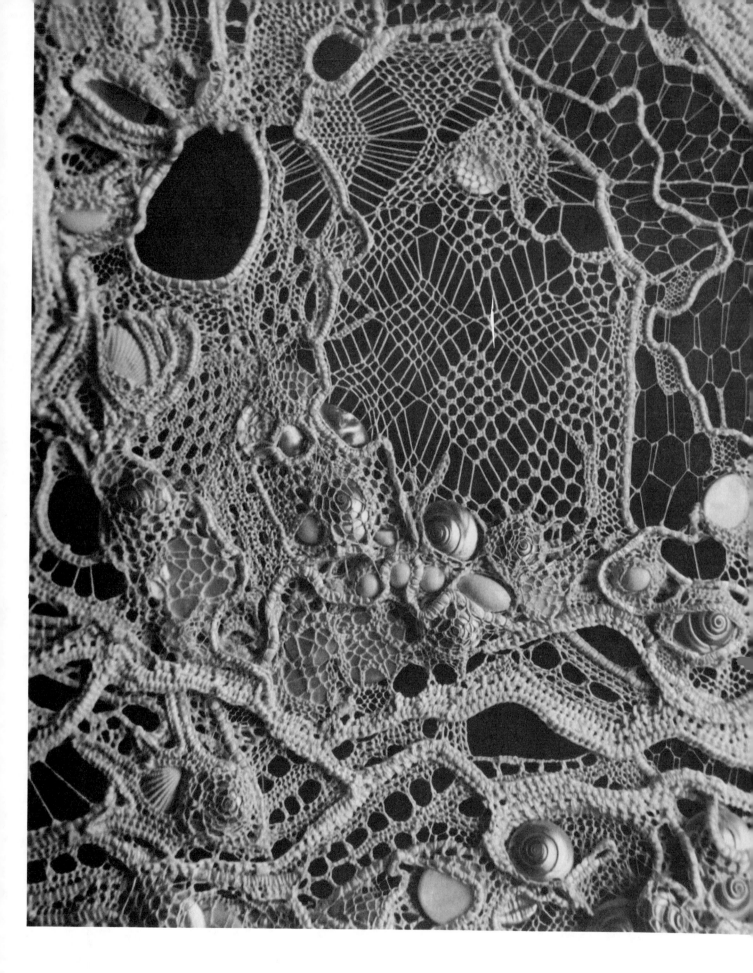

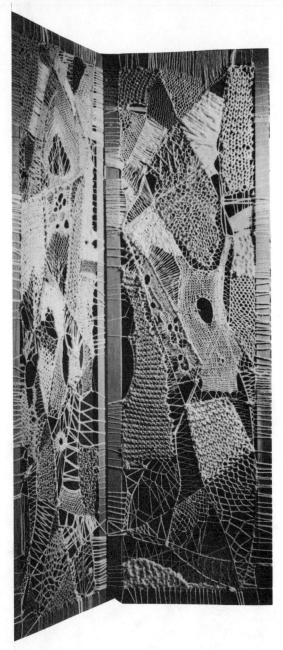

Two-fold screen by Evelyn Svec Ward. Stitchery, knotting, netting. Burlap, cord, Mexican maguey; wool, jute, linen, synthetic cotton, and cotton chenille threads. 61 x 36 inches. Courtesy: Artist.

Opposite page: "Untitled," Otto Thieme. Needle lace on plexiglas. Cotton, linen, rattail, beads, shells, mother-of-pearl, buttons. 18 inches square. Courtesy: Mr. and Mrs. Ken Wessler, Chicago.

"Red Box," Marie T. Kelly. String, muslin, acrylic. Courtesy: Artist.

"To Touch," Virginia Bath. 1971. Relief needle lace and relief embroidery. Linen, wool, silk, with wood, metal, ceramic, and amethyst additions. 40 x 62 inches.

"To Grow," Virginia Bath. 1970. Needle lace and relief embroidery. Wool, linen, silk, metal, mica. App. 30 x 72 inches. Courtesy: Art Institute of Chicago. Mr. and Mrs. John V. Farwell III, restricted gift.

"Foam," Virginia Bath. Needle lace, machine lace, embroidery. Linen, cotton, wool, with wood, ceramic, shells. 48 x 20 inches.

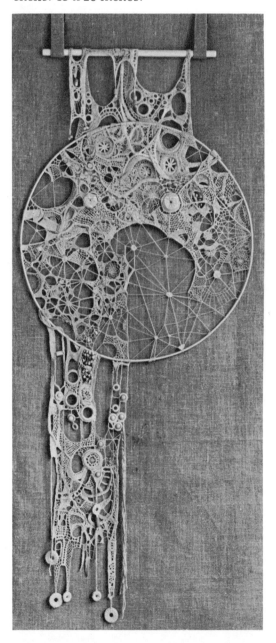

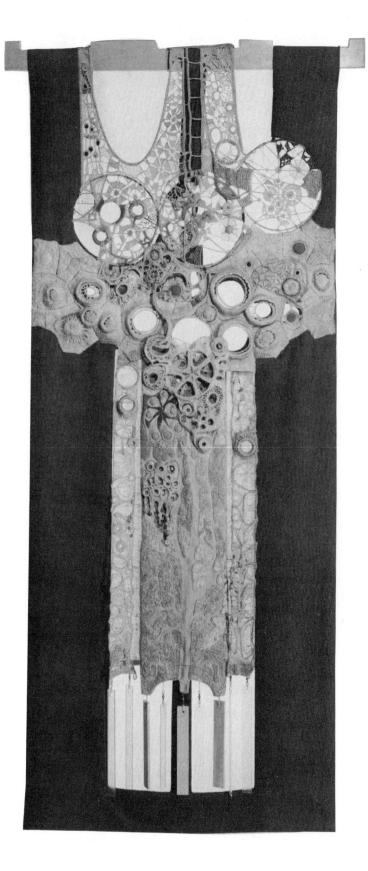

Techniques for Making Needle Lace

In the section that follows are the major stitches of needle lace, as well as directions for beginning the lace and some suggestions for craftsmen and artists who wish to incorporate needle lace into their work.

Preparing the Lace Foundation

For reproducing a *reticella* design, choose a piece of linen that has smooth warp and weft threads of similar weight. It is not necessary to make the lace over a pattern, but a design should be worked out in advance and referred to as work proceeds. Any of the *reticella* patterns in the book can be used for such reference without further drawing or scale changes. It is wise to determine the center of both fabric and pattern and work from the center outwards, and it may be helpful to sew a line of running stitches at midpoint on the fabric. After the outer contour of the opening has been determined, threads should be counted and carefully withdrawn, and the opening should be secured with overcasting stitches. It is usual to leave four threads for the bars of the grid, but the material you use may require more. Two threads will make a very fragile ground.

After the threads have been withdrawn in one direction, you may find the work easier to handle if you mount it on paper. Distortion of the threads is avoided if the work is sewn onto its foundation at this point.

Although in the nineteenth century smooth-surfaced fabrics were used directly under the lace, parchment over two layers of sturdy linen was used for earlier lace foundations. Heavy wrapping paper is a very satisfactory substitute for parchment. Two layers of paper will make a good base. Before the linen is sewn onto it, the paper can be crumpled thoroughly to make it more pliable and then smoothed out carefully. The linen is sewn onto the paper with close running stitches or, if necessary, with back stitches. When the lace is complete, it is cut off the paper (or paper and cloth) between the layers. Basting threads are picked out of the lace. Sometimes a pair of tweezers is helpful in removing stubborn threads.

With the linen ground stabilized on its paper backing, groups of threads can be cut out. Not all the threads that eventually will be removed need be cut out at the beginning of the work. The fabric will have maximum stability if some of the squares are cut for work and embroidered before another group is cut out. If warps and wefts are of different or irregular threads, squares should be determined by eye, not threadcounted.

Today's machine-woven linens are often made with threads that are not as tightly spun as those of old hand-woven linen, so if you choose to use the withdrawn threads for the lace, you should be prepared for more than usual breakage as you work. To minimize this, be sure that the threads that you use are smooth. Pick off nubs of fiber that could catch in the needlework and break the thread. Before threading the needle, give the thread a few twists. Use a needle with an eye large enough to allow the thread to slip through it easily, and do not work with overlong lengths of thread.

For maximum strength, the cut ends of threads that were overcast before cutting should be buttonholed. Edges that are overcast only are not washable except with the greatest care. Bars of the grid can be darned (or needlewoven), buttonholed on one side, or buttonholed on both sides. Picots should be worked into the bars as they are buttonholed or darned. Sometimes it is expedient to work parts of the pattern as the bars are worked, but for good alignment it is usually best to make the fillings after the bars have been covered.

This method of preparing your working base is used to make all the types of needle lace I have presented here, with whatever variations are required by the design. For *punto in aria* and other curvilinear designs, the outline threads are first couched onto the base.

Fabric prepared for drawn-thread work and cutwork. The upper rows will be overcast so that threads can be cut out. The lower row has no overcasting. It will be worked without removing any additional threads.

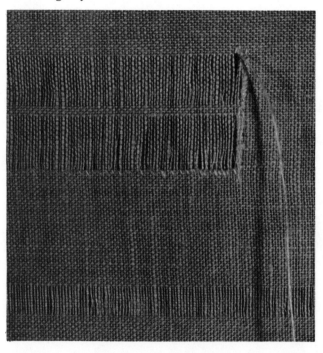

Remove needle lace from its foundation by cutting between layers of cloth.

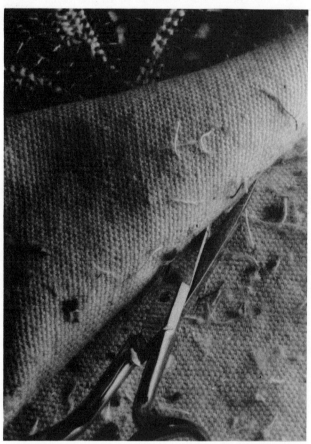

Reticella *being worked into the fabric. Threads withdrawn from the fabric are being used for the lacemaking.*

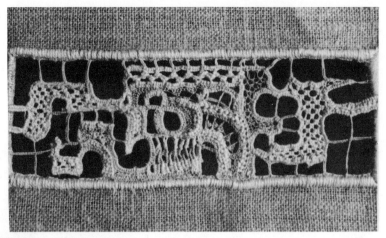

A simple lace insertion, its pattern derived from continuous fil de trace couched onto the foundation without prior planning.

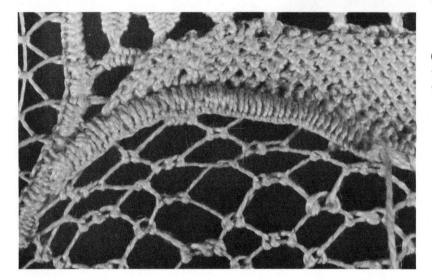

Cordonnet being made by buttonholing over a padding of couched threads.

Needle lace also can be made on threads stretched in a frame or on any basic, firm shape. The picture on this page shows threads stretched over a piece of Plexiglas and a simple project made with threads stretched around a glass jar. A double thread was tied tightly around the neck of the jar, and the other threads were tied into that one.

Detail of jar.

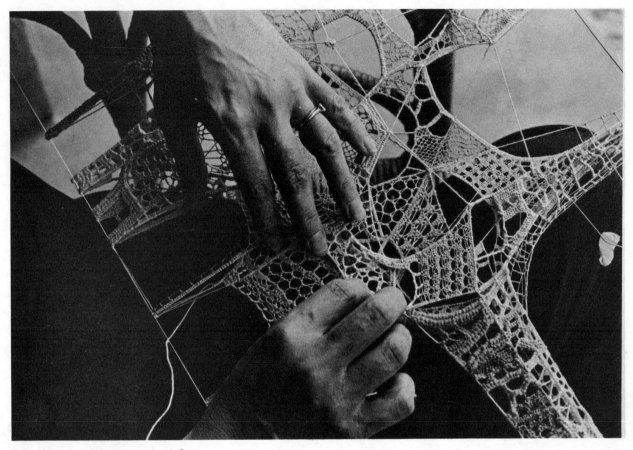

Lace being made over plexiglas.

Jar. Stout yarn was tied around this glass jar and needle lace stitches were worked into the intervals in bright colors. Buttonhole stitch over cabone rings adds relief. Lid top has a Tenerife-type wheel worked over cardboard glued to it.

Unfinished lace construction. V. Bath.
Close stitch in the third dimension.

Hangings of Needle Lace

As some of the preceeding pages show, needle lace can be used to make a wide variety of fabric sculptures and hangings. A few hints may save the artist who wishes to make a needle lace piece from costly and time-consuming errors.

In general, materials for needle lace should be durable and cleanable. If you wish to add objects to the composition, select things that won't stain the background fabric when cleaned or that can be removed and put back easily if they are not suitable for washing or dry cleaning. Wire used to shape parts of a construction should be rustproof, or should be painted before the lace is made.

In making large pieces that are to hang, you may need weights. Dress weights, drapery weights, or chains can be concealed, but the same purpose can be achieved by using wood or plastic tassels or other slightly heavy objects where weight is needed.

Relief embroidery is an excellent counterpoint to needle lace. English lace of the seventeenth century and the great *gros points* of Italy and France underscore this point. The link between the two techniques is the use of detached buttonhole stitch. Thick padding can also be used in the relief work.

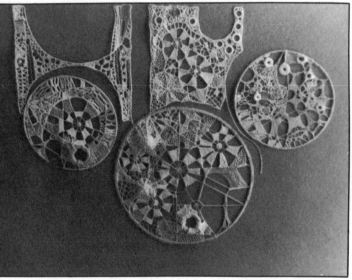

Sections of a large needle lace wall hanging before assembly.

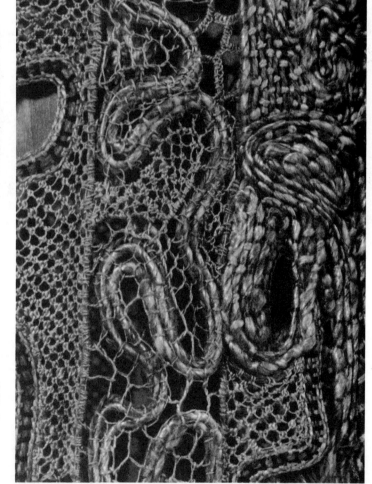

Wall hanging (detail). The same yarn used on the right for couched embroidery is laid into the buttonhole stitch in areas of guipure lace.

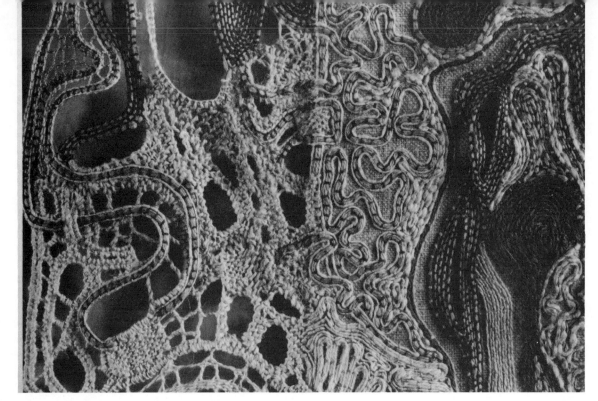

Wall hanging (detail). The relief embroidery on right, the punto avorio in the center, and the guipure lace on the left were all made with the same threads.

Detail of "Craters," needle lace wall hanging.

Needle Lace and Clothing

Needle lace still has possibilities for clothing. The colors of a tweed or stripe can be duplicated and worked into a simple or intricate pattern. Strong patterns in the fabric need not rule out the use of lace. A brilliant paisley may suggest motifs that can be arranged around a curve for collar and cuffs and then duplicated in colored wool in needle lace. Another fabric may suggest a contrasting lace. For the heavy double-woven wool shown here, I reversed the color scheme for the collar and cuffs. The simple latticed stems of the pattern in the woven cloth intertwine intricately in the collar, and the thick lace is accented with circles centered with wooden beads. Hats, headbands, and any items of clothing needing close fitting can be made with needle lace. Individual parts are made, then assembled for the shape. In the hat pictured here, there are four assembled parts plus a knit band. An oval piece was made for the crown, and three segments that made a truncated cone when put together complete the shape.

Handbag by Virginia Bath. Knitting and reticella. Wool with brass ornaments, carbone rings. Detail 6 x 7½ inches. Courtesy: Mrs. Kenneth Bath.

Vest-over-blouse, Bucky King. Needle lace and hand weaving (tapestry). Courtesy: Artist.

119

Hat by Virginia Bath. Wool guipure, no cordonnets. Knitted band.

Collar and cuffs by Virginia Bath. Relief needle lace with wooden beads. Wool and silk on dress of double-woven wool.

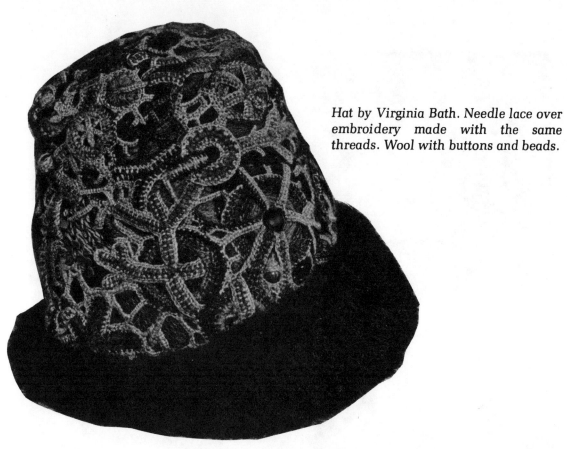

Hat by Virginia Bath. Needle lace over embroidery made with the same threads. Wool with buttons and beads.

Collar and cuffs. Virginia Bath. Guipure in wool and silk; for a printed wool dress.

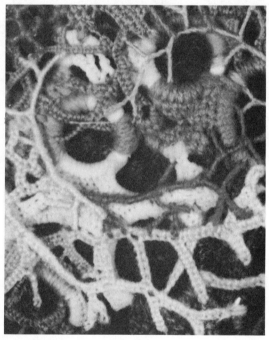

Handbag by Virginia Bath. Relief needle lace. Wool and synthetics with suede, carbone rings, glass beads. Handle and bottom of bag knitted, top crocheted. Couched suede edge. Courtesy: Mrs. Russell C. Bath.

Collar (detail), Natalie Novotny Green. Colored felt and wool yarn. Courtesy: Artist.

Stitches for Needle Lace

The main stitch used in making needle lace is the buttonhole stitch, which is also called close stitch, or *punto smerlo*. A knotted version of the buttonhole is called *punto a festone*. But although the buttonhole stitch is the dominant stitch used, the forms that the buttonhole stitch takes are so many and ingenious that they should be enumerated for the aspiring maker of needle lace.

Another technique basic to needle lace, as it is to all types of lace, is needleweaving. The weaving stitch is referred to as *darning stitch, in-and-out stitch, punto di Genoa, punto stuora,* or *armaletta.*

Sampler. The openings cut into the ground of this embroidery were buttonholed around the edges and filled with a variety of practice stitches.

Point de Bruxelles

This is the basic buttonhole stitch of needle lacemaking, and it is the basis for many of the stitches in this section. The first row of stitches is worked onto the foundation thread, and each succeeding row is worked on the buttonhole loops of the row above. The direction of the work is reversed with each row.

Point de Bruxelles may be worked with such variations as the double stitch shown here, or it may be decorated with spots of buttonhole stitches.

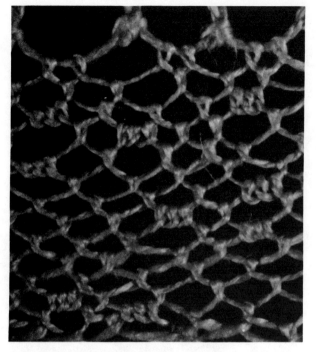

Brussels stitch with spots made with buttonhole stitch clusters.

Looped picots.

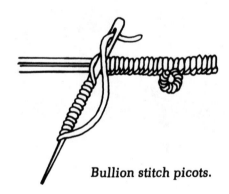

Bullion stitch picots.

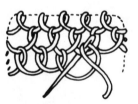

Brussels stitch.

Single Brussels stitch.

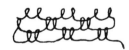

Double Brussels stitch.

Buttonholed ring picots.

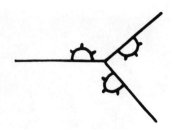

As these patterns for arrangements of fancy picots show, the buttonholed picot has almost infinite variations. Picots like these were used to decorate the edges of many of the laces in this book.

Picots

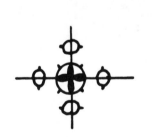

Mesh Stitch 1

For this stitch the preparation for the first row can be accomplished in various ways, depending upon the construction of adjacent areas. To work the stitch by the simplest method, make two close buttonhole stitches on the foundation thread, leave a loop of thread, and then make two more close buttonhole stitches. In the return row, make a buttonhole stitch in the first loop above, leaving the thread slack. Then make a second buttonhole stitch in the loop. If desired, you may make a third or fourth buttonhole stitch in the loop as well. The stitches made in the loops should be drawn up close to one another to give a compact appearance. Repeat the second row, reversing the direction of work with each row.

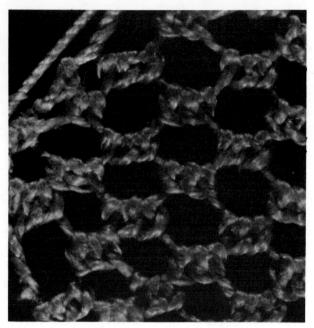

Point de Sorrento

Point de Sorrento can be worked straight across an area or from a corner in diagonal rows. To work diagonally, start with a loop across one corner. Carry the thread down one side to the point where the second row will begin, and make a pair of buttonhole stitches in the loop. Overcast the thread on the opposite side. In the next row, make four buttonhole stitches in each long loop. In the next row, make two buttonhole stitches in the longer loops. Continue to increase the pattern as needed on each side. The work alternates from left to right and from right to left.

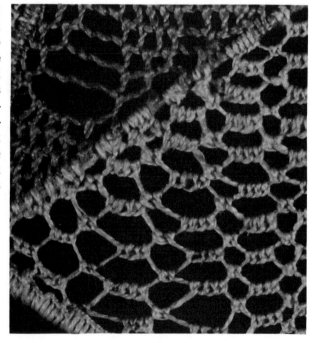

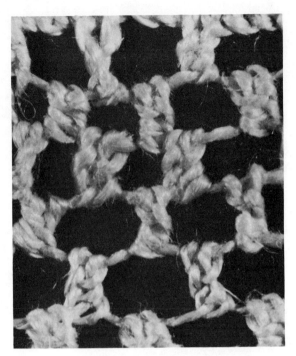

For the first row, make two buttonhole stitches close together, leave a long loop, and then make two more buttonhole stitches. In the return row, make two buttonhole stitches in the loop above and one or more buttonhole stitches in the loop just made in the row being worked. Repeat across the row. The following row is made in the same way, but with the direction of the stitches reversed. Made in small scale, this stitch looks very much like *vrai réseau* of Flemish bobbin lace *(Chapter 3)*.

Mesh Stitch 2

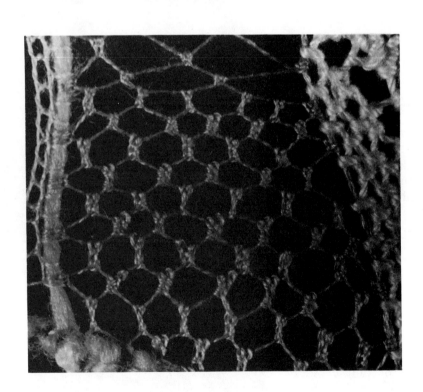

Point de Feston

In early laces, these stitches were worked close together, making a substantial mesh. Begin work on the left with a row of stitches made as for *point de Bruxelles,* but, as you work each buttonhole stitch, put in a second stitch just below the first. The second buttonhole stitch, drawn up tightly, acts as a knot to secure the first stitch. The second row is worked from right to left with stitches made in the same manner.

Buttonholed Mesh

Some of the finest meshes in old Venetian and other laces were made by this demanding technique. To make mesh in this way, begin the work on the left with a buttonhole stitch, and immediately buttonhole back along half the length of the loop with eight or nine stitches. Then, make a second buttonhole stitch and buttonhole it in the same way. When you complete the row, secure the thread on the right side of the span. On the return journey to the left side, buttonhole the remaining uncovered portions of each buttonhole stitch. You may want to make a buttonholed picot at the point where one large buttonhole stitch meets the next. After you work the picot, overcast or buttonhole the working thread into position for the next row of large buttonhole stitches. Place each of these large buttonhole loops so the thread is attached in the center of the lower portion of the loop of the buttonhole stitch in the row above.

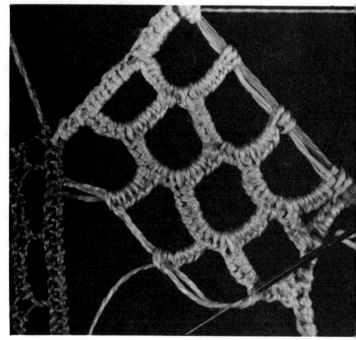

Notice that in the photograph each of the large buttonhole stitches is doubled. Each was made twice so that the total weight of thread on which the smaller stitches were worked would be heavier than the thread used to make the small stitches. Form is more firmly established when stitches are worked in this way, and the little bars do not twist as they do when the buttonhole covering is made of stitches of the same weight as the base thread.

To make any bar or loop of buttonholed thread lie flat, bring up the needle for one buttonhole stitch on the inside of the loop as it is made. Then make a second buttonhole stitch on the outside of the loop. This second stitch puts the working thread in correct position to begin the row of small, covering buttonhole stitches.

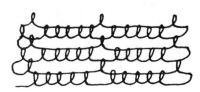

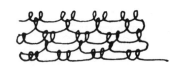

Filling Stitch 1

Open filling patterns with vertical stripes are easy to work. The type shown here is the simplest of all. To make it, begin with a row of buttonhole stitches worked close together. After the thread has been carried down the right perimeter with two buttonhole stitches, make the second row by working a buttonhole stitch in the loop of each sixth loop of the row above, working from right to left. Make the third row by fastening the thread to the left perimeter with one buttonhole stitch and working across from left to right, making five buttonhole stitches in each long loop of the second row. To make the fourth row, bring the thread into position with three buttonhole stitches on the right perimeter and make one buttonhole stitch between each group of five stitches in the row above. Essentially, the fourth row repeats the second row, and the fifth row repeats the third.

Normally this filling stitch is worked quite compactly; in the photograph the stitches have been left spread apart for greater clarity.

Filling Stitch 2

To make this filling pattern, begin with a row of close buttonhole stitches or work into existing adjacent work. In the first row, alternate groups of two buttonhole stitches with spaces large enough for three stitches. Work from left to right. In the second row, working from right to left, make three buttonhole stitches in the loops left between groups of stitches above, and make one buttonhole stitch in the loop made between the two buttonhole stitches of the first row. In the third row, working from left to right, make two buttonhole stitches, one on each side of the single buttonhole stitch of the row above. Do not make any buttonhole stitches in the loops of the groups of three stitches in the row above; this row essentially repeats the first row.

In this picture, the thread has been carried to position by buttonholing onto a *fil de trace*, but in other work you may prefer to overcast the thread into position.

Point de Brabançon

Point de Brabançon is one of the fancy striped filling patterns that are made by skipping stitches in regular sequence. To make it, alternate pairs of buttonhole stitches with long loops in the first row, which is worked from left to right. In the second row (right to left) work seven buttonhole stitches into each long loop and one buttonhole stitch into the loop of the pair above. In the third row, work one buttonhole stitch on each side of the single stitch in the previous row, but none into the loops of the seven-stitch groups. Essentially, the third row repeats the first row, and the fourth row is like the second.

Usually this stitch is worked very compactly. In this picture the stitches have been left loose so that the construction can be seen.

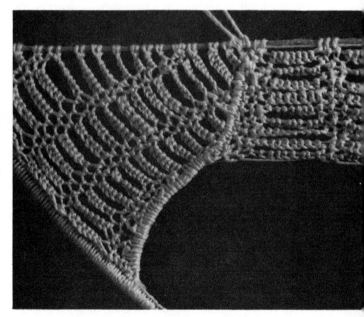

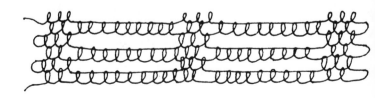

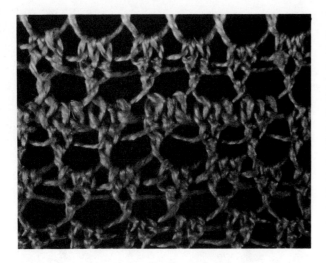

To begin patterns like these, make a row of closely set buttonhole stitches. In the second row of the top picture, each sixth stitch was skipped. This work, except for its pattern, proceeds exactly as *point de Bruxelles*, with rows worked left to right and then from right to left. In the third row, work the stitches into each loop made by stitches in the row above, but not into the bridging threads where stitches were skipped. Work the following rows in the same manner until only one stitch remains in each group. Then, in the next row, work buttonhole stitches onto the bridging threads to equal the number of stitches skipped. The number of stitches in this row should equal the number in the first.

When the pattern for this stitch is varied so that a lozenge shape, rather than a pyramid, is produced, the result is *point de Valenciennes* stitch. Obviously, the number of stitches in the first row of each group of pyramids or at the widest point of each lozenge effects the appearance of the stitch, as do the texture and weight of the thread.

Venetian or Tulle Stitch

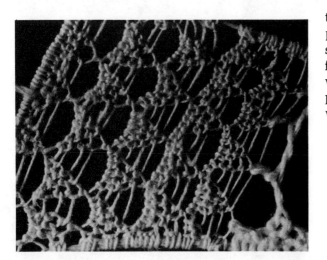

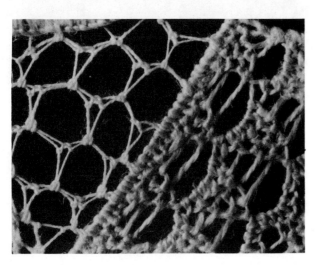

Venetian stitch, or tulle stitch pyramid variations.

Point de Valenciennes

Point de Valenciennes is a fancy filling stitch with buttonholed lozenge shapes. The filling can be dense or open, depending upon the spacing of the stitches and the weight of the thread.

Row 1—Make buttonhole stitches into a *fil de trace* or into a finished part of the lace. Space the stitches alternately quite far apart (wide enough to accommodate seven buttonhole stitches) and closer together (just wide enough for two buttonhole stitches).

Row 2—In the wide loop, make seven buttonhole stitches. Make no stitch in the smaller loop. Repeat across the row.

Row 3—Make six buttonhole stitches in the group of seven above; make two buttonhole stitches in the span between the groups of seven stitches in the row above; and repeat across the row.

Row 4—Make five stitches in six above, three stitches in the two above, and repeat.

Row 5—Make four stitches in the five above, four stitches in the three above, and repeat, keeping the diagonals in line.

Row 6—Make three stitches where there are four above and, for the next group, five stitches where there are four above, maintaining the diagonals. Repeat.

Row 7—Make two stitches where there are three above, and then six stitches where there are five above. Repeat.

Row 8—Make no stitches where there are two above; make seven stitches where there are six above; repeat across the row.

Row 9—Make two stitches where there are none above; make six stitches where there are seven above. (Diagonals now turn in the opposite direction.)

It should not be difficult for you to continue the pattern from this point.

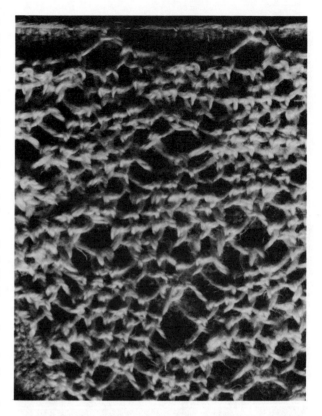

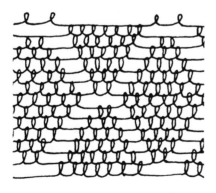

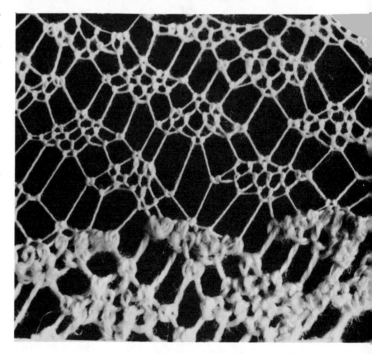

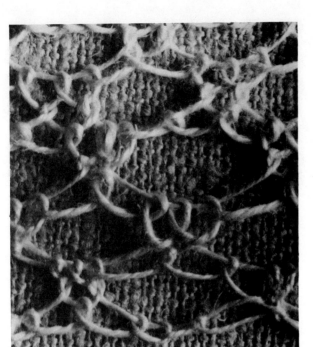

The perforated net stitch begins with a row of rather closely spaced buttonhole stitches, if worked onto an uncovered *fil de trace*. Otherwise, the pattern begins with row 2.

Row 2—Buttonhole stitch in two buttonhole stitches in row above; skip two buttonhole stitches in the row above; repeat.

Row 3—Buttonhole stitch three times in the loop made by the skipped stitches above, and make one buttonhole stitch between the two buttonhole stitches of the row above.

Row 4—Buttonhole stitch in the two loops made by the group of three buttonhole stitches in the row above, and skip to the next group of three above for the next two buttonhole stitches, in effect repeating row 2.

Repeat rows 3 and 4 for the pattern.

The effect of the perforated net stitch varies with how tight it is worked.

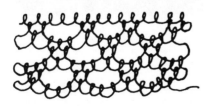

Spotted Filling Stitch

Begin this filling stitch by working groups of three buttonhole stitches alternating with spaces equal to the space required for the three stitches. To make the first row, which is worked from left to right, work three buttonhole stitches into the perimeter, and then make one or two stitches under the initial three and in the loop. (The picture here shows two stitches worked into the loop.) Skip a space and repeat the process. Make the second row (right to left) in the same way, but work the groups of stitches onto the loops remaining in the row above, where spaces were left. The third row is like the first.

Point de Venise

The stitch called *point de Venise* is worked on the odd rows, going from left to right. Work four tight buttonhole stitches onto each large, loose buttonhole stitch before you fasten the next large stitch into the perimeter. For even rows, work from right to left. In these rows, the buttonhole stitches do not have extra buttonhole stitches worked into them.

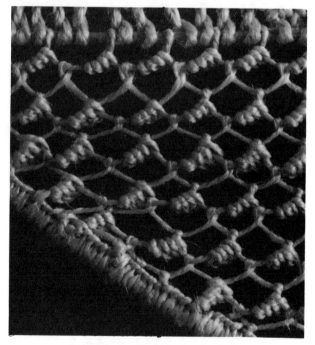

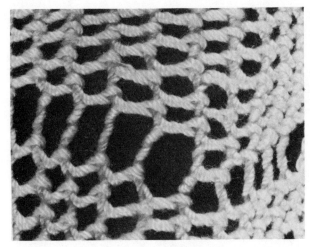

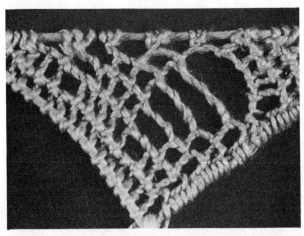

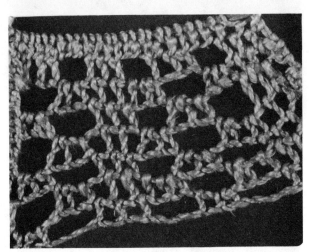

Begin *point d'Espagne* on the left. Bring the needle through the upper perimeter of the space to be filled, as you would for making a buttonhole stitch. With your left hand, hold the thread in a long loop to the right of the stitch that will be made. Weave the needle through this loop, first over the thread and then under it. Draw up the thread rather loosely to keep the stitches quite long. Continue the stitches to the right edge of the work. Overcast the thread to secure it and then twist the thread once into each loop made by the stitches of the row above until the thread is again on the left margin. For the third row, overcast the thread along the edge of the adjacent work until it is in position. Work the third row as you did the first.

Point d'Espagne can be worked from left to right in the first row and from right to left in the second for a less wiry filling called *double tulle*. Double tulle is often worked in fancy patterns, the variety of which is limited only by the imagination. The middle picture shows a version in which a progressively larger number of stitches were skipped, forming a pyramid. To make the version in the bottom picture, work the first row by alternating three stitches with a space about equaling that occupied by the three stitches. In the second row, skip a space under the first group of three stitches. Work three stitches into the space above; two stitches into the loops of the second group of three in the row above; and three stitches into the second open space of the first row. This leaves a space under the third group of three stitches in the first row as the pattern is repeated. The third row is like the first, and the fourth row is like the second.

Point d'Espagne

Greek Stitch

This large mesh can be used for backgrounds. Begin by working a row of stitches made in the manner of *point d'Espagne* from left to right. Space the stitches apart somewhat and keep the thread slack. For the second row, made from right to left, twist the thread four times around each loop (in overcasting stitch) so that the loop rounds. The third row is like the first and the fourth like the second. Unless the loops are fully twisted with thread, you will not form the hexes properly. As each left to right row is made, new stitches should be positioned to be in the center of the loop above.

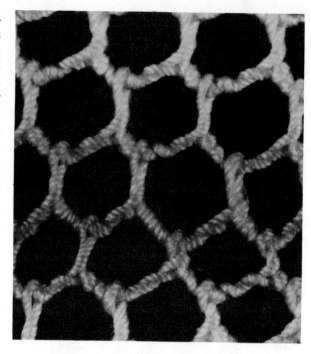

Point de Grecque

Point de Grecque is worked from left to right. To make it, work three *point d'Espagne* stitches close together on the upper edge. Leave a loop and work three more stitches. Continue alternating stitches and loops until you reach the right side. Overcast the thread back to the left side for the second row. In the second row, make three *point d'Espagne* stitches in each long loop of the row above, and work loops under the three stitches of the previous row. For an open, graceful filling, loops must be generous and even.

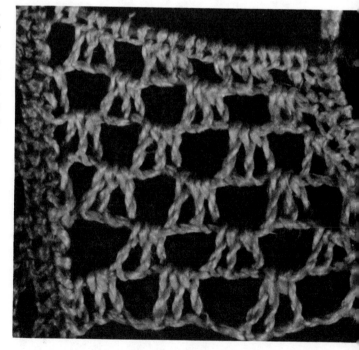

Called *point d'entoilage* in old laces, this stitch is used for cloth portions of lace. Begin working on the left. The first row consists of buttonhole stitches spaced somewhat loosely across the area to be filled. When you have completed the stitches to the right side, carry the thread back across to the left side and secure it at a point on a level with the bottom of the loops of the buttonhole stitches you made in the row above. Then repeat the first row; catch the laid thread into the stitches as you work them. Work every row from left to right.

Venetian Cloth Stitch 1

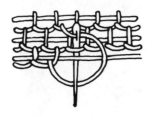

Work this indispensable stitch exactly as you worked the Venetian cloth stitch 1, but work the buttonhole stitches close together, making a very dense toile. Because you work all the buttonhole stitches in the same direction, the cloth has a very neat appearance and is quite textureless. This stitch was used for *point de gaze* and other laces as well as for Venetian lace. Another name for the stitch is *point noué*.

Venetian Cloth Stitch 2

Point de Grains

Point de grains, or seed stitch, looks like a group of connected picots or bullion stitches. In this picture, the stitch has been worked from left to right and then returned from right to left. Begin the stitch by attaching a long, loose buttonhole stitch to the upper perimeter of the area to be filled. Into this buttonhole stitch, work four additional buttonhole stitches, completing the first seed. Repeat the process for the pattern.

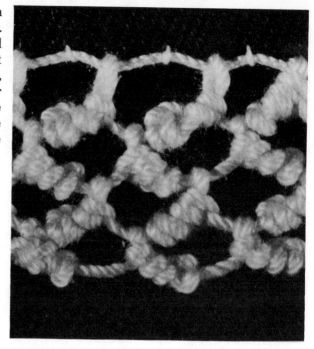

Filet Stitch

Like shuttle-made nets, this imitation of filet ground begins with a single mesh in one corner and is worked diagonally. Lay a loop of thread across one corner and overcast the thread into position for the next diagonal row. If desired, keep the loops even by pinning temporarily as the knots are made. Make a knot in the center of the first loop by carrying the thread over and then under the needle, as in the top picture, and then drawing it up tightly.

Care should be taken to keep the meshes even. A mesh made in this way can be decorated with any of the stitches used to decorate network, including *point d'espirit*.

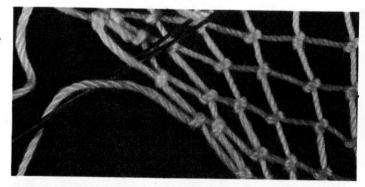

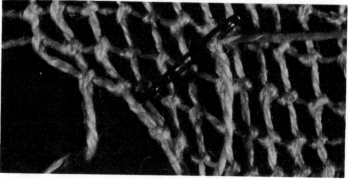

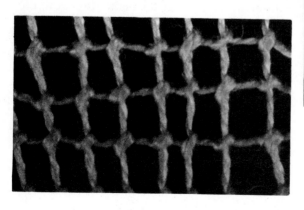

The stitch called *point d'Angleterre* has small wheels against a rectangular or square grid. To make it, lay double threads across a span in one direction in the spacing you want for the grid. While work is in progress, you may hold these threads in a vertical, horizontal, or diagonal direction, depending on your convenience. When you lay the crosswise threads of the grid however, you must lay them one at a time, always from left to right. The thread then passes from right to left. As it approaches each crossing, the thread is woven around the threads of the crossing twice (or as many times as desired) and is then carried on to the next crossing, where another wheel is made. As the thread moves from wheel to wheel, it crosses the thread that was previously laid in the same direction. When the row is finished, the thread is brought into position (by overcasting) for the next row, laid from left to right, and then worked back from right to left with wheels woven around each crossing.

In the most delicate examples of *point d'Angleterre*, only one thread is laid in the set of foundation threads. On the second passage of the thread (as the second row of wheels is made,) the thread is tightly twisted around the thread of the first passage.

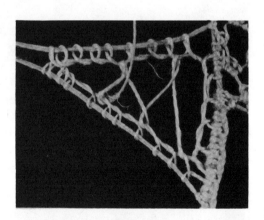

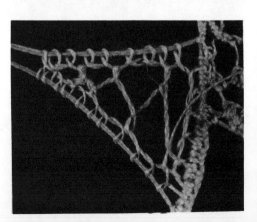

The stitch called *point Mechlin* begins with herringbone stitches in a framework that usually spans a narrow area. The herringbone stitch is overcast to strengthen the zigzagged foundation. As the overcasting stitches approach each angle of the herringbone stitches, the thread is worked around the angle, then buttonholed close all around to form a small ring.

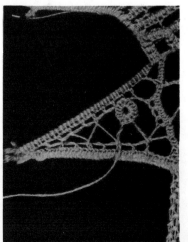

Spot-Circular Mesh Filling

This contemporary filling is akin to the snowflake and *oeil de perdrix* fillings that are to be found in both needle and bobbin laces. It consists of a series of spots with spokes radiating from each. To make it, section off with twisted bars the section to be filled. In each segment, work buttonhole stitches around the perimeter. Sometimes these buttonhole stitches are given an extra twist, as in *point d'Espagne*, and sometimes they are buttonholed along half the distance of their loops, but they are always overcast when the row is complete, and the overcasting thread is drawn up so that the corners of the shape are rounded. In this photograph, an outer row of buttonhole stitches was buttonholed halfway. A second row, inside the first, is buttonhole stitches with an extra twist. The remaining oval was filled with cloth stitch.

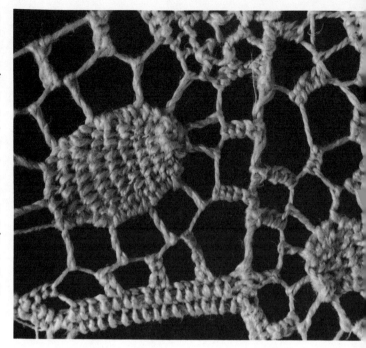

Point de Reprise

Point de reprise is identical in appearance to darning stitch, matting stitch and *armaletta*, stitches used in network, mixed laces, and even in bobbin lace. Sometimes this work is called needleweaving. In needlepoint laces the stitch is worked over a framework of threads. Often these are laid onto the area in herringbone stitch, overcast to reinforce the framework. Usually the area filled is quite small and the stitches are worked from side to side across the narrower dimension of the opening. Sections of the area transversed with the herringbone stitching are closely darned, forming triangular motifs. In other laces threads may be laid straight across an opening and a thread darned between pairs or woven into three or more threads.

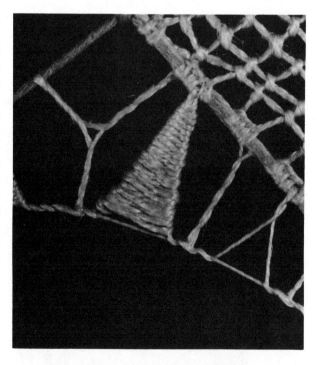

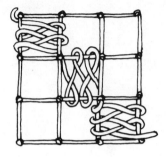

Needleweaving and darning on net are similar to these needle-lace techniques.

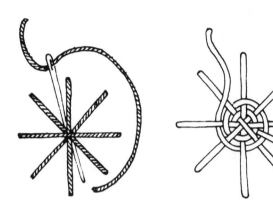

Woven wheels worked in darning stitch. Note Step 1 for the placement of the extra spoke needed for continuous weaving. Wheels also can be made with back stitch or stem stitch. When working with either of these stitches an uneven number of spokes is not required.

Point de reprise fillings are limited only by the imagination of the worker in the invention of laid thread frameworks for the stitch. To make the filling pictured here, lay three threads at intervals to cover the space to be filled, making the spacing even or irregular, depending on the design wanted. In laying the threads, be sure that a regular weaving sequence is maintained as the threads working in one direction cross those laid in the other direction. Then work a thread in *point de reprise* over all the laid threads. As you approach the woven intersections, overcast the working thread along one of the threads until the woven section has been passed. The *point de reprise* stitches may be worked loosely, as in this picture, or they may be packed close together for a solid filling with regularly spacing openings.

Point de Reprise Filling

Close Stitch with Openings

Small openings, usually in geometric arrangements, often can be found in areas of close (buttonhole) stitch. Work the openings into the cloth by skipping two or more buttonhole stitches as you work from left to right. The placing of the motifs is accomplished by counting stitches in the row above. When the working thread has reached the right boundary of the area being worked, lay it across to the left side. As you work the next row of buttonhole stitches (again from left to right), cover the laid thread and the bridging threads that remain where stitches were skipped in the row above with the buttonhole stitching. If you are going to skip stitches directly under other skipped stitches, twist the working thread around the laid thread and the loop from the skipped stitches as you come to these points. Carry the working thread, twisted around the laid thread, to the right. At the right edge of the opening, resume regular buttonhole stitching. If you are going to resume buttonhole stitching under the skipped stitches, add as many stitches as you previously skipped.

For very large areas or for complicated patterns, the design for the openwork can be drawn on the pattern under the work and followed without threadcounting.

Triangular Mesh Filling

You may make this filling with pairs of buttonhole stitches spaced either close together or farther apart. If you space the stitches apart, keep the spacing even by pinning the loops made between the pairs of stitches, using a ruled line on the pattern as a guide. Begin work on the left side, one stitch length below the upper perimeter thread. Make two buttonhole stitches on the upper thread. Leave the working thread in a slack loop, or pin it in place. Leave or pin a second loop and make a second pair of stitches on the upper thread. Continue this process across the first row. On the right perimeter, buttonhole the thread to secure it before you return it, as a laid thread, to the left side. On the left, buttonhole or overcast the working thread into position for another row. In making pairs of buttonhole stitches across the new row, catch both the laid thread and the loop between the buttonhole stitches of the first row into the stitches.

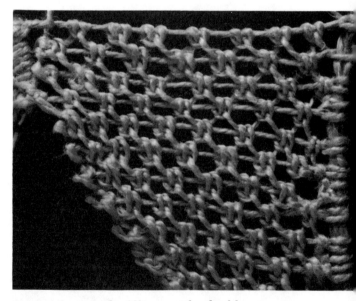

Triangular mesh filling with double buttonhole stitches.

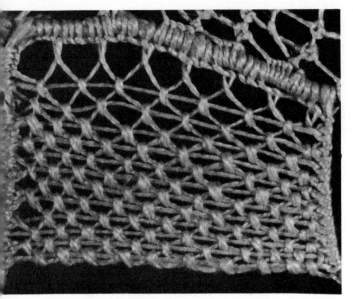

Point Turque can begin with a single loop in a
corner and be worked in diagonal rows, or a
row of loops can be buttonholed along one
edge of the area to be filled. The second row,
which goes from right to left, is simply a laid
thread put across the work at the lower edge
of the loops. The third row consists of knots
and loops. Make the knots at the point where
the laid thread and the loops of the first row
touch. Pass the needle under both loop and
laid thread and pass the working thread over
and then under the needle. Draw up the knots
tightly but leave a loop between them. Some
workers keep the loops even by pinning them
in position temporarily while the knots are
being made.

Point Turque

Filling Stitch 2

To make this attractive and rather bold filling, alternate groups of three buttonhole stitches with rather long loops. If it is difficult to keep the length of the loops even, mark their positions and pin them temporarily as work progresses. Begin as far down on the left edge of the space to be filled as the length of the loop is to be. Allow a little space at the end of the top row. Make three closely spaced buttonhole stitches; then make another loop. Continue with loops and groups of three stitches across the row. Bring the working thread down on the right side of the space by overcasting. Then make three buttonhole stitches in each loop until the working thread is on the left edge again. The thread between the stitches is not looped, but drawn up tight. In the third row, make three stitches into the three above, and leave loops between the groups of three stitches. Work the fourth row as you did the second.

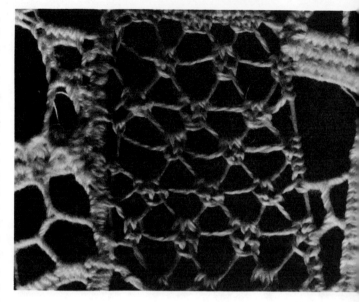

Hollie Stitch

Hollie stitch begins with a thread fastened at the right, laid across the top of the span to be filled, and secured at the left. The same thread is used to work hollie stitch from left to right. To make hollie stitch, begin with a buttonhole stitch, but leave it slack. With the left thumb hold a U-loop. Then weave the needle through the loop and the buttonhole stitch.

To make reserved-design patterns of hollie point, skip stitches in pairs following a thread-count diagram. Written stitch-by-stitch directions, which can be found in old lace books, are very long and involved. It is simpler to work following a pattern drawn on the foundation. Wherever lines occur in the pattern, skip two hollie stitches. In the next row, try to avoid putting two skipped stitches directly under two in the row above. Usually patterns for old hollie work avoided skipped stitches in vertical columns. A vertical line was generally zigzagged. Diagonals were more usual. In openwork areas a typical arrangement was a checkerboard of skipped and worked stitches.

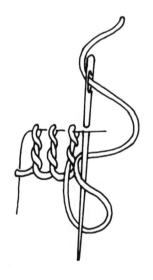

Bars (legs, *brides*) used in needle lace may be very delicate or quite substantial. To make a fragile, cordlike bar, overcast along one edge of the work to a point at which a bar is needed. Lay the working thread across the span at an appropriate angle (usually a right angle), insert the needle, and as you return the thread to the overcast edge, twist it around the stitch just made one or more times. Then continue overcasting to position for the next bar.

More substantial bars can be made by buttonholing the returning thread. Both twisted and buttonholed bars can be embellished with picots.

In arranging bars in large openings, large buttonhole-like stitches can be spaced around the edge. The stitches are like buttonhole stitches except that each is given an extra twist, which tends to enlarge it, and the working thread is twisted once into each stitch after the row is complete. When the thread is pulled tight, a row of precise meshes appears.

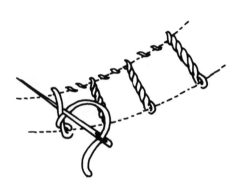

Bobbin Lace

It is customary to speak of needle lace as a lace composed of one thread and bobbin lace as composed of many threads. Bobbin lacemaking relates to weaving as needle lace relates to embroidery and is like weaving on a warp-weighted loom in that both are techniques in which many threads are in play simultaneously and are kept in order by the use of weights (or bobbins). In bobbin lace threads are twisted, plaited, and

A lacemaker at work in Bruges.

A Belgian lacemaker (Bruges) uses a convex lace pillow with up to 1,200 threads, sometimes more.

interwoven. Their solid parts look exactly like woven cloth. However, in the earliest examples solid areas were minimal, and the laces, frequently metal or stiff silk, look little different from the *passements* (braided trimmings, *passementeries*) that were their immediate antecedents.

How bobbin lace evolved is not known, but it seems to be related to several early thread-manipulating techniques. Many scholars consider the plaited work on Coptic headcoverings found in Egypt a forerunner of bobbin lace. This plaiting was made by a method similar to that used to make Scandanavian *sprang*, in which the worker stretches threads on a frame and then, with her fingers, twists them around one another

Doily of bobbin guipure. Belgium (Bruges), 1967.

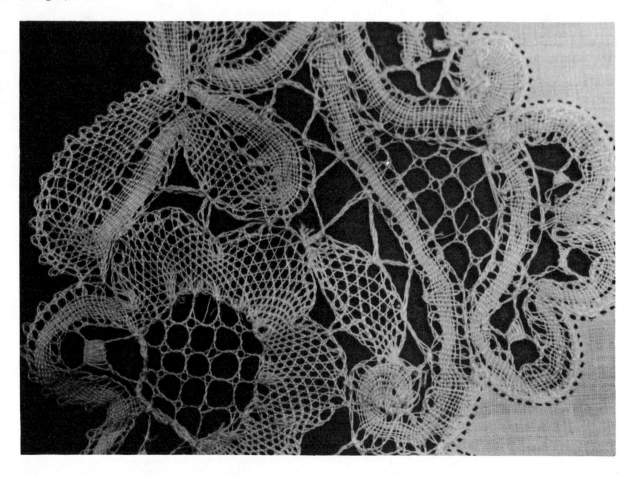

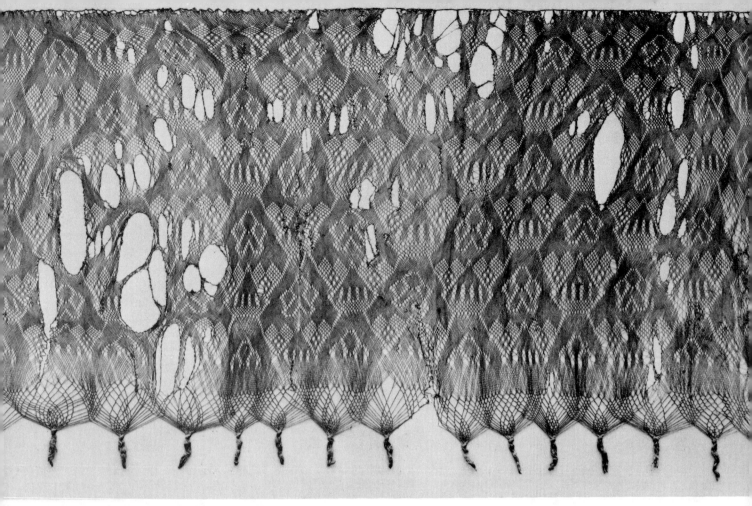

Border of sprang. England (London, Finsbury), c. 1450-1500. Courtesy: The Metropolitan Museum of Art. Gift of George F. Lawrence, 1928.

in orderly sequence so that a pattern is formed. The twists cause changes of position at both ends of the stretched warp. As the worker finishes each row, she holds the threads in position by slipping a stick between them. Then she makes another row. Patterns can be introduced by varying the order and direction of the twists. A distinctive characteristic of plaited work of this type is elasticity. It is the fact that the fabric is constructed of twisted threads that relates it to bobbin lace.

Other writers see connections between early macramé and bobbin lace. In the working procedures used, there are similarities between the two techniques. Both are laces in which many threads are in play simultaneously. Both are methods used to finish the fringed edges of fabrics. One researcher, Mrs. Nevill Jackson, thinks that when the pillow was introduced for *macramé*-making, bobbin lace was only a few steps away. The presumption is that in time the threads were plaited rather than knotted, a less tiring procedure, and that bobbins were introduced to keep the threads in order.

Many early bobbin laces were made according to patterns for needle lace, which were at that time still tied to the vertical and horizontal patterns of cutworks and *reticella*. These sixteenth-century bobbin laces made much use of plaits in their simulation of the effect of needle lace "points." (Compare the pictures here with those in the "Needle Lace" chapter.) The open, geometric patterns of these sharply zigzagged bobbin edgings can be seen on the lace ruffs of sixteenth- and seventeenth-century portraits.

When Venice was the leading center of needle lacemaking in the sixteenth and seventeenth centuries, Genoa headed the list of bobbin lacemaking cities. By the fifteenth century gold thread was being imported into Genoa from Cyprus. From Genoa *passements* (braided trimmings) made of Cyprian gold threads were widely exported. Simple bobbin trimmings developed from the plaited *passements*. As technique grew more complex, figures made with the threads needed to be pinned down to hold their form as work advanced. It is not surprising that the earliest true bobbin laces were made of metal thread. Genoese laces were widely exported and were in use in England and on the Continent until the third quarter of the seventeenth century, when they finally began to decline.

In the early seventeenth century, bobbin laces were also made in Milan. Milanese bobbin laces were similar in design to the Venetian needle laces made in the same period.

In Flanders, bobbin lacemaking began early. Both bobbin and needle laces of the finest quality were being produced in Brussels and the Brabant in the sixteenth century. Woodcuts made in 1580–81 by Martin de Vos, De Bruyn, and Van Londerseel show pillow lacemaking in progress. Queen Mary of Hungary, the sister of Charles V, became Governess of the Low Countries in 1530. Beginning with her rule, lacemaking was taught in the schools of the region, continuing even during the religious persecutions and economic upheavals of the sixteenth century.

The laces of Brussels and the Brabant were popular from the outset. By 1662 so much Brussels lace was being purchased in England that Parliament passed legislation forbidding its importation. Still, Charles II used a great deal of it himself. In an effort to meet the competition, English lace manufacturers brought foreign lacemakers into their companies. In addition, European lacemakers were among the many religious refugees who went to England in the seventeenth century.

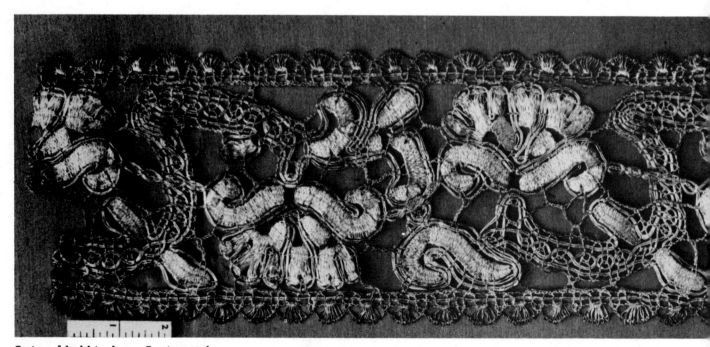

Strip of bobbin lace. Spain, 17th century. Courtesy: The Metropolitan Museum of Art. Rogers Fund, 1909.

Smuggling was a serious problem. It was not difficult to hide small quantities of lace in coffins, parasols, books, bakery goods, and even on babies. Larger amounts required different means of concealment. It is generally believed that the lace called *point d'Angleterre* (a term originating in French inventories, according to most theories) was really Flemish bobbin lace that was brought into England illegally and listed as English point on bills of lading. However, Mrs. Nevill Jackson argues that *point d'Angleterre* originated as an English lace and that the Flemish product was ordered as a means of filling commissions that could not be accommodated by English craftsmen. However and wherever they came to be made, most of the laces known today as *point d'Angleterre* were made of Flemish threads, according to Flemish patterns.

In France, both bobbin and needle lacemaking were established in the Normandy lacemaking region. Around Dieppe and Le Havre, lacemaking was a prevailing industry from the 1660s on. Often the wives of sailors were lacemakers. By the end of the seventeenth century there were 20,000 women employed in the industry, and in the eighteenth century production increased. Many different kinds of lace were made.

For about three centuries making bobbin lace was a clean, genteel occupation for thousands of women. Women who made lace were paid in cash for a highly marketable commodity. Some were well-paid, but most worked for low wages for overlong hours in ill-lit rooms. Some went blind at an early age, and the poor working conditions threatened their health. Still, women continued to weave webs of increasing fragility through wars and political upheavals, often keeping households stable when men could not find work or during wars when their husbands were wounded or away at battle.

Although lace now seems a luxury, hardly a product to depend upon for support in hard times, in the seventeenth and eighteenth centuries supply could barely meet demand. Not only women, but young boys, men too old to pursue more arduous work, and fishermen beached by heavy weather made lace. It was not until fashionable gentlemen stopped wearing laces in the late eighteenth and early nineteenth centuries that any significant decline in the industry occurred. Unlike needlepoint lace, a preoccupation of ladies of leisure as well as of professional lacemakers, bobbin lace apparently had little appeal as a pastime for gentlefolk.

Bobbin lace samples. Courtesy: Mary McPeek.

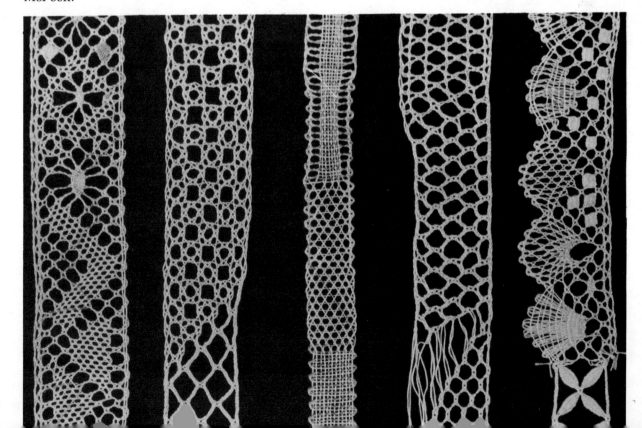

The mode of production did not change very much over the years, but the manner of selling was a different story. Until the middle of the seventeenth century, peddlers sold laces. Buyers were especially vulnerable after a good meal, and evening hours at eating places were good moments for the lace sellers. From Elizabeth's time on shops and private lacemakers worked on special orders for the privileged. Laces were also sold by their makers or their families at fairs. In Italy the business began to centralize. Agents of lace firms met the cottage lacemakers at a central market to collect the laces for sale.

The French Revolution disrupted most of France's important lace centers, scattering the workers. The day of the awesome techniques of the eighteenth century was at an end. Simpler laces continued to find a market, but technique was disintegrating, the final blow coming with the introduction of machine-made net.

In many places lacemaking schools were established to stave off the economic depression that was prevalent in the nineteenth century. In the Italian town of Burano, for example, the winter of 1872 was particularly severe. With fishing fleets unable to take to the sea, other means of livelihood for the town had to be found. At first fishermen's nets were made—a poor endeavor, since there were no customers for nets. Then a lacemaking school was established by Princess Chigi-Giovanelli and Countess Andriana Marcello. Burano had been an important lacemaking center as early as the sixteenth century, but its industry had declined. By 1882, eight years after the establishment of the Burano school, there were 320 lacemakers in Burano making needle and bobbin laces of many kinds. Other Italian towns undertook similar ventures, leading to the *Industrie Femminili Italiane*. In New York, when hard times threatened Italian families, another school was set up where teen-aged Italian girls copied lace and lace-like embroideries.

In Czechoslovakia, Austria, and Hungary, arts and crafts schools undertook the designing of new patterns for old techniques. In Hungary Archduchesss Isabella, Countess Ilona Batthyany, and others involved themselves in a home lacemaking industry, with the help of the government. A good business in bobbin lace was started.

In 1904 there were still 47,500 lacemakers in Belgium, the majority in East and West Flanders. There were 160 lace schools, three-quarters of them in convents. The industry was divided into three levels: the contractor, the middleman, and the lacemaker, who was a cottage worker. In many instances the "middleman" was a convent. Pierre Verhaegen wrote that a lacemaker was paid about ten pence for an eleven-and-one-half-hour workday.

Czechoslovakia, like Belgium, is one of the countries where lacemaking continues to be taught in schools today, and the maintenance of the lace industry in the twentieth century in that country has been systematic. In the early twentieth century, the State Institute provided artistic training in an effort to promote cottage industry, and there were similar ventures at the Dětva, Bratislava, and the Źadruha, Prague. The State Institute supervised thirty-three courses in various lacemaking regions. The girls and women who took the courses made their own designs and also copied complicated patterns sent out by the Institute for them to work. Flax, wool, silk, and linen threads were used. Colors and gold and silver were introduced into geometric and simplified floral designs. Madame Sedláčková-Serbousková was an outstanding designer. Also in the vanguard was Madame Paličková-Mildeová, whose patterns are acclaimed all over Europe.

The works of Emilie Paličková are known to many people through the exhibition of her work at Expo 58, Brussels. The evolution of her design parallels that of many painters and graphic artists whose exhibiting years began in the second decade of the twentieth century. Many contemporary Czech lacemakers were students of or have been influenced by Madame Paličková.

Lacemakers in countries like the United States, where no formal training on an accredited level is available, should find the experience of a professional lacemaker in Czechoslovakia of interest. In Prague a young woman may study at the School of Applied Arts in the special studio for lace. Later, she can go on to work in the Institute

Doily of bobbin lace. Russia, 20th century. Courtesy: Mary Lou Keuker.

Design adapted from a collar by Frau Hoffmaninger (one repeat only).

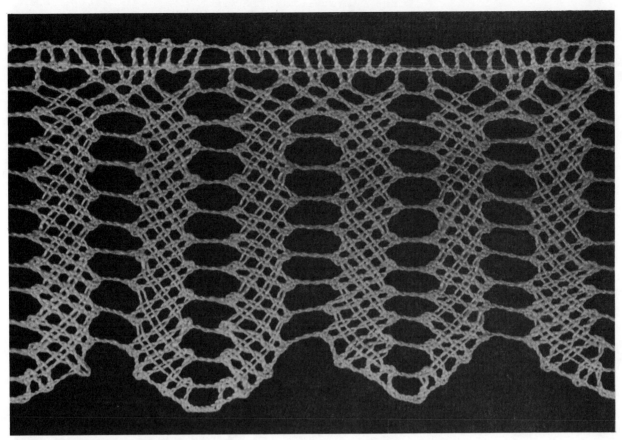

Border of bobbin lace. Contemporary,
Germany. Made for sale.

of Housing and Clothing Culture, where she can learn, among other things, how to design for machine techniques and knitted laces. With schooling finished, she may decide to be a teacher, or she can design for industrial production of lace curtains, dress laces, or similar items. Very likely she will continue her interest in hand-made laces.

After the last splendid art nouveau designs of the early twentieth century, the development of lacemaking as a modern art seems to end, despite the fact that at certain unique centers a few exquisite traditionally designed laces continued to be made and that in a few more places good, simple laces that could be sold at low cost have been made on an industrial basis.

Possibly lace was a victim of the "less-is-more" philosophy, or perhaps it suffered because it was a reminder of autocracy. The dwindling demand for lace was finally erased, in the United States at least, by the Depression. Who could afford imported luxuries then? Still, many people over fifty can remember seeing bolts of good handmade lace in dry goods stores as late as the early forties. Satiny bobbined edgings and insertions in many widths and patterns were still available for finishing embroidered linens and for other uses, but they were going out of style rapidly.

But now more and more textile designers are again studying laces for reasons other than their historical significance. A limited number of these craftsmen already have begun to show how traditional techniques of bobbin lacemaking can be used to create a contemporary phase of the art.

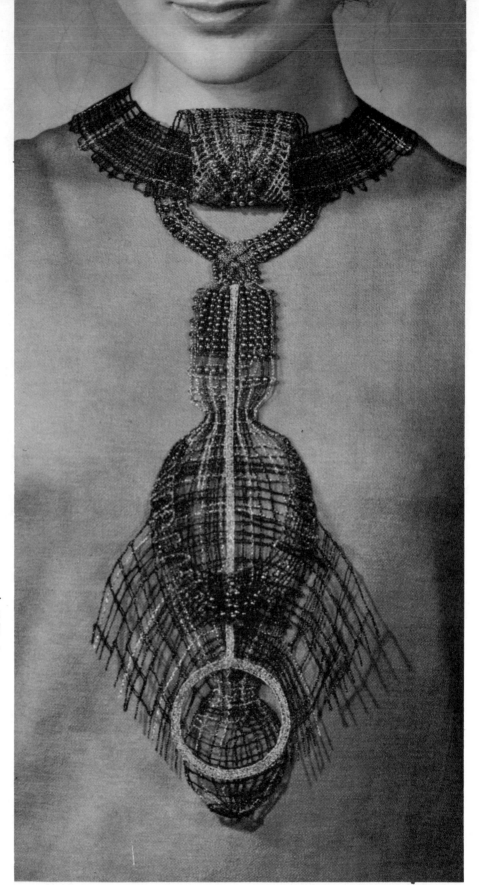

Jewelry by Marie Vaňková-Kuchynková. 1971. Bobbin lace. Gold threads, old gold threads, yellow line, pearls. Courtesy: Artist.

Photo by Jar. Sirový

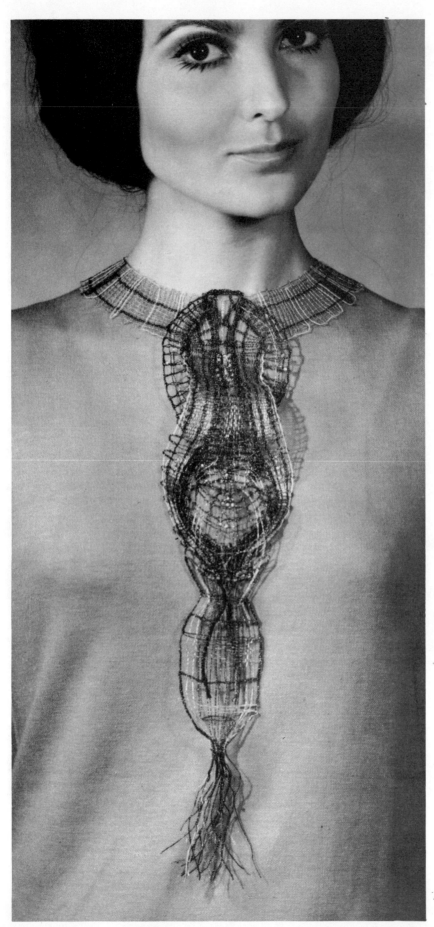

Jewelry by Marie Vaňková-Kuchynková. 1971. Bobbin lace. Old gold, gold threads, black line, pearls. Courtesy: Artist.

Photo by Jar. Sirový

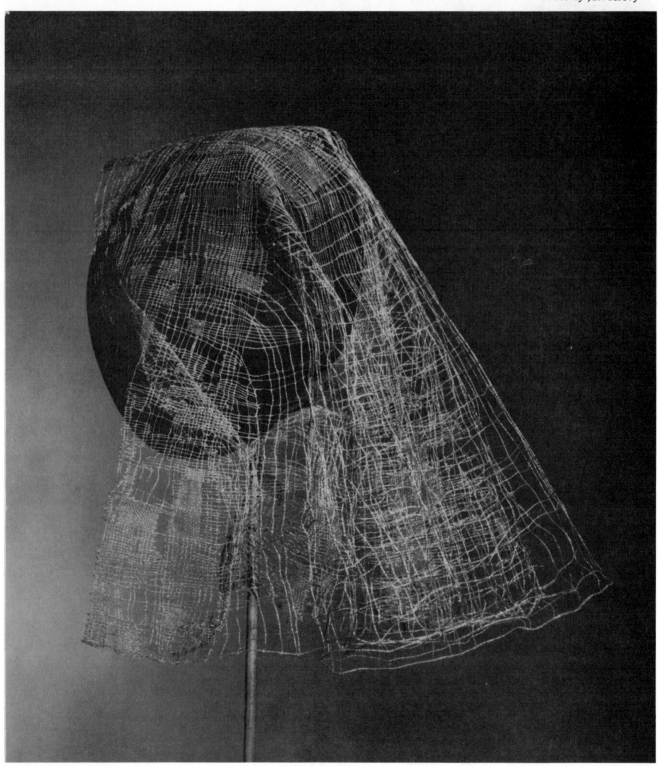

Headcovering by Marie Vaňková-Kuchynková. Bobbin lace. Gold and silver threads, pearls. Courtesy: Artist.

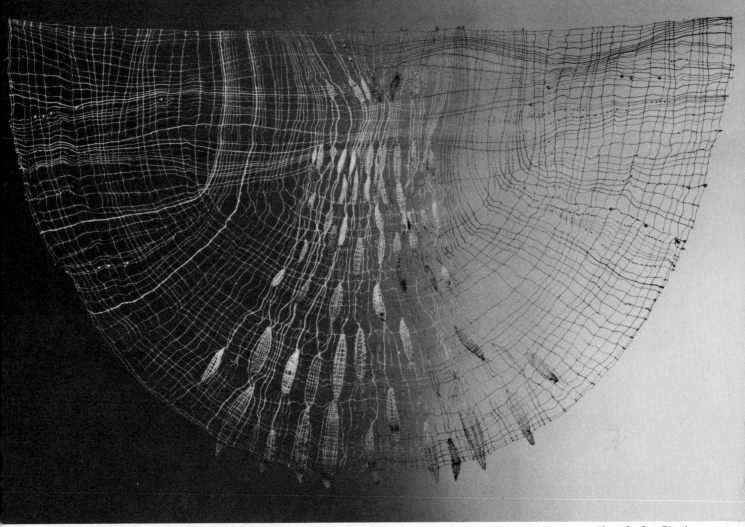

Photo by Jar. Sirový

Headcovering by Marie Vaňková-Kuchynková. Bobbin lace. Gold and silver threads, natural linen, pearls. Courtesy: Artist.

Bracelet by Jaroslav Prášil. 1971. Bobbin lace. Flax, pearls. Courtesy: Artist.

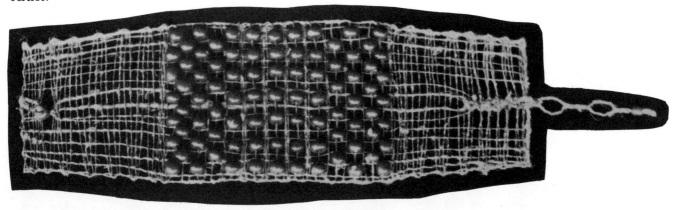

Photo by Jar. Siroý

Tablecloth by Marie Vaňková-Kuchynková. 1972. Bobbin lace. Lace made of threads of the machine-made material. Courtesy: Artist.

Curtain by Jiřina Trojanová-Pavlitová.
1964. Bobbin lace. Flax. Courtesy: Artist.

Sampler by Judith W. Carr. Bobbin lace. Linen. 6 x 19 inches. Courtesy: Artist.

162

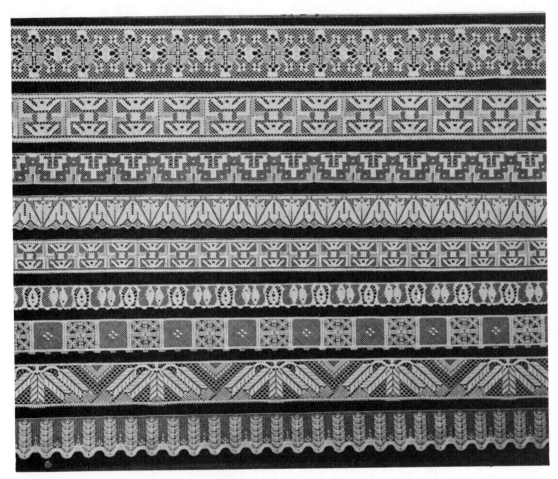

Borders of bobbin lace. From Fören-
inger Svenska Spetsar, Linköping,
Sweden. Designers, top to bottom:
Märta Afzelius, Märta Afzelius, Elin
Peterson, Birgit Lennartsson, Märta
Afzelius, Märta Afzelius, Greta Sand-
berg, Greta Sandberg, Greta Sandberg.
Courtesy: Föreninger Svenska Spetsar,
Linköping, Sweden.

Patterns and Designs for Bobbin Lace

The design of bobbin lace is affected crucially by the two different techniques that are used in making the lace. The first technique, the one most closely allied to the origin of bobbin lace in *passementerie* and braid making, is called *straight lace, fil continu,* or *one-piece lace.* In this lace, solid portions, background, and fancy fillings are all made simultaneously. All the bobbins that will be used in making the lace are hung onto the top of the pattern at the beginning of the work. The design must therefore be worked out in entirety before work is begun. Although individual methods of making straight lace patterns differ in the amount of working detail they show, all carefully indicate every point at which a pin will have to hold intersecting threads in place. From the pattern a pricking is made as a guide in placing pins as the actual work proceeds. Most simple straight-lace procedures are carried out by beginning in the upper left corner and working from pinhole to pinhole in diagonal rows until the lower right corner is reached. Often the work zigzags around elements of the design, an entire area being completed before the adjacent, differing configuration is started.

Since in most straight laces no bobbins are added or taken away in the course of the work, patterns must be worked out in such a way that cloth stitch elements can be added satisfactorily as the mesh ground ends and the cloth area begins. If the mesh is very open, the cloth parts will be loosely woven, because there are few bobbins available. Thus, there is a relationship between mesh and cloth that must be taken into account in making the design and in choosing the thread for it. For example, *Chantilly* is a straight lace that has a delicate mesh ground requiring few threads. The cloth parts of *Chantilly*, therefore, are very open; in fact, an outlining thread is introduced to accentuate the delicate contours. On the other hand, *Binche* and *Valenciennes* laces have closely worked cloth areas, comparatively speaking, and correspondingly, the grounds for these laces require a great number of threads. Therefore, necessity as well as esthetics governs the combination of ground, fillings, and mesh in these laces.

The straight laces include sixteenth-and seventeenth-century Venetian, Genoese, and other Italian bobbin laces, *Point de Paris, Binche, Valenciennes, Mechlin, Lille, Chantilly, Blonde, Dieppe,* Buckingham Point, Bedford, Maltese, *Cluny,* and *Le Puy* laces, as well as the Italian, Russian, and other domestic laces that are made universally.

The second type of bobbin lace is called *free lace, à pièces rapportées,* or *pieced lace.* Two simple techniques not used in straight lace make the difference. The first process has an ambiguous name: "sewing" or *crochetage.* This term does not mean stitching with needle and thread, but a joining of threads using a needle-pin or, although experts frown on it, a crochet hook. In making free lace the tool is in constant use. By this method parts of lace are joined and new bobbins are hung in. A series of sewings can maneuver bobbins from place to place, avoiding the necessity of cutting them off. This process is called "rope sewing." The effect it produces is sometimes mistaken for a *cordonnet.*

Another technique used in free laces involves *raccroc* stitch (*point de raccroche*). The introduction of this stitch, which was invented by M. Cahanet, was revolutionary in the development of free laces. *Raccroc* stitch is used to join widths of mesh invisibly. Before its invention, mesh areas were not very wide, from about three-quarters of an inch to a few inches, depending on the technique being used. After *raccroc* stitch came into use these narrow widths could be joined and designs of larger scale could be made. *Raccroc* was worked so expertly that it is usually impossible to detect without magnification.

With these two procedures, sewings and *raccroc* stitch, very large laces could be attempted. Not only could the lace be made in parts, but it could be made by a group of specialists, most of them, as the industry evolved, having no idea how the finished lace would look. That eighteenth- and nineteenth-century laces are so cohesive in scale and technique is remarkable, considering the blind assembly line process that produced them. At the top of the industrial organization were designers and merchants who had no real contact with the actual lacemaking. A middleman parceled out various jobs and saw to it that the lace parts conformed to the design. Workers, constantly repeating their own specialties, became fast and adept.

Some of the pieced laces include seventeenth- and eighteenth-century Italian and Spanish laces of the continuous braid type (Milanese, *Maglia di Spagna*, and others having motifs touching or on bar or net grounds); Brussels, *point d' Angleterre*, and other eighteenth-century Flemish pillow laces with *vrai droschel* ground and various fillings; Brussels appliqué; *Duchesse*; and Honiton.

The designs of the early straight laces were geometric or had reversed repeats. A limited number of basic, geometric motifs appear in domestic laces, although these motifs, (lozenges, spirals, spiders, leaves or seeds, triangles and others), are combined in an infinite number of ways. When floral patterns originally appeared in straight laces they were starkly simple and geometrically abstract, but in time lacemakers learned to adjust patterns and threads so skillfully that naturalistic and exceedingly complicated patterns could be worked.

Obviously, in straight lace the easiest pattern to work is a narrow edging or insertion, because it involves comparatively few bobbins. Most straight laces are rather narrow yardage, but extraordinary flounces of complicated design were also made. As a rule, the large bobbin laces, shawls, dresses, parasol covers, mantillas, and other articles were free, pieced laces. Jabots and lappets were excellent shapes on which to work out compositions not possible on an edging, but not too large to be made as straight lace. These popular eighteenth-century items of dress were made in both types of bobbin lace and, of course, needle lace as well.

The mechanical nature of bobbin lacemaking tended to flatten and simplify needle lace patterns, which, when worked as intended in needle lace, usually had raised effects. For example, notice that there is not a great deal of difference in the underlying pattern of relatively flat Milanese bobbin lace (page 169) and sculptural needle-made *gros point* (page 75). Both reflect the prevailing mood in Italy for long, rather narrow, undulating leaves in synthetic pattern, scrolls, and fanciful figures.

Genoese and Other Early Plaited Laces

The drawn-wire and other metal laces of Genoa were simple in design. Patterns were geometric and did not strain the stiff "threads" into unduly intricate configurations. An amount of *cartisane*, a material similar to the "plate" used by embroiderers, was worked into some designs. This material was a flat, metal strip. In general the more *cartisane*, the less desirable the lace, because often the thick strips were used to fill in the pattern quickly. Better laces were worked more carefully and with smaller threads. Metal-wound threads with a silk core were also used. The same type of pattern used for these laces was used for polychrome *guipures*. (*Guipure* in this case meaning a lace "without a background," as defined by E. van Overloop. In French terminology the word sometimes may designate a lace with a net ground.) Instead of pure metal, metal on parchment, or silver gilt over the fiber core, workers used colored silk wound onto the core to make the polychrome laces.

The most easily identified of the Genoese laces are those in which the designs are produced largely of four-thread plaits. At first the makers of bobbin lace used needle lace patterns. They carefully copied the triangles and seedlike shapes of *reticella* using matting stitch, called *armalletta*. A characteristic form for the stitch to take was a pointed oval. The shape is variously described as an oat, a seed, a grain of wheat, a leaf, or a paddle. It has even been called "fat." The stitch appears in many laces other than those of Genoa, particularly in Milanese, Torchon, and nineteenth-century Maltese, the designs of which were based on the earlier Genoese laces and even earlier needle-made *reticellas*. In English the stitch is most commonly called "leaf stitch."

The first Genoese borders had pointed or Van Dyked edges as did the needle laces, but later deep scallops replaced the points. The linen threads used for Genoese laces came from Sàlo and were said to be "fat in body." In *La revolte des passements*, the French poem so valuable for its listing of and comments on the laces of its day, Genoese threads were said to have *le corps un peu gros*.

Point de Gènes Frisé or *merletto a piombini* was widely imitated. In Spain it was called *Hispano-Moresque*, or Greek lace. A Spanish version, also plaited, had rounded points and curvilinear motifs set against a rectilinear ground.

A splendid coverlet, thought to have been made for Philip IV of Spain, is Flemish work. Although it is a free rather than a straight lace, I have included it with the Genoese laces because it is very Latin in spirit and design, as if the designs in *Le Pompe* (1557) had been carried to their logical conclusion. The border of the coverlet has points, reflecting early needle lace design that preceded scalloped borders.

Designs adapted from Genoese plaited laces.

Border of bobbin lace. Italy (Genoa), early 17th century. Courtesy: The Metropolitan Museum of Art. Rogers Fund, 1909.

*Cover (detail). Bobbin lace. Flanders.
Thought to have belonged to Philip IV
of Spain. Courtesy: Victoria and Albert
Museum, London.*

Panel of Milanese à brides. Italy (Milan), 17th century. Courtesy: Victoria and Albert Museum, London.

Milanese and Other Continuous Braid Laces

Milanese laces (*punto de Milano*) are strong in pattern and essentially simple in technique. Although they are pieced laces, they are not as technically complicated as the pieced laces of Flanders. The reason for their relative simplicity can be seen most easily in the earliest type of Milanese lace, which had highly stylized ornaments devised of thick serpentine outlines and decorative fillings. The heavy outlines were handled as continuous line designs, the thick line never varying much in width. This type of design was translated into lace by rendering the wide contour as a continuous tape of cloth stitch (see page 245). The tape was made with a row of meshes along each edge, and into these meshes the background bars or net were worked, keeping the edge of the cloth part of the tape clear of the ridges and irregularities that would have appeared if the groundwork had been hooked directly into the cloth stitch part of the tape.

Thirty-six or thirty-eight bobbins were often used in making the braids of the original Milanese laces. Seven pairs were used for the cloth stitch, and six pairs were used at each side for the openwork. Continuous braid laces have been made at other times and in other places using far fewer bobbins. Nineteenth-century versions made in rural Russia, Spain, and elsewhere were sometimes made with twelve bobbins.

Braids of Milanese laces and others similar to them were not always of unvarying width. Extra bobbins could be hung in at the center of the tape to swell the line, or the bobbins could simply be spread a little for a slight variation. The plain cloth tape could be enlivened with holes and stripes made by twisting threads in certain ordered sequences.

Some Milanese laces, usually early ones, had no background. These laces were designed in such a way that the motifs touched in enough places so that the lace was perfectly stable. In these laces, called *Raphaellesca*, extra meshes can be detected. The extra meshes are usually the reason for the special charm of *Raphaellesca*; they tend to "round out" the background shapes, simplifying them and reducing the dominance of the primary shapes. The result is a pleasant abstraction of the familiar scrolling leaf and stylized flower composition ever-present in Italian laces.

Many early Milanese laces had cloth stitch braids that varied little. They were decorated here and there with little holes and zigzags of twists. When the motifs did not touch as in *Raphaellesca*, their backgrounds were series of plaited bars zigzagged from motif to motif and sewn to the motif each time that motif and plait touched. Within the motifs a variety of fancy fillings were used—leaves, squares, dots, and bars worked in matting stitch. Other fillings were variations of the "spider" motif. Instructions for some of these fillings appear in the instruction section of this chapter.

Eventually Milanese laces, like all laces of the eighteenth century, were grounded with mesh instead of bars. In Milanese laces the *réseau* appeared about 1664, when the lace was also characterized by its straight edge. Various grounds were used, among them the *réseau* called *round-meshed Valenciennes*, which is seen in the eighteenth-century example presented here.

There was a shortcut form of Milanese, too. To make it straight tapes were woven first. These were basted to the pattern, gathering or pleating to make curves and turns. The fillings and grounds were needle made. Such laces were called *Milanese au lacet* or *mezzo punto*. They can always be recognized by the gathers in the tapes and by their needlepoint fillings.

Continuous braid laces were made in many places besides Milan. Fine ones were produced in Genoa, and they were also especially good in Spain and Russia, where they were frequently rendered as straight (*fil continu*) lace edging having broad scallops. The

Sleeve (detail). Milanese à reseau.
Italy (Milan), 18th century.

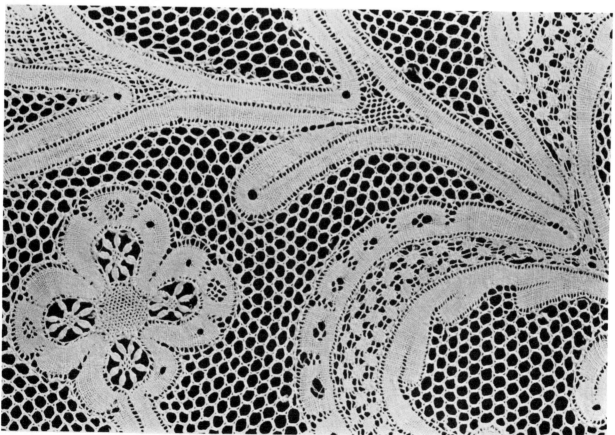

design usually runs a repeated, symmetrical, serpentine course in a never-ending broad line.

The Russian laces made in continuous braid technique are especially interesting to the contemporary lacemaker. The implements used to make them have changed little since early times, when they were pinned with thorns and made with simple stick bobbins. No doubt no one makes laces with thorns anymore, but the bobbins have sensibly remained straight and unadorned, because the intricate convolutions of Russian designs require endless sewings, which are most easily made with a straight bobbin.

The Russian laces have some interesting adaptable features. Sometimes two colors are used in hanging on the passive threads. Bridges or bars may be made with cloth stitch instead of with twists, and they may have picots. Designs not unlike those of Milanese may be made in two or more colors on a white or colored ground. Roosters, double-headed eagles, peacocks, lions, and trees of life were favorite motifs in these boldly patterned laces. For example, in one Russian lace a large rooster with an outline of cloth stitch had a filling of large leaves arranged checkerboard fashion. In other laces the sizes of threads used may not be uniform. A heavy gimp thread laid down the center of the continuous tape gives some laces a unique look. Other braid laces differ in being made rather loosely in thin threads, which gives this type of lace a diaphanous look.

Pattern for bobbin lace adapted from photo on opposite page. Note details showing where cloth stitch should be interrupted and half stitch substituted.

Border of Milanese à reseau. Italy (Milan), late 17th-early 18th century. Cardinal's Coat of Arms. Linen. 6½ inches wide. Courtesy: Art Institute of Chicago. Gift: Mrs. Edward E. Ayer.

Design for contemporary continuous braid lace in the manner of the table mats of Emilie Palicková.

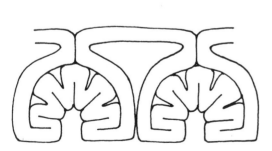

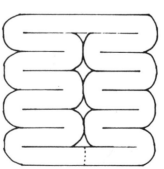

Pattern derived from Russian lace.

Pattern derived from Russian lace.

*Doily by Mary McPeek. Continu-
ous braid with plaiting.*

Fragment of bobbin lace. Italy, 19th century. Courtesy: Art Institute of Chicago.

Brussels, Brabantine, and Other Complex Free Laces

The earliest bobbin laces made in Belgium were apparently continuous braid types having motifs touching or with bar grounds, now sometimes called "pillow *guipures*," and technically about the same as those made in Genoa and Milan. Some of this early lace (*kant*) had a heavy gimp outline (*trolle*), and therefore it was called *trolle kant*.

Later Brabant pillow laces have slightly shaded effects produced by working cloth and half stitches closer and closer together or farther and farther apart. In some areas of the lace cloth stitches may be very densely packed. It is possible to manipulate threads in this way when the lace being made is a free lace. Bobbins can be cut out or hung in at will. In the complex designs of these laces, it was best whenever possible to avoid cutting the bobbins off. Therefore, when it was necessary to move a group of bobbins from one position to another, a rope sewing was made (see page 247). This technique produces a slightly raised effect along the course the bobbins travel, an effect that may be as decorative as it is useful. Rope sewings are subtly employed in Flemish laces and possibly are confused at times with *cordonnets*. In addition, these laces have rich fillings, such as *fond à la vierge* (maiden's net) intricate interchanges of threads called *armures*, or fillings spotted with buds or shells.

For compositions involving this amount of detail, shaded and textured drawings were sometimes made to show the effect of the fillings. An explicit line drawing that showed exactly where each ornament was to be was always made. Such a drawing was a necessity when the work could be carried out by more than one lacemaker. With several people at work on a single lace item, a large piece could be planned.

Bar-grounded laces were discontinued about mid-eighteenth century. The ground consisting entirely of bars disappeared from fashion so completely that after 1761 it had to be specially ordered. Instead a *vrai réseau* or *droschel* ground was used. Usually this hexagonal ground was worked with meshes twisted on four sides, the other two sides plaited four or more times. The ground was made in sections about three-quarters of an inch to an inch wide and about seven inches long. After the introduction of *point de raccroc* it was possible to piece together sections of *vrai réseau* imperceptibly. The joining was made with a needle; in English the process is called *fine joining*. *Raccroc* was a specialty of the lacemakers of Brussels and Bayeux. Instructions for the *raccroc* stitch are on page 256.

Sometimes the grounding of a lace was a mixture of net and bars, and needle-made grounds were used also. If the ground was made with a needle, the phrase *à l'aiguille* was added to the name of the lace. If a bobbin ground was used, the phrase *au fuseau* was added. A needle-made ground was three times as expensive as a bobbin ground. Not only the grounds of bobbin laces were made sometimes *à l'aiguille*; flowers in the assemblage might also be needle made.

In making the intricate motifs of Brussels lace, two sizes of pins were used. Large pins were used at margins to keep edges straight, while smaller pins were used within the design to keep spacing even.

Maximum efficiency and proficiency were achieved by alloting one process only to each worker. Each specialist, working the same part of each lace repeatedly, eventually learned to complete complex techniques very rapidly.

Since some of the workers saw only the parts of the lace that they made themselves, the cohesiveness of the design as a whole depended upon the ability of the overseer to exact work made precisely as indicated by the designer. Thus, this technique, so full of potential for individual expression, remained relatively unexplored, because the goal was, of necessity, uniformity.

Relief effects were a natural development in a lace that is an assemblage of parts. Cordonnets, rope sewings, and lace-over-lace built the surface to delicate, embossed richness. The laces were even modeled. A bone tool was used to shape leaves.

For the earliest Flemish laces, patterns intended for needle lace were translated freely. The only texture they were allowed was an outriding thread along the edges of motifs into which the sewings were made. These early designs were usually symmetrically arranged leaves oriented around a central axis. By the middle of the seventeenth century, inconspicuous repeats, not necessarily symmetrical, appeared. In the last quarter of the century thin, scrolling designs were used, sometimes as the thick contours of a motif having an inner motif or fancy filling. Plaited bars were the usual ground. Meshes came later, and the area of the background in relationship to the motif increased. Net grounds were delicate, and the designs of Brussels laces of the Louis XVI period and the Empire frequently look like *run net* (running stitches embroidered into net, generally with floss thread).

Lappet of point d'Angleterre à reseau. Flanders, early 18th century. Linen, 4½ inches wide. Courtesy: Art Institute of Chicago. Gift: Mrs. Edward E. Ayer.

Flounce of bobbin lace. Flanders, early 18th century. 23 inches wide. Courtesy: The Metropolitan Museum of Art. Bequest of Catherine D. Westworth, 1948.

Valenciennes and Binche, Complex Straight Laces

Valenciennes and *Binche*, both complex straight laces, are technically similar and easily confused. *Belle et eternelle Valenciennes* is a dense, solid lace with cloth portions that have the texture of fine cambric. Since straight lace (*fil continu*) is made entirely by one person, the technique is completely uniform. Both *Binche* and *Valenciennes* are based upon the laces of Antwerp (see M. A. Malotet, *La dentelle à Valenciennes*).

Although this type of lace also was made at Ypres, Menin, Alost, Courtrai, and Bruges, the lace made in the town of Valenciennes, called *vrai Valenciennes*, was said to have a particularly fine quality (see M. Dieudonne, *Statistique du department du Nord*).

Valenciennes was a part of the ancient province of Hainault in the Netherlands. It became French in the late seventeenth century. The laces of Valenciennes became famous about the middle of the seventeenth century. They flourished under Louis XIV, were favored by Madame du Barry, and enjoyed their best years from 1725 until 1780, when there were 4,000 lacemakers in Valenciennes and surrounding towns. By 1790, men having stopped wearing laces, there were only 250 lacemakers left at Valenciennes, and by 1851 there were only two.

Binche has been documented from the later years of Louis XIV, and was under royal edict from 1686. This extremely popular lace was mentioned in many eighteenth-century inventories, often as *guipure de Binche*. By the nineteenth century, Binche laces were also in decline. Pierre Verhaegen wrote in *Les industries à domicile en Belgique* (1912) that there were only nine makers of *Binche* remaining.

Before the late seventeenth century the patterns of *Valenciennes* and *Binche* were indefinite. Then rich ground patterns and baroque designs began to develop. Since they

Border of Valenciennes. France, early 18th century. Courtesy: The Metropolitan Museum of Art. Gift by Subscription, 1909, Blackborne Collection.

Border of Binche. Flanders, c. 1700. Courtesy: The Metropolitan Museum of Art. Gift by Subscription, 1909, Blackborne Collection.

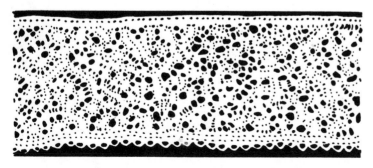

Algarabia lace border, Spain. Ambiguous pattern said to be based on design of paving blocks.

were straight laces made with fine threads, the *Vals* and *Binches* had a great many threads to accommodate in the making of the grounds. Fancy grounds with patterns called buds, shells, snowflakes (*fond de neige*), or eye of the partridge (*oeil de perdrix*) frequently were used. Each of these patterns has a needle lace counterpart made in an entirely different way, but having the same general design. Buds were symmetrical and shells were asymmetrical. Partridge eyes, like both buds and shells, had holes in the center; snowflakes did not. *Armures* were intricately worked spotted patterns. On pages 263 to 269 instructions are given for the techniques of these grounds and fillings.

According to L. W. van der Meulen-Nulle, the cloth sections of *Valenciennes* give the impression of paper. While this is true of the later *Vals*, some of the earlier ones are worked more openly. The relationship between the number of threads in the cloth sections and fillings permitted more threads to the cloth areas than were available to most straight laces, because both the plaited *Val* grounds and the fancy snowflake or bud fillings used large numbers of bobbins. Despite this the effect of some of the earlier laces is open and thin, with Binche more loosely worked than *Val*. Highly textured grounds and the lack of outlining *cordonnets*, or gimps, give the lace a flatness and a cohesiveness of design and abstraction that is completely appealing. In both *Binche* and *Val* only a row of open meshes outlines the design. The "line drawing" effect of open rows of meshes against extensive cloth work characterizes Regency examples of *Binche* particularly.

The designs of *Valenciennes* and *Binche* laces were so complicated and closely worked that a great deal of time was needed to complete them. Using the exceedingly fine, pinkish thread of *Val*, a worker could complete only about an inch and a half a day. With all the work in one piece the number of bobbins on a pillow at one time might be enormous. Imagine a pillow with three to six hundred bobbins attached, the approximate number that a pattern two to three inches wide would require. Work was slow even in areas filled with simple-appearing *Valenciennes* square or round mesh. This sturdy ground, the round version appearing in earlier laces and the square in later examples, had from two to five plaits on all sides, the number depending upon the town in

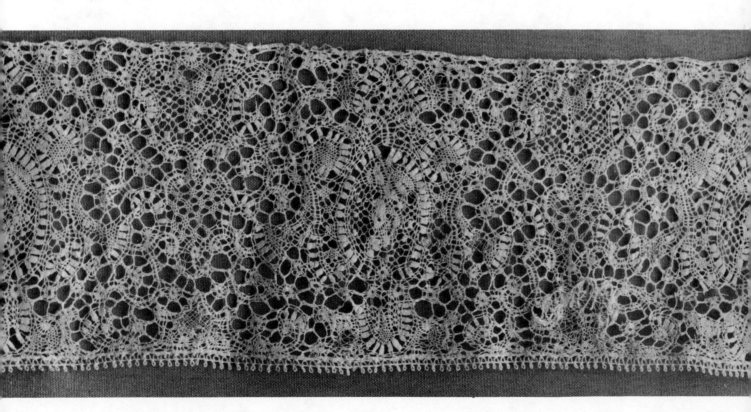

which the lace was made. Even with the low wages paid to workers these were expensive laces.

Fond à la vierge was one of the many pretty fillings used in *Binche* and *Valenciennes* laces. When worked in tiny scale, these were torturous techniques, and it is no wonder that lacemakers willingly abandoned them. Nevertheless, the laces continued to be made in simplified versions. The industry moved to Antwerp, but the laces were made in numerous towns. *Point de fée* carries on the tradition.

Round-meshed *Valenciennes* ground was made at Harlebeke, Bailleul, Courtrai, and Bruges. The sides were plaited, but in making the intersections outer pairs were twisted twice, inner pairs were cloth-stitched, giving a rounded appearance. *Valenciennes* square mesh ground varied with the town in which it was made. Plaited types are the most common, although there were both twisted and plaited versions. The mesh of Ghent and Menin was braided two and a half times, Courtrai workers braided three to three and one-half times. At Honfleur only one and one-half braids were used, while at Bruges, Ypres, and Alost four or four and one-half braids might be used, occasionally five or five and one-half. In Dieppe a version was made in which three, rather than four, threads were plaited.

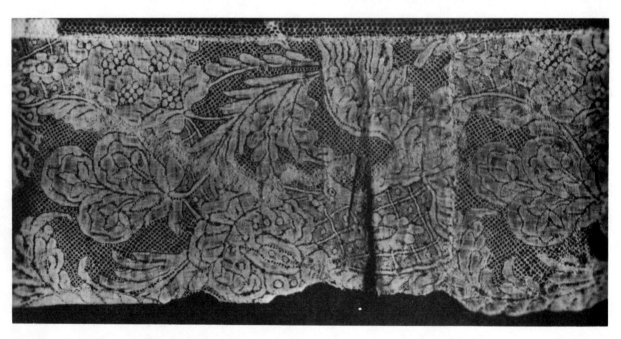

Border of Binche. Flanders, 18th century. Courtesy: Art Institute of Chicago.

Lappet of Binche. Flanders (Binche), first half of 18th century. Linen. 4 inches wide. Courtesy: Art Institute of Chicago. Gift: Mrs. Edward E. Ayer.

Lappet of Binche. Flanders, 18th century. Courtesy: Victoria and Albert Museum, London.

Mechlin

Mechlin is a clear, light one-piece lace with a flat, silky gimp outlining its motifs, sometimes called *broderie de Malines* because of its embroidery-like appearance. A straight lace made entirely by one person, it required a great number of bobbins. A competent worker could make about fourteen inches in a week. *Mechlin* was an expensive lace.

Mechlin was popular at the court of Louis XV. In France before 1665, all Flemish laces were known as *Mechlin*. The lace was made at Antwerp, Lierre and Turnhout. According to Savary, the name was also given to laces made at Bruges, Courtrai, Dunkirk, and Ypres. Turnhout was the center at the time of the final failure of the industry after nineteenth and twentieth century efforts to revive it had proved fruitless. *Mechlin* was a favorite of Queen Anne, Queen Charlotte, and Princess Amelia, as well as of Napoleon.

Like *Valenciennes* and *Binche*, *Mechlin* developed from a simple straight-edged lace of ambiguous pattern and then it passed through a stage of awkward floral patterns. With the development of the *Mechlin réseau* designs began to clarify, eventually growing more spare, graceful, and *rococo* in feeling. Leaves, flowers, and other motifs were worked in cloth stitch, but more loosely than in *Valenciennes* or *Binche*. The *Mechlin réseau* requires only two pairs of bobbins at each head pin, instead of the four required for *Valenciennes*. Therefore the cloth areas were more open. The silky gimp thread worked around the edges of motifs helps to define the contours of the designs and gives them slight relief. A sprinkling of dots was a feature of some *Mechlins*, as it was of Antwerp laces.

Mechlin was a summer lace. Its fine texture and softness made it show off to best advantage when worn over color. It was much used as insertion and as ruffling. Laces especially meant for gathering, called *quilles* or *plisses à la vielle*, were designed. *Mechlin* was used also for the *campane*, an insertion bordered on both sides with ruffled edges. In the eighteenth century many laces, including *Mechlin*, had border designs, scalloped or with shallow waves, and spotted grounds. This type of design helped to stiffen the edge of the eventual ruffle, at the same time keeping the edge to be gathered free of very much bulky cloth work in the lace. Rich fillings were used, many of them the same as were used for *Valenciennes* and *Binche*. Other fillings were quite simple.

The *Mechlin* mesh is similar to Brussels ground, but openings are smaller, because fewer plaits are used. Sometimes *fond chant* is used instead of the *Mechlin* ground.

Flounce of Mechlin. Flanders, 18th century. 8 inches wide. Courtesy: The Metropolitan Museum of Art. Gift of the Estate of Mrs. Irving Lehman, 1950.

Chantilly, Las Blondas, and their Star-Meshed Antecedents

A group of laces whose grounds grew ever more fragile developed after the introduction of the six-pointed star (or hexagon-triangle) mesh. These first star-meshed laces led toward the last great technical achievements of the bobbin lacemakers—the *Chantilly* and *blonde* laces. Compared to *Chantilly* and *blonde* lace, *Valenciennes*, *Binche*, and *Mechlin* were substantial fabrics.

The laces of Antwerp have already been mentioned. The manufactory in Antwerp was established in the seventeenth century, and laces with both bar and mesh grounds were made. Because of the plaited edges of their motifs, these laces, like *Mechlin*, were thought to look like embroidery. The usual design was a vase with flowers. The flower and vase pattern continued to be made in Belgian *bequinages* of the nineteenth century and in Spain, where the design is called *jarro*. Early seventeenth-century versions of the pattern in *Flandres* lace had the same symmetrical, branched pattern, but a *cinq trous* (five hole) or square mesh was used. The Dutch version, *potten kant* or *potte kant*, had the same motif but a more open ground.

The lace known as *Lille* originated in France in the eighteenth century and was in great demand in the nineteenth. It had a ground made with twists only, and, like all laces with this fragile ground, its delicate cloth stitch areas were defined with a thick gimp. By the nineteenth century, the lace was being made in cotton as well as linen.

Fan of Chantilly. *France, third quarter of the 19th century. Courtesy: Victoria and Albert Museum, London.*

Mantilla of blonde. Spain, 19th century. Silk. 82½ x 31½ inches. Courtesy: Art Institute of Chicago.

Old *Lille* usually had straight edges and heavy border patterns. Later designs tended to have more scattered patterns and scalloped edges. Sometimes the *Lille* ground was strewn with square dots. Belgian and French *Lille* usually had tiny patterns; hence it was much used for baby clothes and for women's caps and dresses.

Lille laces also were made in Denmark at Schleswig-Holstein and in England in Bedfordshire and Buckinghamshire. The best of the English *Lilles* were made in Buckinghamshire in the seventeenth and eighteenth centuries. These laces were called Buckinghamshire *trolly* because they had a heavy gimp thread; they should not be confused with later Buckinghamshire laces that were flat and based on Maltese patterns (page 196). English workers tended to add more decorative stitches to their *Lille* laces than did Continental workers. Buckinghamshire edgings and insertions usually are one-half to two and one-half inches wide.

The clarity of the *Lille* ground results from the absence of plaits. To make this ground, two pairs of bobbins are hung onto each head pin. Each pair is twisted one to three times. French lacers twisted once; English lacers twisted two or three times, producing the effect that gives their mesh its name, *wire ground*.

The lacemakers of Spain worked similar grounds. Catharine of Aragon was thought to have brought the six-pointed star ground (called *kat* stitch as well as *wire ground*) to England upon her marriage to Henry VIII.

Point de Paris, originally made in the environs of Paris in the eighteenth century, got its name when the industry moved to Belgium. The grounds of *point de Paris* were

186

Borders of Potten kant. Antwerp,
Flanders, 18th century. Courtesy: Victoria and Albert Museum, London.

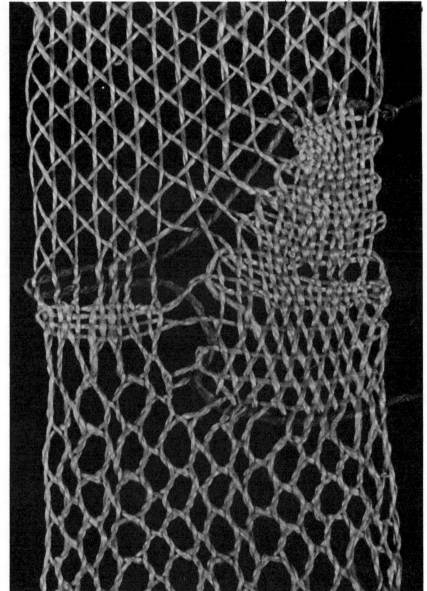

Method of construction for Chantilly. Gimp outlining motif in whole and half stitches. Tulle ground below, ground having no whole stitches.

Insertion of bobbin lace by Mary McPeek.

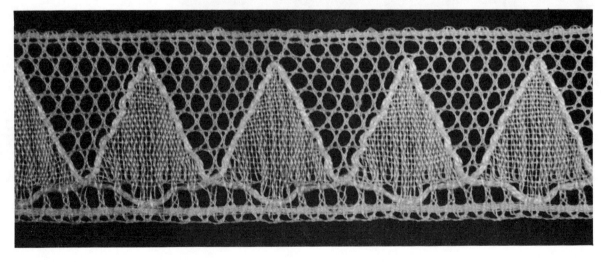

especially fine, and the motifs had a gimp outline for definition. Flowers, baskets, birds, and cherubs were the unvarying motifs. The ground of *point de Paris* is somewhat different from the star-mesh grounds of laces of other cities, but it is similar in its delicacy.

Catherine de Roban, the duchesse de Longueville, established a manufactory at Chantilly in the seventeenth century. She brought workers from Dieppe and Havre. The first laces that were produced were narrow yardages. Later *guipures* began to be made, not only in linen, but also in black silk thread. Familiar ground and filling designs were used. Linen threads were never used for the black laces of Chantilly and Bayeux; instead, workers used black grenadine, which is easily mistaken for linen because it is not shiny.

Chantilly ceased to function as a royal manufactory in 1793, a victim of the French Revolution. Since they were producers of articles of luxury, both patrons and workers were executed. Many of the French lacemakers fled to Spain, where *Chantilly* patterns began to appear among the laces of Cataluña. In Barcelona, versions were made called *randas barcelones*.

The Chantilly industry was reestablished successfully at Caen and Bayeux in 1835, achieving even better laces than before. Verhaegen reports that by 1851 there were forty-nine schools in Grammont teaching lacemaking of the Chantilly type.

Items of large scale were made: gowns, capes, shawls, and parasol covers as well as the smaller, more familiar collars, cuffs, flounces, coiffures, mitts, and fans. Large articles were shipped to Spain and America. At the beginning of the nineteenth century, there had been little interest in Chantilly laces; the white *blondes* were the rage of Paris. By 1835 black lace had returned to favor, and during the Second Empire great Chantilly laces came out of the Normandy region. The long mourning periods observed in the nineteenth century were responsible in part for the demand for black lace, especially in the Latin countries.

Blonde laces can be of any color, but the name derives from the original ivory shade of the silk threads, imported from Santander and Nankin, from which they were made. *Las blondas* were made in Chantilly and Caen as well as in Spain. Frequently they were black. The term was applied both to pillow laces and to embroideries made on machine net that looked much the same as the pillow lace. Examples of embroidered net should be called *bordados*.

Silk laces had been made in the south of Spain at least as early as the seventeenth century, but the large floral designs that are associated with *blonde* laces were not introduced until about the time of the First French Empire, the first decade of the nineteenth century.

Blondes were in demand in the court of George II. Marie Antoinette, who favored *blonde* lace, did not know the big, satiny flower designs that were loved so much in the nineteenth century. Goya repeatedly painted this lace, letting flowers float about the face and arms of his sitters. In fact, this floating effect was just what was so appealing about the lace, which had the same fragile ground as Chantilly. Obviously, *blondes* were not sturdy laces.

As worked in the *blonde* laces the ground consisted of meshes made of two twisted threads, and there were no whole stitches. *Blondes* were straight laces. The mesh did not provide sufficient thread for a compact filling, so heavy, lustrous floss threads were introduced into the cloth areas. A gimp (*nutrido*) was introduced a little apart from the heavy part of the lace, but outlining it.

The *blonde* lacemaking industry flourished until the introduction of machine-made net in the nineteenth century, when embroidered versions began to be made. For a while black laces escaped this competition, but in time excellent copies of both *Chantilly* and *blonde* laces could be made by machine.

Duchesse, Honiton, and Other
Later Free Laces

Duchesse is Belgian; *Honiton* is a product of England's Devonshire country. Both are relatively recent laces based on Flemish work of the seventeenth and eighteenth centuries. The two laces are similar in technique, and, although at times a pattern of one may be confused with that of the other, their designs and threads differ.

Point Duchesse, which appeared first in the 1850s, was made of finer thread than that used for Honiton. *Duchesse* flowers and leaves were worked in cloth stitch with a few half stitch accents, the motifs highlighted with rope sewings. A late version of *Duchesse* also included needle-made elements. Duchesse is obviously simpler and less impressive than Brussels and other earlier laces, but at its best it is a strong, straightforward expression of lace technique.

The flowers and sprigs of Honiton were originally worked as a straight lace, but later the parts were made separately and applied to a ground. Honiton began as a fine, costly lace, but in time it was abbreviated to a *guipure* lace.

The women of Devonshire have made bobbin lace since before the sixteenth century. Orginally they produced a simple "bone" lace. Unable to afford bobbins, they used sheeps' trotters, hence the term "bone lace." It is said that they used fishbones for pins. In the lace collection of the Art Institute of Chicago there is an extraordinary example of Devonshire lace, dated 1661 and made for Catherine of Braganza. Apparently it was used for a collar of the type that was worn low on the shoulders. The lace is a border five and one-half inches wide, and it has been shaped into an "L." The inscriptions, *C1661B* and *Carolus Rex*, appear in the detail. Elsewhere there is an inscription reading *C B Baronet*. (It is unclear why Charles made Catherine a baronet when she was already the daughter of a queen.) The motifs of this lace are Tudor roses, Prince of Wales feathers and crowns, and oak branches. Traditionally the oak leaf symbol is attached to Charles II, who hid from Cromwell in an oak tree.

Barbe of Honiton. England, 18th century. 4½ inches wide. Courtesy: The Metropolitan Museum of Art. Gift of Samuel S. Howland, 1906.

Collar of Bath Brussels (?). England (Devon), 1661. Inscription: Vive le Roy, Carolus Rex (twice), CB Baronet, and C 1661 B. Linen. 5½ inches wide. Courtesy: Art Institute of Chicago. Gift: The Antiquarian Society.

*Caps of bobbin lace. England (Devon),
first half of 19th century. Courtesy:
Victoria and Albert Museum, London.*

The coarse thread with which this lace was made is typical of early English lace. Laces as wide as this one are generally listed as Bath Brussels or *Point d'Angleterre*. The designs were translated to the early tape configuration which was made with thirty bobbins. In this one the use of a réseau at such an early date is noteworthy.

The appearance of the Devonshire laces changed as imported threads and patterns began to be used. Better tools were introduced, and the industry was organized. Through the efforts of lace merchants, philanthropists, and lacemakers such as John Rodge, Mrs. Minifie, and Humphrey of Honiton, the laces became known. The pride of the Devonshire lacemakers was Honiton.

Honiton reached a high point between 1780 and 1820, when piece-workers achieved near machine-like precision, but the introduction of machine-made net was the beginning of the end for Honiton. Performance and design declined, although Honiton revived briefly in the late nineteenth century during the years of the international expositions.

Most of the work of the nineteenth century consisted of premade sprigs joined with buttonholed bars. Sprigs were also applied to net. If the *réseau* was hand made, the lace

*Cuffs of Honiton. England (Honiton),
c. 1900. Designed by Lewis F. Day.
Courtesy: Victoria and Albert Museum, London.*

Border of Duchesse. *Belgium, late 19th or 20th century. Courtesy: Barbara Smith.*

Lappets of Duchesse. Belgium (Brussels), late 19th century. Courtesy: Museum of Fine Arts, Boston.

was very expensive. More often the sprigs were applied to machine-made net. Honiton was usually made in white linen, although it was also made in black ingrain silk, a material that took dye well.

In Belgium, the *point de'Angleterre* of the nineteenth and twentieth centuries had either a needle-made ground or the exacting *vrai droschel* made in extremely fine thread, a *réseau* requiring joints of *point de raccroc* every inch or so. In the 1820s the new machine-made bobbin net enjoyed a vogue for a while, but when it became commonplace, needle-made grounds again began to be used. The laces were called *rose point*, or *point de gaze*. *Duchesse* was made relatively quickly by the same method as *point d'Angleterre*. Another lace was called *rosaline*. It was made much like *Duchesse*, but it had decorative edges along cloth stitch borders. The effect was produced by twisting the last pair of bobbins three times before putting in the edge pin. The ornamental effect of this lace was heightened by adding needle-made "eyes," or small, buttonhole-stitched rings.

A comparison of photographs will show that English lace of the free type was bold and inventive in the eighteenth and nineteenth centuries. In the twentieth century, lacemakers were still occasionally making copies of Italian laces. The curving motif against geometric ground of *reticellas* seems to echo in the laces of Honiton even as it shouts in the Maltese laces. Honiton was a reigning lace in Victoria's day and was used for her wedding dress, as it was for the bridal attire of Queen Alexandra and Queen Mary.

Torchon, Cluny, Maltese, and Other Simple, Straight Laces

Most of the completely hand-made laces produced today are narrow edgings of straight lace in *torchon* or related techniques. Torchon is the simplest of the straight laces. A variety of *torchon* called *beggar's lace,* or *gueuse,* was made early in France. Saxony lace, made from the seventeenth century, the legacy of the religious emigrants, was a *torchon. Torchon* is the French word for dishcloth; *torchere* means to wipe. The ground of *torchon* is the most quickly made of all the lace grounds. Seed stitch, squares, and spiders are used in *torchon.* Half stitch alternates with cloth stitch in the solid parts of the lace. *Point de la vierge* is one of the most frequently seen fillings, but rose grounds of many variations also appear. Fans worked along edges are distinctive in this lace, which also may feature scrolling devices worked in cloth stitch. The most characteristic designs, however, are strictly geometric and based on the diagonals that naturally develop in the making of the lace. Except for its picots, *torchon* can be copied perfectly by machine.

In the nineteenth century there was a nostalgic review of past arts and crafts. In the reprise of lacemaking two interesting laces, *Cluny* and Maltese, developed. From the standpoint of the ongoing development of lace their coming may not be regarded as an altogether good thing, but at the time they were introduced they were life-saving measures for some economically stricken communities. Unfortunately, in the case of Maltese in particular, lacemakers capable of working more demanding techniques turned away from the making of better laces to help supply the demand for the popular new laces.

Cluny was named for the *musée de Cluny,* where the sixteenth and seventeenth century laces from which it derived were first studied. Designs were derived from geometric needle laces. The makers of *Cluny* could be found not only in France and Belgium, but all over Europe and in the Orient as well (the oriental production was entirely for export).

Cluny is similar to *torchon* and Maltese laces, but its designs are more expansive and curvaceous. *Cluny* laces made in Luxembourg sometimes have *cordonnets* or fans made with heavy cords, a technique called "incrustation."

In an economic improvement effort in 1833 Lady Hamilton Chichester sent lacemakers from Genoa to Malta. Maltese women had been making lace since the sixteenth century, but now early needle lace designs were copied with bobbins. The new Maltese laces derived from *reticello,* Greek lace, and similar geometric laces. By the

A Bruges lacemaker at work on torchon edging for handkerchiefs, the corners shaped as she works.

time of the Great Exhibition of 1851, imitations of so-called "Greek lace" were a fashion craze. Plaited laces, led by Maltese *guipure*, were so prized that patterns were kept under lock and key. It was at this point that expert lacemakers began deserting more exacting techniques to make Maltese. Despite this infusion of talent, the quality of the lace deteriorated.

The same black and cream-colored silk threads that were used for the Spanish *blondes* were used for Maltese (the deep tan color that the existing lace so often has now is the result of discoloration). Cotton threads also were used. The patterns usually were set against a gridwork of plaits, sometimes worked with "pearls," or picots. The solid parts were cloth stitch. Some pieces had a little raised work. At first large and complicated projects were undertaken, but by the late nineteenth century only narrow edgings were being made.

Torchon, Cluny, and Maltese laces all are characterized by the limited number of motifs used, although these few were arranged and varied in many ways. Maltese has countless arrangements of seed stitches, as well as designs featuring the Maltese cross. *Cluny* and Bedfordshire Maltese laces have raised work, scallops in cloth stitch, and open plaiting designs with picots. *Torchon* was the least fanciful; among its designs were alternating circles and bars, alternating circles and flowers or stars made of leaf stitches, single or double zigzags, scallops, scrolls, lozenges, open lozenges with spider or leaf-star fillings, rows of spiders, broken lozenges in various arrangements, and fans.

These laces were made in many rural areas. In England, Maltese and *torchon* were made in the Midlands and in Nottinghamshire and Bedfordshire. Sometimes colored or metal threads were worked into them. In Russia, heavier threads sometimes were introduced for accent. Russian women also made linen *torchons* with very fine thread in a very loose *toile*. Lace was made from the fringed edges of embroidered cloths. In

Tablecloth of Cluny. Russia, 19th century. Lace squares alternate with squares of cross stitch. About 59 inches square. Courtesy: Art Institute of Chicago.

Flounce of Maltese lace. 19th century.
Courtesy: Victoria and Albert Muse-
um, London.

Sweden shelf borders were embroidered with simple satin stitch borders; these have cleverly made lace edges. The fabric was unraveled along the edge and the threads of the fringe were used for the hangers of a bobbin lace pattern. Threads were sectioned off into groups, and each group was worked separately in the same bobbin lace pattern, which was of *torchon* type. Another idea for the handling of embroidery and torchon comes from the Parish of Leksand, Dalecarlia, where a neck scarf may be made with embroidery and lace insertion made by the same pattern.

Torchon laces may also be made in metal. The simple maneuvers and the straight lace techniques do not abrade metal threads as more complicated lace methods would. Early metal laces were often versions of *torchon*.

Parasol cover of Maltese lace. 19th century. Courtesy: Art Institute of Chicago.

Contemporary Bobbin Laces

At the present time most makers of bobbin lace are craftsmen also interested in weaving and other phases of the textile arts, people accustomed to, and intrigued by, designing within technical limitations. Thus, it is the straight techniques that one most often sees in contemporary work. The free techniques, less "pure" in the technical sense, probably would appeal more to artists with a background of painting or sculpture, since they permit greater freedom of expression. Of the contemporary laces shown here, most are of the continuous braid variety (straight or free), or are straight laces. An exception is the curtain by Jiřina Trojanová-Pavilitová, in which individually-made botanical motifs are grounded with mesh, added later.

Marie Vănková-Kuchynková, some of whose work appears here, studied in the studio of Madame Paličková, the great Czechoslovakian lacemaker. She now designs for industry, but she also experiments with new forms in hand-made bobbin lace. She says that her basic concerns are texture, material, and presentation. Vănková-Kuchynková's prizewinning lace jewelry and structures called *space lace*, well known in Europe, were shown at Montreal's Expo 67 and 68 and at the Fifth Biennial of Tapestry at Lausanne (1971). She won a Silver Medal in the International Exhibition of Fancy Jewelry, Jablonec, Czechoslovakia.

To stiffen her three-dimensional laces, Marie Vănková-Kuchynková uses dissolved Plexiglas or relies on the inherent stiffness imparted to the lace by the technique. She makes the laces herself or has them made to her design on a cylindrical pillow, but she is also experimenting with pillows of other shapes to add new forms to her space laces.

When she expects to make the lace herself, she makes only a general design, without internal details, believing that the best procedure is to express oneself directly in the technique, rather than transferring a drawing into another technique. Even when she makes a large piece, and it is necessary to involve another craftsman, she provides only a rough sketch with annotated structures, thicknesses, and colors, but not with every crossing of the threads. She tries to avoid a mechanical transposition of her design by having her associate thoroughly acquainted with her methods rather than by demanding adherence to a precise design.

Most contemporary lacemakers work with similar ideas in mind, if, in most cases, with less assistance and less formal training in technique. Brigita Fuhrmann designs in small scale first, then enlarges her design to actual size. Sometimes she makes the lace directly on the larger drawing, sometimes she makes another, clearer cartoon. Like Vănková-Kuchynková, she does not draw in every detail of construction. She says, "I am, of course, getting inspired by historical examples, but I am trying to avoid copying the historical approach."

Some of the laces shown here are distinguished by their choice of materials and show that not only other yarns and threads than are usually associated with lace may be used, but also such materials as vinyl tape, video tape, marlin and nylon filament fish line, and all sorts of other materials. Other artists combine bobbin lace with embroidery, needle lace, or other fiber constructions.

Some contemporary lacemakers continue in the tradition of precisely preplanned design, but the forms they use may have little relation to the designs of past times. Madame Freydecká's three crucifixions are compositions in which no detail has been left to chance. The figures were carefully synthesized for the lace idiom and combine solemnity of conception with richness of technique.

Bobbin lacemaking has much in common with loom-weaving. While most looms keep warps in tension by stretching them between two beams, there is a very ancient type of loom, still in use some places, on which the warp threads are kept manageable by weighting the threads. The weights serve the same purpose as bobbins, which not only hold long lengths of thread neatly and cleanly, but also serve as weights to keep tension even and threads separate.

While in weaving warp threads can be made to travel diagonally and weft threads can be manipulated into various twists and turns, in the end the loom sets limits to invention. A maker of bobbin lace can interweave threads more intricately, setting up a little loom of pins wherever needed as work progresses. In some stitches, passive bobbins, or hangers, are the equivalent of warps; active bobbins, or workers, are the equivalent of wefts. Solid parts of the lace design, made in cloth (*toile* or *whole*) stitch, look exactly like loom weaving, except that two threads instead of one made each edge turn. For fancy fillings (*modes, jours*), and background net or mesh (*fond, réseau*), the interaction of bobbins is more complex.

Panel of bobbin lace. Belgium (Bruges), contemporary. Courtesy: Technisch Instituut H. Familie, Bruges, Belgium.

Panel of bobbin lace. Belgium, contemporary. Courtesy: Technisch Instituut H. Familie, Bruges, Belgium.

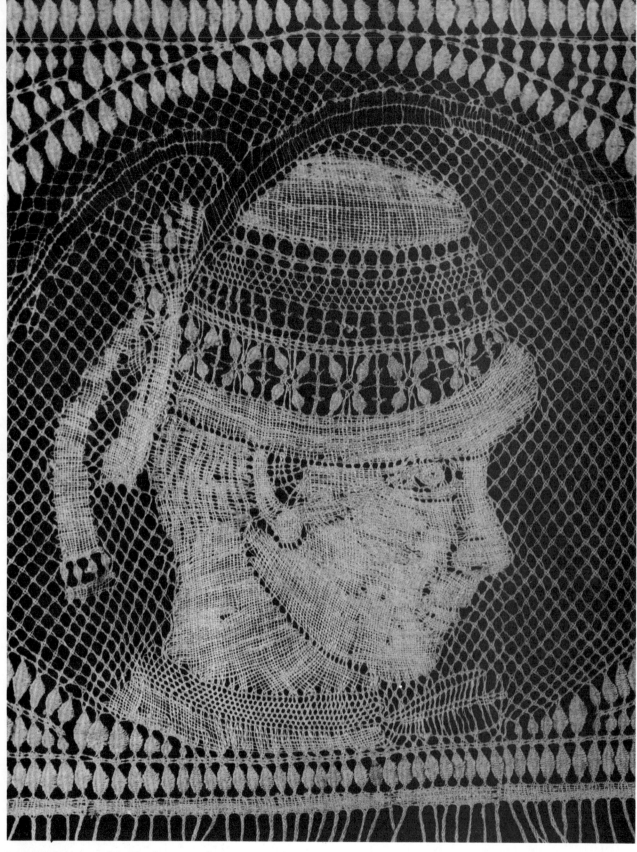

Detail of curtain by Blanka Hanušová.
1958. Flax. Courtesy: Artist.

Doily. Russian, *20th* century. Courtesy
Mary Lou Keuker.

*"Sphere," Brigita Fuhrmann. Bobbin
lace. Metal thread and wire. Courtesy:
Artist.*

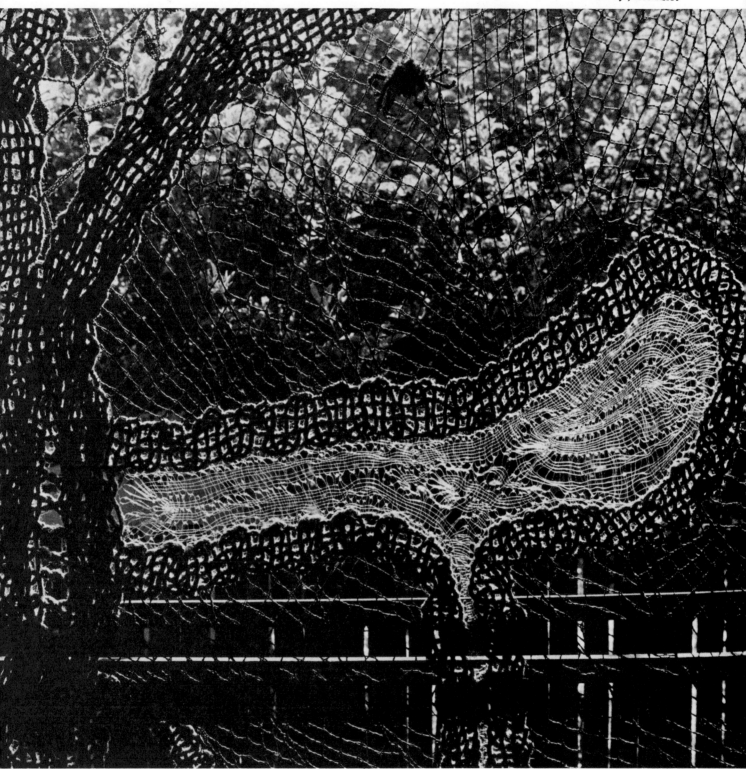

"Life Cycle," Kaethe Kliot. Bobbin lace. Marlin, wax linen, nylon monofilament. Courtesy: Artist.

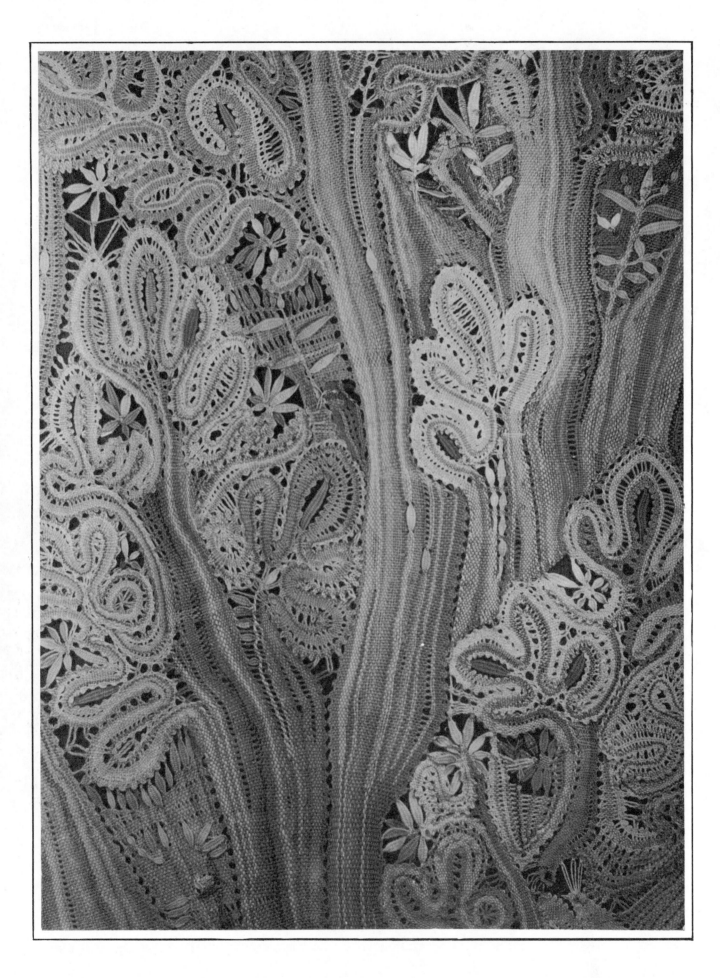

"Tree of Life," Lida Krěcǎnova-Koc-
manová. Bobbin lace. Wool. From
wedding room in Mlada Boleslav.
Courtesy: Artist.

Photo: Foto-Yysoká škola umělecko prùmyslavá

"Ostrava," J. Sikytová. Three strips,
one behind the other. Flax. Courtesy:
High School of Applied Arts, Prague.
Special Studio for Textile, Prof. A.
Kybal.

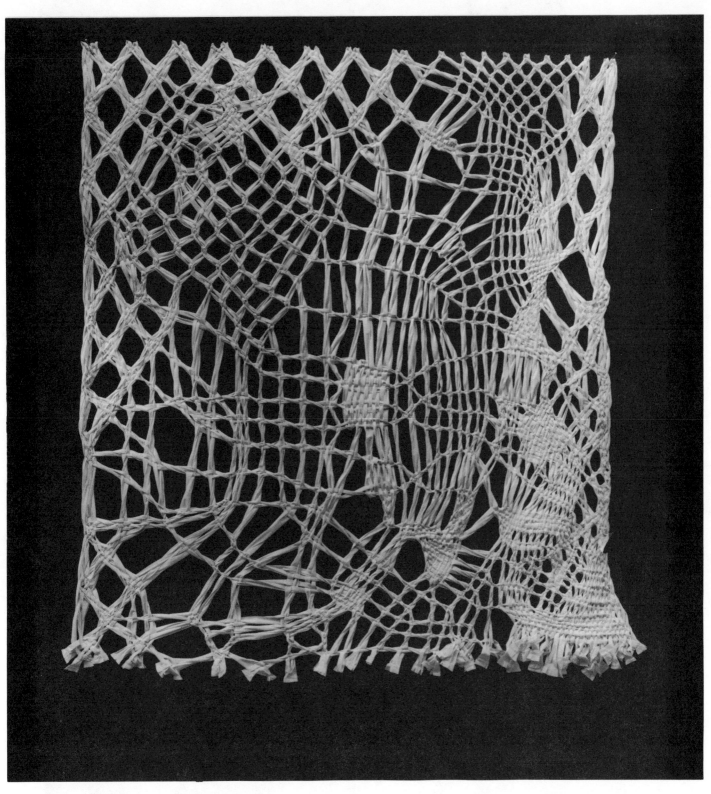

"Small White Lace," Ed Rossbach. Bobbin lace. Vinyl tape. Courtesy: Artist.

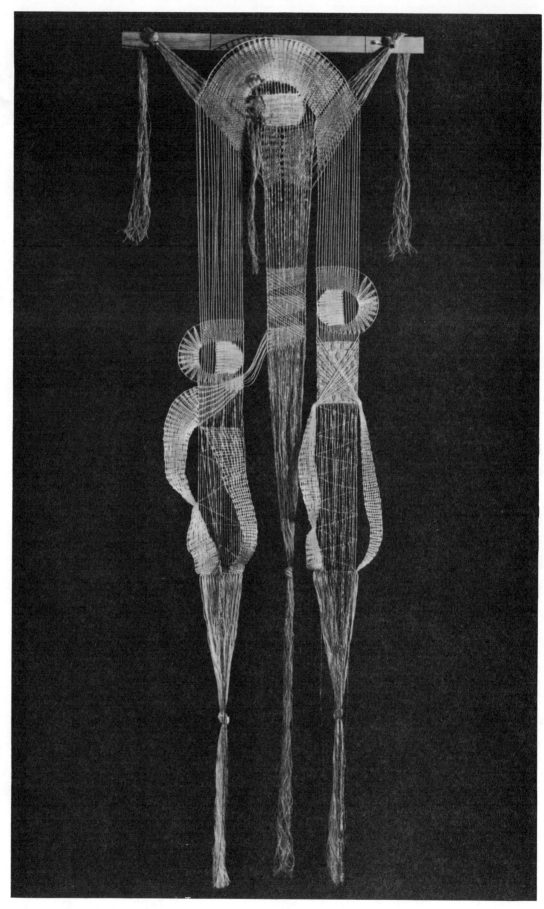

"Crucifixion," M. Frydecka. Bobbin
lace. Courtesy: Artist.

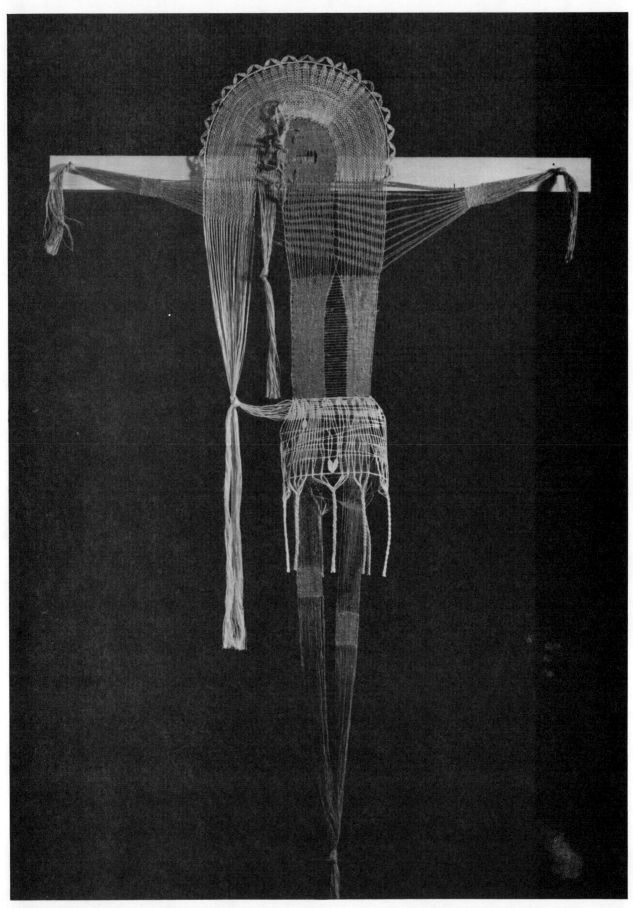

"Crucifixion," M. Frydecka. Bobbin
lace. Courtesy: Artist.

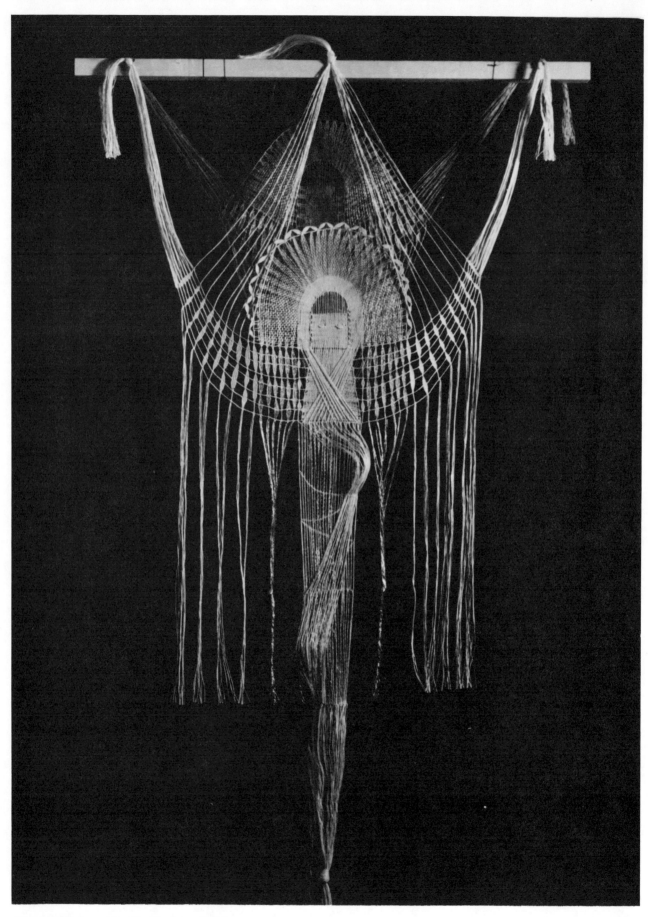

"Crucifixion," M. Frydecka. Bobbin
lace. Courtesy: Artist.

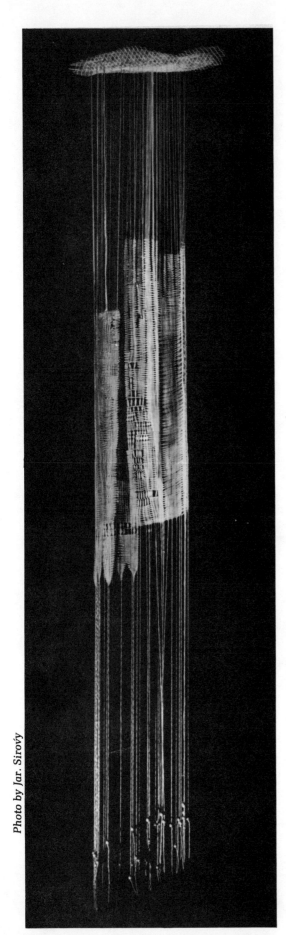

Hanging by Radka Vodáková-Šrotová. 1969. Bobbin lace. Flax. Courtesy: High School of Applied Arts, Prague. Special Studio for Textiles (Prof. A. Kybal).

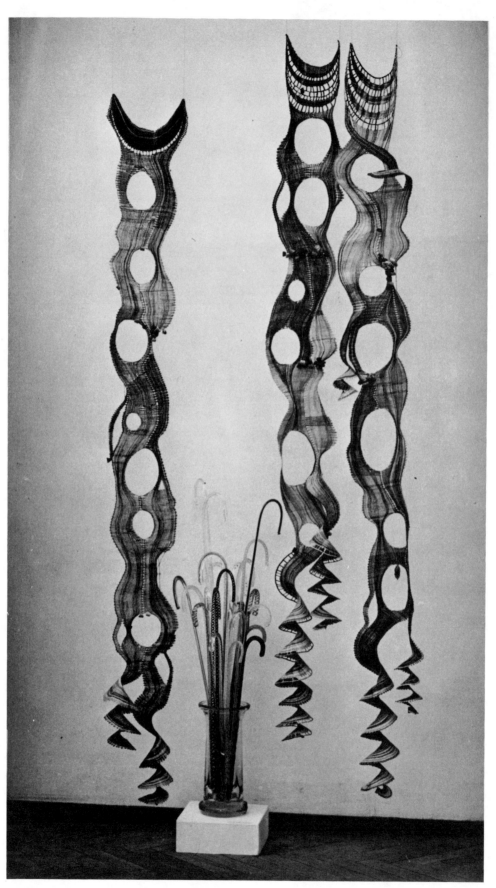

*Hanging by V. Solcová. 1972. Bobbin
lace. Flax. Courtesy: Vlasta Solcová,
Prague.*

Decorative handmade bobbin lace by
Marie Vaňková-Kuchynková. 1969.
Made on a specially-formed pillow.
Black and white line (thread). Cour-
tesy: Artist.

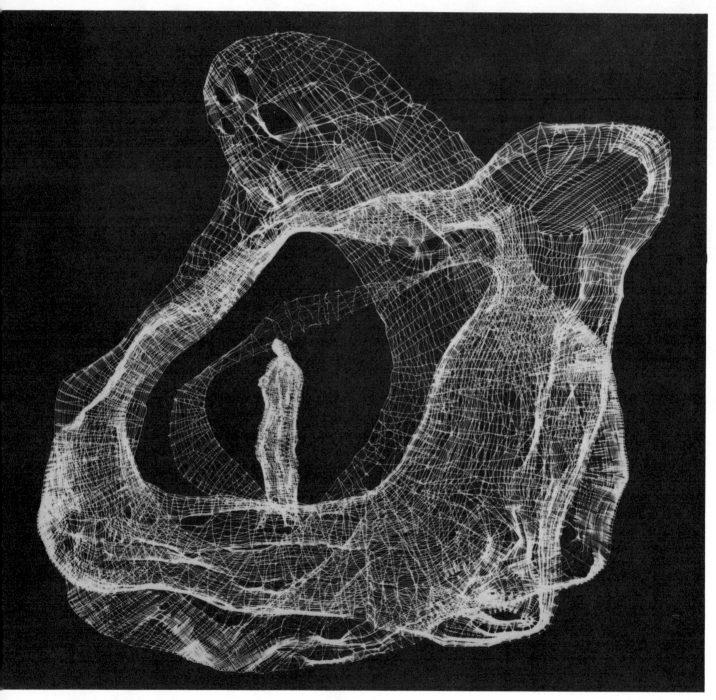

"Music theme: Leoš Janáček: In Mist,"
Milča Eremiášová. 1967. White flax.
Courtesy: Artist.

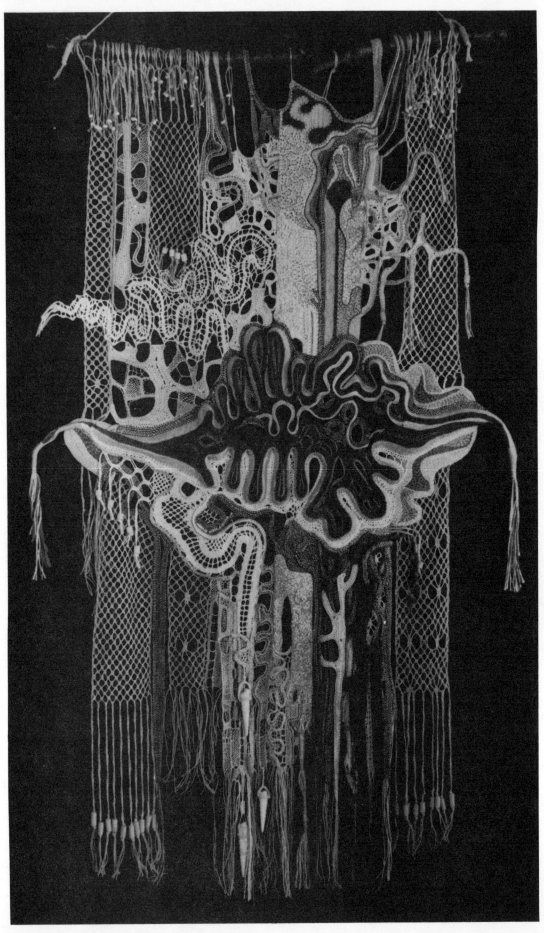

"Fossils," Virginia Bath. 1972. Embroidery, needle lace, bobbin lace. Linen, wool, silk, ceramic, shells.

Techniques for Making Bobbin Lace

Bobbins

Bobbins and Pricker. Left to right: Pricker; sheathed bobbin; English bobbin with beads, appropriate for straight laces; Belgian bobbin, appropriate for sewings and free lace.

Most bobbins are made of wood or bone, although some are of ivory, metal, or glass. Bobbinmakers seem to have been extraordinarily discontent with leaving bobbins plain. Unadorned bobbins certainly work best, but decorated varieties abound. Bone or ivory bobbins have *piquéd* designs of dots and zigzags, names, inscriptions and sentimental messages burnt in or carved, then rubbed with dye or pigments. Sometimes the carving is extremely intricate, involving caged balls, bobbins, or other little forms within detailed Gothic windows or similarly precisely tectonic openings. Some of these were oriental work intended for the European market. Glass bobbins having spiraling designs in colors were made at Murano. French bobbins with heavy turned shanks were fitted with metal rings. In Spain, special bobbins were made for metal lacemaking. Fancy carved bobbins were favorites of Spanish and Portuguese lacemakers. Ivory bobbins were used by Peniche women. At first glance, many bobbins seem to be frivolously decorative, but the material from which they are made and their shapes are primarily matters of function. The shape varies according to the need for tension on the thread, which in turn varies with the type of lace being made, the size and the amount of thread to be wound on the bobbin, whether or not sewings will be made, and other considerations. The size of the narrow neck of the bobbin, where the thread is wound, is longest for bobbins used in making straight, one-piece laces in which the threads are continuous throughout (*fils continu*). When sewings are to be made, the overall shape of the bobbin must be fairly narrow or tapering. The bobbin must be smooth because it will have to pass through loops of thread during the lacemaking process. Bobbins with ornaments that could catch in the threads would be inappropriate and annoying to handle.

The weight of the bobbin together with the type of pillow that is used, can help the lacemaker achieve proper tension. A heavy, unsupported bobbin will tug at threads; although in some laces, it may assist the lacemaker by pulling threads into position after the stitches are made. Heavy, falling bobbins are also less likely to come unwound. On the other hand, if a very fragile thread is used, as in Brussels laces, too much weight could break the thread; so for fragile laces the bobbin is light in weight, and the pillow is fashioned so that the weight of bobbins is supported by it. When weight is wanted the bobbin may be made of heavy wood, may have a bulging or ball-shaped shank, or may have metal rings or inlays added. Loops of glass beads, buttons, or other ornaments may also add weight; loops of beads also serve to keep the bobbins lying flat and to prevent them from rolling. Hooded or sheathed bobbins keep threads from unwinding, and they also keep the thread clean.

Most bobbins now available for sale are made for traditional types of lacemaking. They may be too light and hold too little thread to be used for coarse, heavy lace. For some yarns and threads a large sheathed bobbin may suffice, but it is also possible to improvise by using short lengths of dowels with notches cut into them at one end around which the noose may be tightened.

A yarn winder may be helpful when winding long lengths of thread on smaller bobbins.

The remarkable threads of most early laces were linen and had either one or both of two important characteristics. First, they were even and smooth. These laces required precise technique that was possible only if each successive stitch looked exactly like the last, a feat requiring a thread that would produce identical stitches. Second, some of the threads were incredibly fine. The fact that some of them could only be spun in moist, dark cellars has become legendary. Frail and easily destructible until strengthened by the close weaving of the lace, they were seldom more than twenty inches long. In fact, one way certain laces are identified is by the frequent joinings of threads. *Threads*

Today the objectives of lacemaking do not require such incredible threads. Lacemakers are likely to experiment with threads of various textures, not caring as much for exact technique as for unusual effects. Those who wish to work in traditional methods can find excellent lace threads not only in linen but in cotton. Some of the cotton threads are very smooth and fine. For most lacemakers, even those who work with traditional patterns, there is a certain fascination in seeing how the old design looks made in a different scale, with a different thread, and perhaps, in a different color. Time is limited for most people who are interested in lacemaking, and no one should imperil eyesight by making lace. For these reasons, what one might call *macrolace* has a great deal of appeal. Laces of large scale are, in fact, made in the teaching of lacemaking. All sorts of cords, yarns, twines, ropes, and thread can combine in such laces. In addition to traditional linen, silk, cotton, and wool lace threads, all sorts of synthetic, plastics, and other recently developed materials can be used.

A word of caution about color is in order. Because it has open construction, lace is exceedingly light-vulnerable. Value relationships are subject to change according to the prevailing lighting conditions. The problem is not as crucial in bobbin lace as it is in needle lace—because knots must be avoided, the temptation to make arbitrary color changes is less likely to occur. Nevertheless, care should be exercised in planning extreme contrasts of color.

A look at the photographs of lace in the process of being made is sufficient proof that no one type of pin is used universally. The ornate, glass-headed pins that one occasionally sees are more ornamental than functional, although a round-headed push-pin can be more pleasant to use than ordinary pins. Brass pins tend to bend; nickel-plated tin pins, if they can be found, are more sturdy. Long pins are helpful in holding bobbins out of the way. Very short pins, or pins that can be pushed down to the heads into the pillow, are necessary in making free laces. Some lacemakers use longer pins at the lace margins and shorter ones to hold the ground meshes in place. *Pins*

Patterns and Prickings

Traditional bobbin lace begins with a drawing. Because in the past the designer and the maker had no direct contact, an exact pattern, predetermined down to the placing of the last pin, was necessary. Improvisation almost never occurred. But today, when designer and maker are the same person, improvisation is possible and exciting new effects emerge. However, if you are a beginning lacemaker, it is wise to work with the patterns for a while, following all the directions step by step until you have grasped the principle of each procedure. Later you will need less guidance and will be able to make a lace from the sketchiest of drawings.

First, you will need to determine the spacing between stitches. Most of the diagrams in this book were worked out on graph paper that had ten squares per inch. The samples were made of stitches two or four squares apart for 10/2 or 20/2 threads. (Usually, the higher the number of thread, the finer it is; many fine laces today are made with 100 or 110 thread. The second part of the number designates the ply; two strands were plied for the threads used.) Make a diagram in the scale you need, following the diagram in this book. For some threads you may be able to make a tracing, but it is a good idea to practice working out the patterns for yourself. In the beginning, work with rather large threads.

When you have finished making your diagram, make a pricking. The pricking will be put on the pillow, and the pinholes in it will be a guide in making the lace. With smooth, colored paper, Bristol board, or lightweight cardboard taped under your graph paper design, make a hole at each point of the diagram, using a pricker (an awl-like, pointed instrument) or a large needle fitted with a dowel or pen-holder handle. Work on layers of newspaper or similar padding so as not to injure the work surface. Always use colored prickings for light-colored or white laces so that the background will contrast with the threads.

Next, pin the pricking on the pillow. If a long length of lace is planned and a cylindrical pillow is to be used, the pricking should be made long enough to go around the pillow, a little longer if necessary to finish the last repeat so that it joins properly with the first. You may need additional padding on the pillow to make the pattern fit exactly.

Prickings can be made in parts for free laces. Usually individual motifs are worked and then joined by working in a background mesh, making a sewing, or joining sections of net with *point de raccroc*. The entire original drawing can be traced and pricked for use in assembling the parts. Any drawing that indicates location of motifs should be rendered in pen and ink; pencil will soil your lace. Prick only the parts of the lace still to be worked. Keep the original drawing for reference.

In the past, when prickings were used over and over, they were made of parchment. Today it is usually only necessary to choose a material that will survive one working of the pattern. Wrapping paper often suffices nicely. A tracing-paper pricking is adequate for colored lace; it has the advantage of being semitransparent, so that any drawing that may be needed can be made on the back of the paper. Another advantage of using a tracing paper pattern is that the diagram can be traced with ink and no actual pricking need be made. As the lace is made pins are simply stuck in position on the proper ink dots. It is sometimes also possible simply to pin the graph paper drawing on the pillow and use it in place of the pricking; however, none of these makeshift substitutions will give the accuracy that can be achieved by making an accurate cardboard pricking.

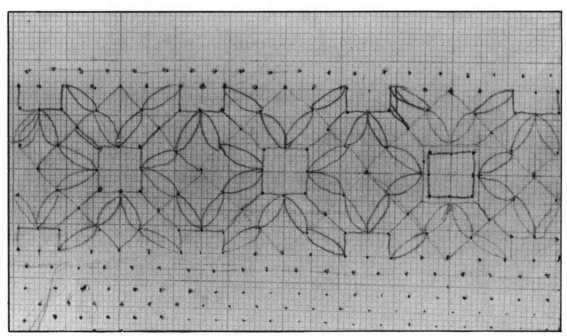

Drawing for insertion by Mary Mc-Peek.

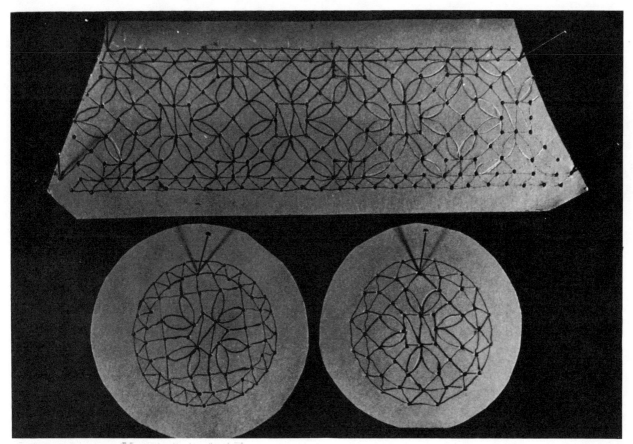

Prickings for insertion made by Mary
McPeek. The lace made from this
design appears on page 238.

Sketch with pricking and finished
lace, showing changes as the pattern
developed. Courtesy: Mary McPeek.

A lace pillow is essentially a large, firm pincushion. An adequate pillow for any type of lace can be constructed easily, but it is important to choose the correct type of pillow. When making a relatively narrow, long straight lace edging use a cylindrical pillow. Whether the pillow you work on is a simple, homemade type fashioned of household odds and ends or a pretty, ready-made pillow, the cylindrical shape will ease your work. A pricking can be made to fit around the cylinder, and you can make lace continuously without shifting the pricking by simply removing the pins and rolling up the finished parts of the lace.

A flat pillow with a large working surface on which a sizable pattern can be seen all at once will serve you well if you are making a free lace, finishing it in parts for later assembly. Sometimes pillows used for this type of work are round and are set on a swivel base, because it is necessary to turn the work frequently.

Traditionally, twelve-bobbin, continuous braid lace (page 236) was made on a muff- or bolster-shaped pillow. The pillow for Honiton was flat. Brussels laces were made on a round, flat pillow. In Saxony, straight laces were made on a long pillow. In Spain, the shape of the pillow influenced the nature of designs in some areas. Where the long bolster pillow, set vertically, was used, panels of pattern were made, then joined, the repeated design sometimes reversing on alternate panels. The same type of pillow was used in Switzerland. The lace pillow of Cataluña is long and slender. The bolster-shaped Arabic *almohada* was held on the knees or cradled in a stand. In Castilla, a prop was made for the pillow, and the lacemaker sat on the floor. For bolster pillows a stand that turns and tilts was helpful when serpentine laces were made. It kept bobbins from sprawling in disorder. Other lacemakers sometimes used a spring stretched across the lower part of the pillow to keep threads separate.

Lace Pillows

Cylindrical pillow for straight laces mounted on a fan-shaped cushion. Courtesy: Christa Mayer Thurman.

The pillow pictured here can be used for small motifs or narrow edgings. It is made entirely of materials that can be found in most households. Construction begins with a fruit juice can, an oatmeal or salt box, or any other sturdy tubular form. If you are using a metal can, remove the ends; if you are using a cardboard box, the pillow will be sturdier if the ends are left on. Use lengths of cotton flannel remnants for padding. Other soft material, such as strips of an old blanket or towels, will also work. The padding must be deep enough so that a pin will hold when stuck into it. Cut long strips of remnants to fit the width of the pillow; then set them aside. Wind small and irregular leftover pieces on the can first. Glue the first layer in place. Lightly baste or temporarily tape subsequent layers to hold the pieces in place. Glue the first dozen or so layers along the edges. Finally, wind on the longer strips that have been put aside, joining each strip carefully to the last with herringbone stitches. The edges of the strips should touch but not overlap, so that the pillow will be as smooth as possible. Use glue sparingly and only at the edges; if used elsewhere it will interfere with pins later. When the padding is sufficiently deep, sew the last layer into place with herringbone stitches. Overcast the side edges of all layers together, passing the needle though the glued as well as the free layers and drawing the top layers down tightly to the sides to compact the padding as much as possible.

To make a cover, measure the circumference of the cylinder and add a seam allowance to give one dimension of the cover. Measure the width of the cover from can rim to

The flannel strips are wrapped on a cylindrical form.

The ends of the flannel strips are overcast together.

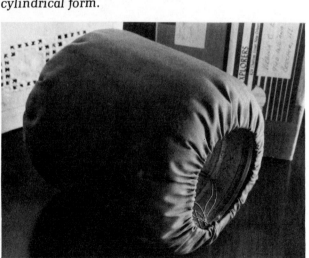

The removable cover is tied on.

The lacemaking in progress.

can rim. Allow extra material at each end to make a casing for the drawstring that ties the cover into position on the can. The cover should not be loose.

This pillow sets in a small cardboard box covered with self-stick vinyl. The box, which can be weighted if necessary, keeps the cylinder from rolling.

The drawback of a pillow of this sort is that it offers no support for hanging bobbins. A more satisfactory cylindrical pillow can be made with a small amount of carpentry.

Begin by making a solid, cylindrical cushion. Determine the size you think will be most convenient for your work, the diameter of the cylinder and width of the cushion. Cut two circles of stiff cardboard with the required diameter. In the center of each make a hole just large enough for a one-inch dowel. Then cut two circles from heavy canvas or other fabric in a color of medium value, making them only enough larger than the cardboard circles to allow for a seam. Cut a rectangle of fabric slightly longer than the circumference of one circle (to allow for seams) and as wide as you want your lace cylinder to be. Machine stitch each of the circumference-length sides to one of the cloth circles. When the three pieces are assembled, put the two cardboard circles inside the assembled cloth cylinder, adhering them in place with white glue, if desired. Then cut through the center of the cloth circles, slitting the material up to the edge of the center hole of the cardboard circle in several places. Turn in the cloth and glue it onto the cardboard on the inside of the cylinder. This will make a neat, turned-in edge.

Now cut a length of one-inch (diameter) dowel long enough to put through the pillow and to allow for handles on each side. The handles need not be more than about an inch long. Begin to pack the cloth cylinder with sawdust, Spanish moss pounded for density, or some other filling. Sand will also work. Do not fill the cylinder completely; put the dowel in place soon enough so the filling packs in well around it. Then completely fill the pillow. Be sure the material you are putting in is very compact. With small stitches close together sew up the side opening on the pillow. Before completely closing the slit, push some more filling in, and finally, close the pillow. If you want a good-looking pillow, finish the ends of the dowel before putting it in place. If sand or sawdust filler is used, glue the cloth cover to the dowel ends to prevent spillage.

Next you will need a small wooden box (bottomless) in which to rest the pillow. Make the box just large enough so that the cylinder will be able to turn in it without binding. Make it high enough so that the dowel ends, which will be rested into two semicircular grooves on the sides, will hold the cylinder so that it turns freely, without dragging. It may be convenient to make the notches for the dowels by drilling a hole in a board wide enough to make two sides and then sawing the board through the center of the hole. The outside of this box is completely covered when the lace pillow is complete, so it is not necessary to finish it, but the inside may be finished, and the edges should be sanded smooth.

You will also need a large circle, oval, or octagon of plywood. The size will depend upon the size of the bobbins you will use, the type of threads you probably will use, and other considerations. In deciding on the size, remember that your bobbins will most likely be about six inches away from your work, and they should rest on the pillow. Keep in mind also that you will not center the box you have made on the pillow; you will place it so that the space at the back is narrower. When you have decided on the shape you want and have it cut and sanded, nail or glue the box where you want it.

The next step is to pile the plywood base around the box with filler. This material should produce a rather unyielding surface on which the bobbins will be manipulated. Pile the filling high enough to fill the space to top of the box and taper down toward the outer edge of the plywood shape. Make a heavy cloth cover to hold the filler in place. Fit the material around the box opening first. The material can be cut and glued neatly to the inside of the box or it can be turned on the edges of the box, stapled in place, and covered with a decorative tape, which can be glued in place. If you use tacks, make sure

A cylindrical pillow for straight lace, mounted on a circular cushion. Bobbins are held in place with a pinned ribbon. Courtesy: Lydia van Gelder.

Brigita Fuhrmann at work at her bolster-shaped pillow.

Brigita Fuhrmann with her lace pillow out of the cradle as the direction of the lace changes.

they will not interfere with later lacemaking. Fit the cover around the dowel notches.

When the box edge is finished, put in more filler if needed before completing the cover. Then, pull the cloth down tightly, and working from side to side and front to back, tack or staple the cloth on the back of the plywood. Be sure the grain of the cloth is straight and that the filler is evenly packed at the edges, making a neatly rounded contour. Be sure to push all tacks and staples well into the plywood. Then, cut a circle of felt and glue it to the bottom.

Rest the dowel ends of the cylindrical pillow in the notches of the box, and you are ready for work. To keep the cloth cover of the pillow clean, keep an extra cloth cover over the cylinder, but under your pricking or pattern. Keep the work covered when the pillow is not in use.

You can make a large, flat pillow by padding a pressed paper drawing board or a piece of fiberboard so that the surface is convex. Taper the padding toward the edges to allow bobbins to hang away from the work without pulling on it. Making a large, flat pillow is a good way to use up old, soft curtains or towels. A blanket provides large pieces of padding. Whatever the filling, it must be pulled tight to form a firm pad. Commercial fillings such as polyester fiberfill are difficult to compact.

Most old lace pillows were filled with straw, hay, bran, or moss pounded to make the filling dense. Presumably sawdust would make a good lace pillow, but obviously it is best not to use such a highly flammable material.

Basic Procedures

Before making any of the meshes or simple laces diagrammed and illustrated, be sure you understand the few simple techniques that follow.

Not everyone winds bobbins in the same way. The objective is to wind as much thread on the bobbin as possible, keeping threads neatly aligned, but not to overload the bobbin, lest the thread loosen and unwind. If the type of bobbin you use does not have a separate notch at the top for the noose, leave a little space at the top of the neck for it. One way to begin winding the bobbin is by holding the bobbin in your right hand until the thread has been secured with a few twists, winding thread toward you and then shifting hands and continuing to wind with the bobbin in the left hand. Or, you can secure the twists with the bobbin in the left hand and shift to the right hand, using your forefinger to guide the thread as you twist.

Winding Bobbins

When the bobbin is full of thread, you will need to secure the thread in position with a noose. This loop is tightened around a special notch at the top of some bobbins or at the top of the neck in others. Holding the bobbin in the left hand, make a loop of the end of the thread with the right, twist twice away from you and slip the noose over the head of the bobbin. Pull the end of the thread to tighten the noose. A noose made this way will allow the thread to feed out as needed with a few twists of the bobbin. It also prevents the thread from unwinding.

Bobbins are almost always used in pairs. While it is possible to knot two threads, it is usually better to wind bobbins on the two ends of a single thread. Hiding knots, especially when a bulky thread is used, is a problem to be avoided whenever possible.

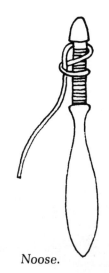

Noose.

Sections of mesh being made for a wall hanging. Top: Torchon with spiders. Bottom: Torchon.

The bobbin winder.

Knots

Two types of knots are used in making bobbin lace. The best way for you to learn these knots is by imitating the interweaving of threads in the drawings on page **40.**

Use the weaver's knot to join threads within the lace. Make the knot, tighten it securely, and leave long ends. You may pin the ends of the thread out of the way during the lacemaking process. Do not clip them until later. Make the knot with a loop from one thread end in one hand. Interweave the other thread end into it as in the illustration.

Use the reef knot to finish off the threads in places where the lace is complete. Making this knot also involves interweaving one loop into another. Unlike in making the weaver's knot, however, the action is symmetrical, leaving a neat, straight turn of the thread at the juncture of the threads when the knot is pulled into place.

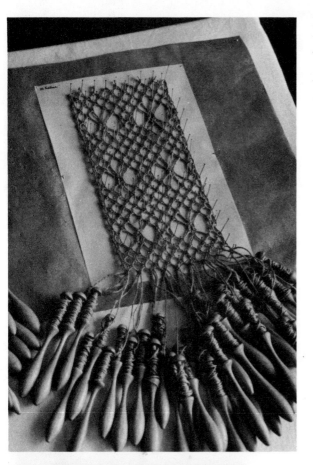

If using pairs of bobbins knotted at the top when beginning a section of lace, stick a pin through the knot to hold the pair in place. Shift these knots to less conspicuous positions by working them to the back of the lace before working very far. Pulling on one bobbin with the pin under the pair, not through it, will allow the knot to shift.

If you use bobbins paired on the same thread, secure the threads with a whole stitch around the pin.

Handle bobbins in pairs, one pair in each hand. Some workers keep palms up, while others have the bobbins under their hands. Usually the hands work simultaneously, but some lacemakers, the Flemish, for example, fan out their bobbins on a smooth surface, then lift them one over the other in sequence.

You will not be working at bobbin lacemaking very long before you will find that you want and need quite a few bobbins on your pillow at one time. Initially the idea of hundreds of bobbins on the pillow at the same time seems too much to deal with. The secret lies in having them all in order and secured while they are out of use, so they cannot move about unless they are in play. Traditionally they are tied with ribbons or tapes pinned over and under successive rows of bobbins. Sometimes pins are used to separate groups of bobbins.

Threads will unwind if the bobbins have too much thread wound on them, if the threads are wiry, or if the bobbin doesn't weight them sufficiently. Keep the noose snug at the top of the neck or in its special notch. Use sheathed bobbins to make wiry and stiff threads more manageable.

Check tension and keep it carefully. The larger the threads, the more the need for an extra tug to keep everything lined up properly. Most grounds and many fillings proceed in diagonal rows. It is wise to stop at the end of each row, to pull all threads into position. Leave a length of about three or four inches of thread between work and bobbins. At the end of a row, check the lengths of bobbin threads and shift all to the left to give working space (if your diagonal is from upper right to lower left).

Lace is easily soiled, so it is wise to take precautions to keep the work clean as it is progressing. Hands should not be oily and should be perfectly clean. Keep the lace and pillow covered as much as possible. Even while work is in progress, pin a cover or "pill cloth" over parts of the pillow not in use. Cover finished portions of lace with a cloth, and keep a piece of heavy paper or cardboard under the bobbins to protect that part of the pillow.

Try to work with good general illumination and a little side light.

Twists

Hang two pairs of bobbins on a pin stuck in your lace pillow. Take one pair in each hand. Working with both hands simultaneously, move the right thread of each pair left over the left thread of the pair. You have made a twist in each pair.

Crosses

Keeping the twisted pairs in your hands, put the right thread of the left pair over the left thread of the right pair. You have made a cross.

Plaits

Now alternate twists and crosses several times. You have made a plait, the first of the many combinations of twists and crosses that make bobbin lace. Twisting and crossing are to bobbin lace what knitting and purling are to knitting.

232

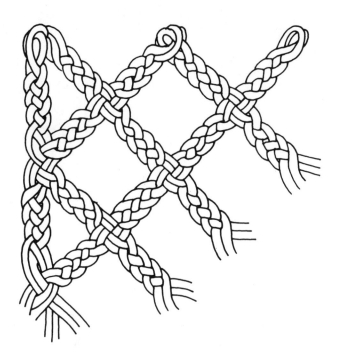

Series of plait crossings.

Method of crossing two plaits.

Method of crossing three plaits.

Border of plaited bobbin lace. Spain,
18th-19th century.

Half Stitch (Demi-point, passé)

Make a pricking like the one shown on page 253. The spacing between points will depend on the size of thread you are using. Twist pairs 1 and 2 once, cross; twist pairs 2 and 3 once, cross, twist pairs 3 and 4 once, cross; continue in like manner to the end of the row. Secure with a pin at the end of the row. Put a pin at point 1, and with the last pair outside it, twist once. Then work right to left in the same manner, twisting and crossing each pair. Notice that after you have made a cross the composition of pairs changes, so aids like numbering the bobbins are useless.

Half stitch is sometimes used as a filling, but more often it is used in conjunction with whole stitch, when a slightly lighter effect is wanted in an area. It produces a lattice-like, fairly close texture in comparison to the woven look of the denser whole stitch.

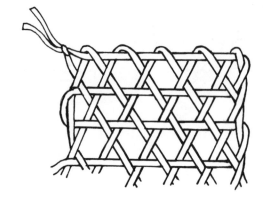

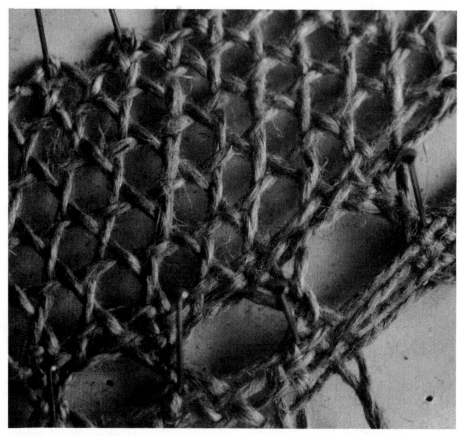

Half stitch maneuvering a curve.

Half stitch often is worked alongside whole stitch to vary the openness of motifs, the half stitch part being more transparent than the relatively solid cloth parts. Put bobbins in pairs at the top of the pattern. Begin work from the left with one half stitch using the first four bobbins. Then join the two right bobbins with the next pair of bobbins to the right and one half stitch (twist, cross) is made. At the end of the row twist the last pair twice after pinning and join it with the next to the last pair (which is twisted only once).

Area of Half Stitch

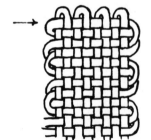

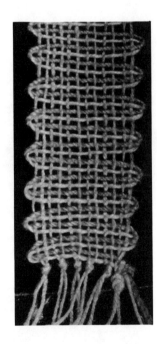

Whole stitch is used to make the solid, cloth parts of almost all laces. It looks exactly like weaving. The stitch is composed of a cross, twists, cross. Hang on two pairs of bobbins at regular intervals across the top of the area to be worked. With pairs 1 and 2 cross, twist, cross; with pairs 2 and 3 cross, twist, cross; continue in like manner to the end of the row. At the end of the row pin to secure. Twist the last pair once to make the turn, then work right to left in the same manner as in the first row.

Whole Stitch

Cloth Stitch Section or Tape

Determine width of tape. Mark left side *a*, right side *c*, midpoint *b*. Hang two pairs of bobbins at *a*. (One pair will be workers, also called leaders or active; all other bobbins are hangers, or passive.) Hang one pair of bobbins at *c* and two or more pairs at *b*, (number depends on width of tape, size of thread). Whole stitch (cross, twist, cross) pair at *a*. Twist inner pair once (or twice, if space is fairly wide), then whole stitch all pairs at *b*, working left to right. Twist last pair on right once (or twice); twist bobbins at *c* once; whole stitch workers and bobbins at *c*. Secure with a pin in the center of the whole stitch on the right margin of the tape. Twist workers (inner pair) once (or twice), whole stitch bobbins at *b*, working right to left. Twist workers once (or twice); twist hangers at *a* once; whole stitch; pin at *a*. Repeat. Other tapes are shown on page 245. To widen a tape extra pairs of bobbins can be added at *b* in the center of those already hanging. Bobbins also can be dropped from the center of the group at *b* to narrow a tape. Openings can be produced within the cloth part of the tape by introducing half stitches or twists in patterned sequence. (See page 170.)

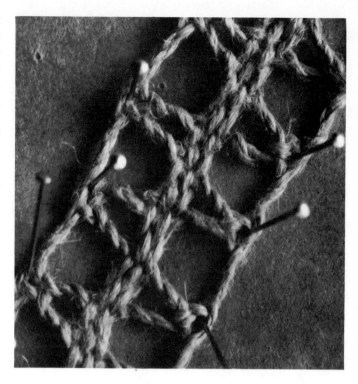

Bobbin Lace Grounds (Reseaux)

There are many different types of meshes that can be made in bobbin lace, each a combination of twists and crosses. Often lacemakers of different towns made a distinctive mesh or a variation of one made in another town. A number of these lace grounds are diagrammed and detailed directions for how to work them accompany the diagrams with some explanatory material about the types of laces in which they were used. The simplest of all the lace grounds is *torchon*, and it is suggested that you begin with this one .

When you have read through the descriptions of the various laces it will be clear how the parts are assembled in making free lace and how the techniques effect designs in a variety of ways.

Plaits and other stitches in loosely spun yarn. Courtesy: Brigita Fuhrmann.

236

Very decorative textured fillings are used in parts of most laces to enrich the texture. Infinite variations developed out of the spider, the eight-thread armure, and other patterns. Lacemakers were very inventive in working out new combinations. In *A Guide for Lacemakers and Collectors* Gertrude Whiting detailed twenty variations on the Trude ground, each the original creation of an American lacemaker.

Bobbin Lace Fillings (Modes, Jours)

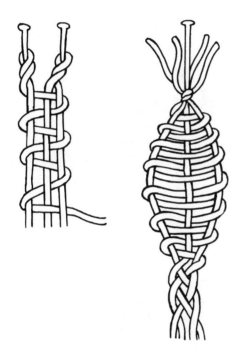

Except for minor variations, the procedures used for leaf stitch, matting stitch, and square dots are the same. For each, four threads are required. To make a leaf, these threads must emanate from the same point. To make a dot or a line of matting stitch, pick up two threads from each of two adjacent points. Of the four threads, three act as hangers, one as a worker. The process is like weaving, the three threads acting as warps, and the worker as the weft that is passed back and forth between the hangers to make a little spot of solid cloth. In making a leaf, pull the first passages of the thread tight to form a point at the top of the shape. As the worker passes back and forth,

Leaf Stitch, Matting Stitch, or Square Dots

Leaf stitch. Courtesy: Mary McPeek.

the tension is lessened, allowing the shape to expand. A little practice is needed before shapes are smooth-edged and all the same size.

The second thread from the left is the worker. Move it over the center hanger, under, then over, the right thread, under the center thread, and over and under the left thread. Before you repeat the action, push the working thread up to lie snug against the threads preceding it. Pack the thread close to assure good substance and shape for the leaf. It may help to count the number of passes of the worker, so that other leaves can be made to match.

Flower centers can be worked in half stitch or they can be handled in various other ways.

Insertion with plaiting, leaf stitch, and half stitch by Mary McPeek.

Single Picots

When bars between motifs are twisted or plaited, single picots sometimes are used to ornament them. Make a loop in the outer thread on the side on which the picot is to occur. Turn the loop so that the bobbin end of the thread is under the thread as it emanates from the plait or twist. Use a pin to hold the picot, pull the thread tight and then continue plaiting or twisting.

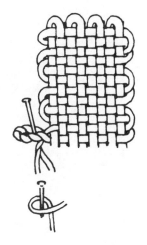

Double picots are usually used to decorate the edges of a cloth stitch tape or area. Make picots with the working pair as they reach the end of a row. Twist these threads five or more times, depending on the size of the thread and the picots. Loop the twisted threads around a pin in the same manner as for single picots, but as you tighten the threads into position, make a similar loop in the second thread and also tighten around the pin. Then the workers resume their function as the active bobbins in the making of the cloth stitch.

Double Picots

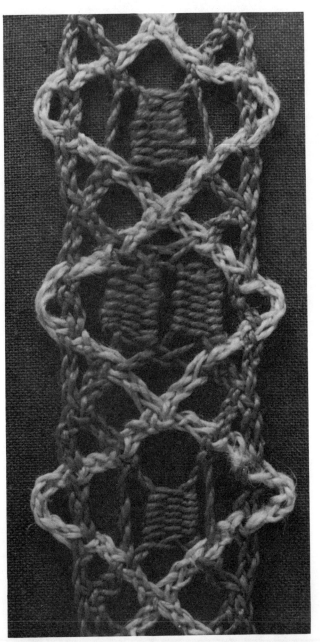

This is a beginner's lace design requiring twenty-four bobbins. It can be made with threads in one, two, or three colors, so that the path of the plaits can be clear even if one has never made lace before. The lace in the illustration was made with two colors. Wind pairs 1, 2, 3, 4, 9, 10, 11, and 12 with gold-colored thread. Wind pairs 5, 6, 7, and 8 with white. To make a three-colored version, wind pairs 1, 2, 11, and 12 with one color, pairs 3, 4, 9, and 10 with a second color, and pairs 5, 6, 7, and 8 with a third color. Make a pricking according to diagram B. Then hang pairs 1, 2, 3, and 4 at a, pairs 5, 6, 7, and 8 at b, and pairs 9, 10, 11, and 12 at c. Then follow the plaiting procedure according to diagram A.

Simple Plaited Lace with Square Dots

1. With pairs 1, 2, 3, and 4, make a whole stitch with two pairs in each hand as pictured.
2. Make a whole stitch as above with pairs 5, 6, 7, and 8.
3. Make a whole stitch with pairs 9, 10, 11, and 12.
4. Plait pairs 3 and 4 twice; plait pairs 5 and 6 twice. (Actually, cross, twist, cross, twist.) Whole stitch pairs 3, 4, 5, and 6. Pin in the center of the whole stitch at 4.
5. Plait pairs 1 and 2 twice; plait pairs 3 and 4 twice. Whole stitch pairs 1, 2, 3, and 4. Pin at 5.
6. Plait pairs 7 and 8 twice; plait pairs 9 and 10 twice. Whole stitch pairs 7, 8, 9, 10. Pin at 6.
7. Plait pairs 9 and 10 twice; plait pairs 11 and 12 twice. Whole stitch pairs 9, 10,

11, and 12. Pin at 7.

8. Plait pairs 11 and 12 three times, put a pin at 8 and keep the plait to the right of it.

9. Plait pairs 9 and 10 twice; whole stitch pairs 9, 10, 11, and 12. Pin at 9.

10. Plait pairs 1 and 2 three times. Put a pin at 10, and keep the plait to the left of it.

11. Plait pairs 3 and 4 twice; whole stitch pairs 1, 2, 3, and 4. Pin at 11.

12. With pairs 6 and 7 make a square dot according to the directions for matting stitch on page 00. Weave the worker back and forth as many times as necessary to make a full dot.

13. Twist pair 5 three times. Plait pairs 3 and 4 twice. With pairs 3, 4, 5, and 6, make a whole stitch. Pin at 13.

14. Twist pair 8 three times. Plait pairs 9 and 10 twice. With pairs 7, 8, 9, and 10, make a whole stitch.

14. Plait pairs 1 and 2 twice; plait pairs 3 and 4 twice. Whole stitch pairs 1, 2, 3, and 4. Pin at 15.

16. Plait pairs 9 and 10 twice; plait pairs 11 and 12 twice. Whole stitch pairs 9, 10, 11, and 12. Pin at 16.

17. Plait pairs 5 and 6 twice; plait pairs 7 and 8 twice. Whole stitch pairs 5, 6, 7, and 8. Pin at 17.

When point 17 has been completed the figure is repeated until point 11 has been finished again. For the alternate two dot motif that begins at point x, make a whole stitch and pin at x. If the thread is rather small it may be wise to twist pairs 7 and 8 and 9 and 10 before making the whole stitch. Then make a dot of matting stitch with pairs 5 and 6 and another with pairs 7 and 8. When the dots are completed, whole stitch pairs 6 and 7 and pin at y. Continue the plaiting as in the first figure.

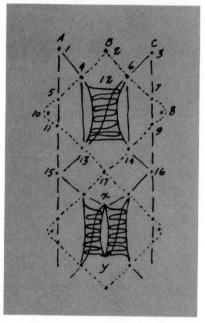

Pricking and working diagram for plaited lace with square dots.

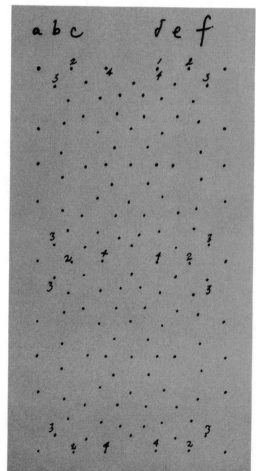

Pricking diagram for plaited lace after Le Pompe.

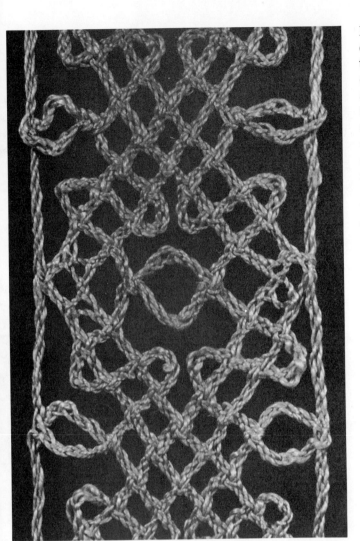

Plaited pattern, after Le Pompe.

Early patterns for plaited laces were not accompanied by instructions for how to work the lace. It was assumed that the lacemaker could figure out the paths of the various plaits and where and how they crossed, an assumption that sometimes left the maker with a considerable problem. The design depicted in the diagram illustrated here was adapted from a similar one shown in *Le Pompe*, published in Venice in 1557. In the original woodcut large holes are shown at the intersections of threads and at the points indicated by picots on my diagram. It is supposed that some fastener larger than a pin, possibly a nail, was used for early lace. If so, the line pattern of the finished plaits would have been studded with decorative holes wherever such large fasteners had been removed.

To write step-by-step directions for plaited laces is possible, but impractical, since they would be so long and complicated that they would be difficult to follow. In fact, all that is needed to understand a diagram for plaited lace is a careful look at how the continuous lines of the pattern intersect. For the *Le Pompe*-derived design, hang six bobbins at *a*, *b*, *e*, and *f* and eight bobbins at *c*. No bobbins were hung at *d*; four of the bobbins at *c* were plaited and carried to *d*, having been pinned to a curve at point 1. At the point marked 2, where only two threads are available, twist and carry the two threads to point 3, sew to the plait at 3 (for sewings see page 000), and then return to 2. At point 4 and in all repeats, but not at the heading, move one plait from left to right, while moving the other plait from right to left. Join the two plaits at an intersection with a whole stitch using double threads. Where the two plaits join on the other side, however, a sewing must be made using doubled threads. A sewing is necessary also at point 5.

The number of half stitches used in the plait between points will depend upon the size of the thread in relation to the scale of the pattern. Make all crossings of plaits whole stitches with doubled threads. Hold pattern curves in place with pins placed at the points showing picots. If desired, make picots in the lace at these points.

Working Procedure for Plaited Lace

Diagram for plaited lace after Le Pompe.

Making a Sewing into a Plait

Sewings are used to tie in new bobbins or to join bobbins to parts of lace with which the bobbins will not intersect. To make a sewing into a plait, draw one thread of the pair to be sewn through the plait. Use a crochet hook to make a loop large enough for a bobbin to pass through. Put the handle end of the other bobbin through the loop and draw both threads tight. Make two or more twists before and after the sewing. The number of twists will depend on the thread and pattern. In a finished lace, two twisted pairs lying side by side look very much like a plait. (See page 247.)

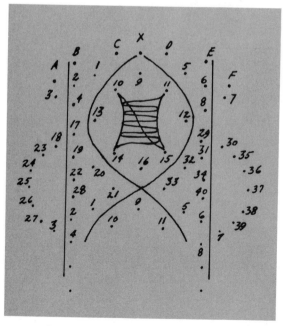

Curving braids joined with sewings to make a fabric. Courtesy: Brigita Fuhrmann.

Scalloped Trimming with Gimps

The trimming shown and diagrammed in these illustrations clearly shows the derivation of bobbin lace from *passementerie*. The sample was made in a glossy, wrapped-core material similar to the silk-wound linen- or silk-cored threads used for early polychrome trimmings. Instead of gimps or cartisane, usual for patterns of this type, a suede thong was worked into the lace as the gimp. The illustrations show variations of this pattern worked in very fine metal thread with heavier gilt gimps and in linen with shiny gimps of contrasting color. The scale is approximately the same for all three laces. Each is about two and one-half inches wide at the widest point.

Hang on one pair of bobbins at a and f, two pairs at b, c, d, and e, and put up the gimps at x. It is usual to enter the gimps in pairs, but one thread will work just as well if it is heavy enough. When pins are stuck following the making of a whole stitch it should be assumed

Pricking and working diagram.

242

that the pin is put in the center of the stitch unless otherwise indicated.

1. Twist pair 3 once; twist pair 4 once; whole stitch pairs 3 and 4; pin at 1; make one more half stitch.
2. Twist pairs 2 and 3 once; whole stitch; pin at 2.
3. Twist pairs 1 and 2 once; whole stitch; pin at 3; make two half stitches.
4. Twist pairs 2 and 3 once; whole stitch; pin at 4.
5. Pass the lefthand gimps through pairs 5, 4, and 3, twisting each pair before passing the gimps through it. Twist pair 7 once; twist pair 8 once; whole stitch; pin at 5; make one half stitch.
6. Twist pairs 8 and 9 once; whole stitch; pin at 6.
7. Twist pairs 9 and 10 once; whole stitch, pin at 7; make two half stitches.
8. Twist pairs 8 and 9 once; whole stitch, pin at 8.
9. Pass the righthand gimps through pairs 6, 7, and 8, twisting each pair before passing the gimps through it. Twist pairs 5 and 6 once; whole stitch; pin at 9.
10. Twist pairs 4 and 5 once; whole stitch; pin at 10; make one more half stitch.
11. Twist pairs 6 and 7 once; whole stitch; pin at 11; make one more half stitch.
12. Twist pairs 7 and 8 once; whole stitch; pin at 12.
13. Twist pairs 3 and 4 once; whole stitch; pin at 13.
14. Twist pairs 5 and 6 once. With pairs 5 and 6 work a square of matting stitch, (see page 00,) weaving as many rows as is necessary to complete a compact square above points 14 and 15. Twist pairs 4 and 5 once; whole stitch; pin at 14; make one more half stitch.
15. Twist pairs 6 and 7 once; whole stitch; pin at 15; make one half stitch.
16. Twist pairs 5 and 6 once; whole stitch; pin at 16.
17. Pass gimps through pairs 3, 4, and 5, twisting each pair before putting gimps through it. Twist pair 3 once; twist pair 2 once; whole stitch; pin at 17.
18. Twist pairs 1 and 2 once; whole stitch; pin at 18; make two more half stitches.
19. Twist pairs 2 and 3 once; whole stitch;

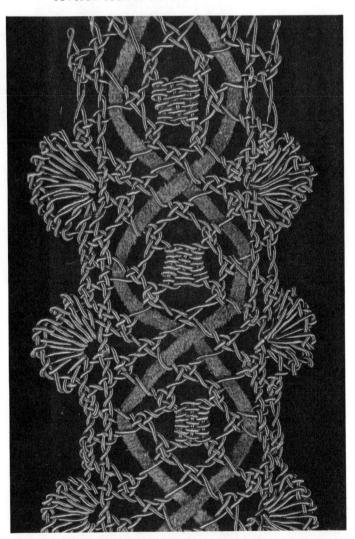

Scalloped trimming with gimps. Silk-covered cord and suede.

pin at 19.

20. Twist pairs 3 and 4 once; whole stitch; pin at 20; make one half stitch.

21. Twist pairs 4 and 5 once; whole stitch; pin at 21.

22. Twist pairs 2 and 3 once; whole stitch; pin at 22.

23-27. To make the sunburst (using pairs 1 and 2): twist pair 1 twice; do not twist pair 2; cross pairs 1 and 2; twist pair 1 once; twist pair 2 twice; cross; pin under last crossing at 23. (Keep the righthand thread of the four pulled tautly to the right; the other three threads move left. Work stitches through 27 in the same manner. If the sunburst requires more stitches for a full effect, stitches can be added.)

28. Twist pairs 2 and 3 once; whole stitch; pin at 28.

29. Pass righthand gimps through pairs 6, 7, and 8 twisting each pair once before passing gimps through it. Twist pairs 8 and 9 once; whole stitch; pin at 29.

30. Twist pairs 9 and 10 once; whole stitch; pin at 30; make two more half stitches.

31. Twist pairs 8 and 9 once; whole stitch; pin at 31.

32. Twist pairs 7 and 8 once; whole stitch; pin at 32; make one more half stitch.

33. Twist pairs 6 and 7 once; whole stitch; pin at 33.

34. Cross gimps; pass gimps through pairs 8 and 9, twisting beforehand. Twist pairs 8 and 9 once; whole stitch; pin at 34.

35-39. To make the righthand sunburst (using pairs 9 and 10): twist pair 10 twice; do not twist pair 9; cross pairs 9 and 10; twist pair 10 once; twist pair 9 twice; cross pairs 9 and 10; pin at 35. Keep the lefthand thread of the four sharply left, the other three pulled right.) Make identical stitches through point 39.

40. Twist pairs 8 and 9 once; whole stitch; pin at 40, half stitch.

Repeat these 40 steps to continue the lace in pattern. Cross the gimps before entering them into the continuing pattern.

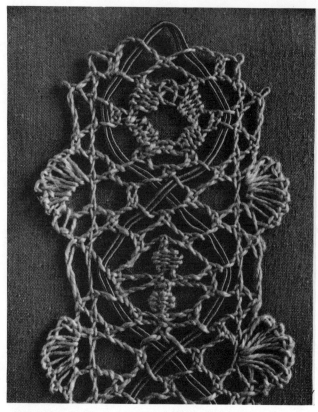

Variation of scalloped trimming made with linen threads and silk cord.

Variation of scalloped trimming made with metal threads.

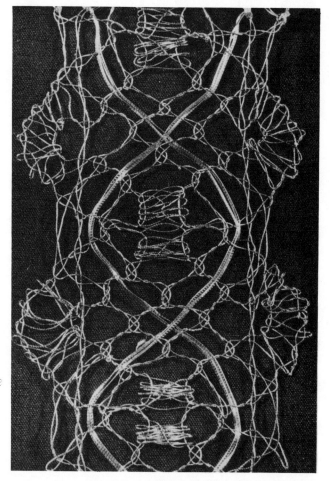

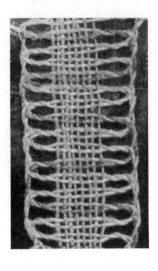

1. Twist pair 1 once. Whole stitch pairs 1 and 2.
2. Twist pair 2 twice. Whole stitch pairs 2 and 3.
3. Whole stitch pairs 3 and 4, whole stitch pairs 4 and 5, whole stitch pairs 5 and 6.
4. Twist pair 6 twice; twist pair 7 once. Whole stitch pairs 6 and 7. Pin at *a*.
5. Twist pair 6 twice. Whole stitch pairs 5 and 6.
6. Whole stitch pairs 4 and 5, pairs 3 and 4, pairs 2 and 3.
7. Twist pair 2 twice; twist pair 1 once. Whole stitch pairs 1 and 2. Pin at *b*. Repeat from step 2.

Cloth Stitch Tape with Plain Edges

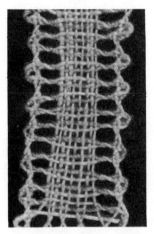

Cloth stitch tape, two edges.

1. Twist pair 1 once. Whole stitch pairs 1 and 2.
2. Twist pair 2 twice. Whole stitch pairs 2 and 3.
3. Whole stitch pairs 3 and 4, 4 and 5, 5 and 6.
4. Twist pair 6 twice. Whole stitch pairs 6 and 7. Pin at *a*. Twist pair 6 once; twist pair 7 twice; whole stitch pairs 6 and 7.
5. Twist pair 6 twice. Whole stitch pairs 5 and 6.
6. Whole stitch pairs 4 and 5, 3 and 4, 2 and 3.
7. Twist pair 2 twice; twist pair 1 once; whole stitch pairs 1 and 2. Pin at *b*. Twist pair 1 twice; twist pair 2 once; whole stitch pairs 1 and 2. Repeat from step 2.

Cloth Stitch Tape with Edge Points

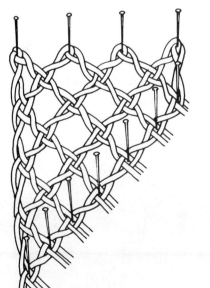

The simplest of the mesh grounds used for bobbin lace has been used from the time of the earliest metallic laces, but it is now called *Torchon* net. It is made with one twist between intersections of threads, which are made with one whole stitch (cross, twist, cross) around a pin. Dieppe ground is almost the same, but it has two twists between intersections and would be a more wiry ground if made with the same threads on the same pricking as that used for a *Torchon*.

Pin a pricking made in the manner of the one in the illustration to a pillow, and hang on

Torchon Ground

bobbins at *a, b, c,* and *d.* There should be two pairs on each pin. You can make a whole stitch around each pin to hold the bobbins in place.

1. Twist pairs 2 and 3, cross, pin at 1, twist, cross.
2. Twist pairs 1 and 2, cross, pin at 2, twist, cross.
3. Twist pairs 4 and 5, cross, pin at 3, twist, cross.
4. Twist pairs 3 and 4, cross, pin at 4, twist, cross.
5. Twist pairs 2 and 3, cross, pin at 5, twist, cross.
6. Twist pairs 1 and 2, cross, pin at 6, twist, cross.
7. Twist pairs 6 and 7, cross, pin at 7, twist, cross.
8. Twist pairs 5 and 6, cross, pin at 8, twist, cross.
9. Twist pairs 4 and 5, cross, pin at 9, twist, cross.
10. Twist pairs 3 and 4, cross, pin at 10, twist, cross.
11. Twist pairs 2 and 3, cross, pin at 11, twist, cross.
12. Twist pairs 1 and 2, cross, pin at 12, twist, cross.
13. Twist pairs 7 and 8, cross, pin at 13, twist, cross.

Continue working diagonally until the piece of net is the size needed. *Double fond torchon* is made with an extra twist in the center of each whole stitch.

Pricking for Torchon and Dieppe grounds.

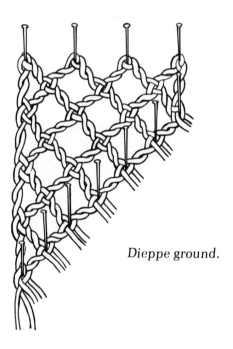

Dieppe ground.

Spiders Many spider fillings are made without being enframed in mesh, and a beginner will make this type most successfully. Prepare the upper half of the lozenge shape into which the spider will be worked by making Torchon or other net diagonally from right and left corners until points *a, b, c, d, e f,* and *g* have been reached. Notice that the pricking will require ten pairs of bobbins, two pairs hung on at each of the head points. The spider is constructed as follows:

1. Twist pairs 5 and 6 three times, whole stitch.
2. Twist pair 4 three times, do not twist pair 5, whole stitch.

246

Spider worked in Dieppe ground.

3. Twist pair 7 three times, do not twist pair 6, whole stitch.
4. Whole stitch pairs 5 and 6, put a pin in the center of the stitch at x.
5. Whole stitch pairs 4 and 5.
6. Whole stitch pairs 6 and 7.
7. Whole stitch pairs 5 and 6.
8. Resume making the net frame. As pairs 4, 5, 6 and 7 are worked down to meet the frame each should be twisted three times to make the lower legs of the spider equal in length to the upper. The action at point h, for example will be: twist pair 3 once (or twice, if Dieppe ground is being made), twist pair 4 three times, whole stitch pairs 3 and 4. (See pricking diagrams on pages 261, 273.)

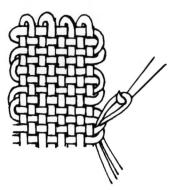

Sewing, Step 1.

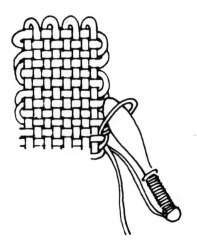

Sewing, Step 2.

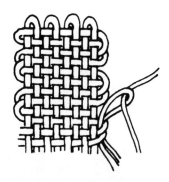

Sewing, Step 3.

Making a Sewing

To make an ordinary sewing, bring the workers through an adjacent portion of the finished lace by drawing one thread of the pair through a stitch that has been pinned, but from which the pin has been removed. Pull a loop through with a needle-pin or crochet hook. Pull the other worker through the loop, the handle-end of the bobbin first. Then twist the two threads together and pull the threads up tight against the lace to which they are being attached. Make twists in the workers both before and after making the sewing. The number of twists depends upon the distance between the two parts of the lace, but two is a minimum.

Sewings can also be made on the bar of an edge mesh when the sewings are made in a mesh-edged tape. Loosen the pins on each side of one of the twisted legs of the mesh, and draw the loop for the sewing up around this leg rather than on the edge. Top sewings are useful when the lace is to have areas in relief.

Double sewings are made to work in a number of bobbins, as, for instance, in preparing to make a filling. Draw a loop of two threads through and put two other threads through the loop. Thus, two pairs emanate from one point, a usual requirement for many fillings.

Making a Pieced Lace

After the individual processes of lacemaking have been learned you are ready to make a lace composition. You can make continuous braid laces without a drawing for guidance, but until you have learned a little about how to handle intervening spaces between the braids, it is wise to work out your design first on paper. Working on paper, you can adjust the course of the braids easily if you see that a span is too wide for a sewing and too narrow to work mesh into. An erasure on a paper sketch is easier by far to correct than a misplaced braid.

Often patterns show pin holes for every pass of working thread in a braid. When you know the scale of the design and the thread that will be used, it is possible to create such a pattern and follow it accurately. But if thread and scale are unknown, it is impossible to predict the best location for pinholes. Therefore, in making your design, work out a pattern something like the one shown on the opposite page. In these sketches the lines represent the outermost edges of the braid, where the pins will be stuck. The solid part of the braid will be much narrower. Where contours of the broad bands touch, sewings can be taken with only one extra twist of the pair before looping it through the opposite braid. Where contours are farther apart, more twists will be needed. If more than two braids meet at a given point, the sewings can be interlocked.

Hold the large spaces between the braids together by working in a network of plaited bars, as in the early Milanese laces, or fill the spaces with a fancy filling or mesh ground. In subsequent sections, various meshes and fancy fillings are shown and working procedures are detailed.

The illustration here shows the partially completed braid outline of a rooster. Notice that an ink drawing has been taped to a rather flat pillow that has been covered with wrapping paper to keep it clean. Before work began the pin holes that would be needed in making the filling and ground were pricked into the drawing, but they are almost invisible. Also notice that the design has been made in such a way that in many places the braids lie close to one another. This is a traditional way of designing. In fact, this rooster is very close in style to the patterns made in Russian laces of the nineteenth century. Other patterns shown at the bottom of page 172 are also typical of Russian work.

When the braid must turn a sharp curve, the edge stitches will bunch on the inner side and strain apart on the outer side. To minimize the difficulty in making such a turn, work around a little circle on the inner side of the curve. This will provide more space for the crowded inner pins and allow, possibly, for an extra pin on the outer edge.

In making this rooster there was no need to refill the bobbins used as hangers, but the workers ran out of thread several times. New thread was joined to the old with a weaver's knot. So that joins could be made with ease, the rooster was made upside down. When the braid outlining the body was complete, thread ends were tied to the beginning threads with reef knots and worked into completed braid. Thread ends should always be left long while work is in progress, even if you intend to clip them at the end of the work. There is always the possibility that an error may be detected, and the extra thread may be needed in correcting the mistake; also, one should take into account the fact that while work is in progress the threads are subjected to considerable pulling and strain.

When the contour of the body was finished, the *point de vierge* filling was put in. A small area of the head was worked in *torchon* ground (page 245). For this two pairs of bobbins were sewn on at each point of the pricked pattern along the top of the head. As pairs reached the sides of the area being filled, sewings were made at these points also. As often as possible, sewings should be taken in loops made around pins rather than on intervening twists. When the head was finished the pattern was changed. Since *point de vierge* also requires two pairs of bobbins at each pinpoint there was no difficulty in

The braid outline of the motif is made.
Sewings join adjacent parts.

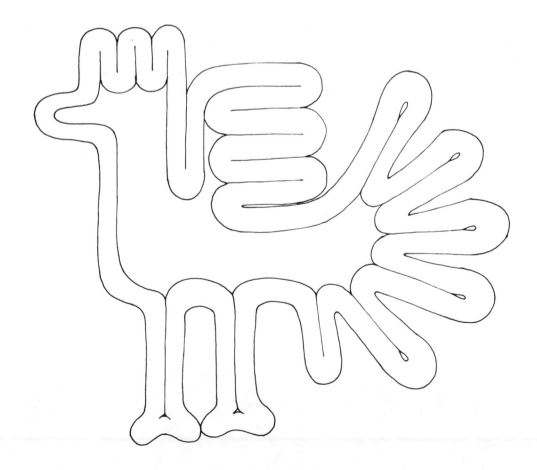

switching patterns. As the form of the body widened, it was necessary to hang in more pairs of bobbins. (Whenever bobbins are hung in, be careful that the pattern of the filling or ground is strictly maintained. This is one reason why a carefully pricked ground pattern is needed.)

When the filling was finished, all threads that could be carried across the braid for work in the ground mesh were sewn into points where they would be useful later in making the ground mesh. Threads no longer needed were tied into the braid after sewing with small reef knots and the end left long, to be clipped or worked into the braid later. It is not always necessary to knot threads, but as you begin making lace, it is a wise precaution.

The making of the ground mesh began with the narrow section of mesh near the bird's beak. There were reasons for beginning at this point rather than at the top or bottom. Since this was a fairly large piece of lace, fifteen by eighteen inches, it was more convenient to work out from the center rather than to reach across the work. More important, by working out from the center a great deal of cutting off of threads was avoided. Threads can be hung onto lace much more inconspicuously and neatly than they can be removed, so it makes sense to plot the course of the work so that cut-off threads are avoided as much as possible. Also, thread ends could be used conveniently along the top and bottom of the work as fringe, or they could be worked around wooden dowels or other hanging devices if it was decided to make a wall or window hanging of the piece.

Therefore, at each point along a horizontal row of pin points just to the left of the beak eight bobbins were hung on. One bobbin of each of the four pairs was hung to the back, out of the way. All the bobbins used were paired by being wound to opposite ends of a single thread. One of each of these pairs was set aside as the mesh making commenced. The other bobbin of each pair was used in making the part of the ground presently in work. Later the work was turned around, and the other bobbin of each pair was used to commence work on the other side. That the work was started in this fashion does not show in any way, except that both top and bottom have thread ends protruding.

To make this lace, 20/2 linen thread was used. The meshes are large, as is the scale of the design. Therefore, it was necessary to improvise in making the netting. Like *Mechlin* ground, the mesh has two stitches at the pins, but it has two twists between pins. The extra twist makes the net a little more wiry and stable than it would have been if *torchon* ground were used for a mesh of this size. In *torchon* the net would have been very soft and pliable. Notice that work on the mesh ground, even when it is confronted with irregular contours, proceeds on diagonal lines, although sometimes these shift from one direction to the other.

In making both the braid and the fillings the work was turned often. Braid pins should be pushed well down into the work, but even so threads will catch annoyingly on the pins of previous work unless they are covered in some way. It is customary to cover any part of the work that is not in progress. In the illustration here, a handkerchief has been folded over a portion of previously made braid in order to provide a relatively smooth surface on which to work.

The sides of this rectangle have been stabilized by hanging in an extra pair of bobbins and working them into the pattern just inside the edge pair. The pattern of the pricking is maintained with the outside pair. The inner pair is twisted and cloth stitched in the same manner as the other pairs, but it is not pinned. At top and bottom three pairs of bobbins were pinned at one side and worked in cloth stitch with the mesh pairs used as hangers. The hangers were then plaited.

Although only fourteen bobbins were required to make the braid, this lace required a total of one hundred bobbins. This was the least number with which it could be completed and meant using bobbins in a most economical way when making the mesh.

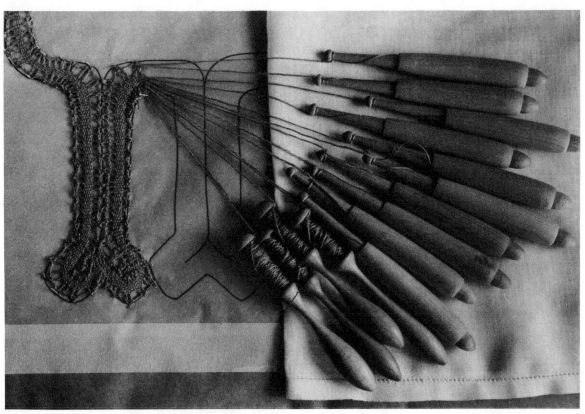

As the bobbins are worked in positions that require them to be manipulated on top of already completed work, a handkerchief or other cloth can be laid over that work to keep threads from snagging in pins.

Mesh is stopped on a narrow margin, and other bobbins are hung onto the motif at a deep indentation, to be worked into position to join the part of the background already made.

Work would have progressed more easily and efficiently with more bobbins, but an attempt was made to learn how few actually would be required to finish the lace. The popularity of designs like the ones on pages 172 and 173 stems, no doubt, from the fact that they can be made with a minimum number of sticks, and, while they involve many sewings, little cutting and ending of threads need be dealt with. Shortly before the rooster was finished, bobbins lying in the center of the work were attached to mesh threads waiting to be worked in. Loose threads of other joinings that lie on top of the work were worked into the braid and clipped off later.

This is neat, pleasant work to do. It can be picked up and put down with little fuss, but care should be taken not to disarrange the bobbins more than necessary. Threads can be shortened and pinned into position under a restraining ribbon to keep them from rolling around. It is traditional, and a very good idea, to keep your work covered.

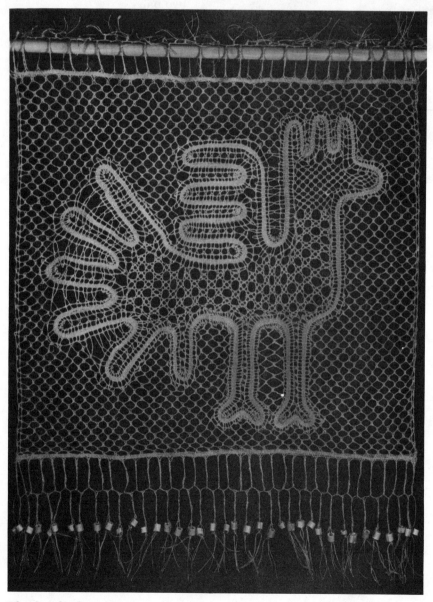

The finished rooster.

Grounds, Fillings, and Edgings for Bobbin Lace

The following are instructions for making grounds, fillings, and edgings that appear on the laces in the "Designs and Patterns" section of this chapter, along with some of the possible variations on the stitches.

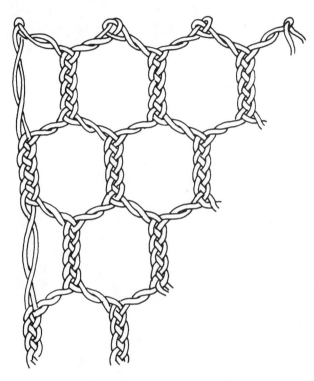

The *Brussels* ground, also called *le réseau droschel, droschelgrund,* and *fondo droschel,* is simple, but time-consuming. It is made on a diamond pricking, work proceding diagonally. Hang two pairs of bobbins at each point across the top of the work.

Brussels Ground

1. Twist pairs 2 and 3 twice, cross, half stitch, pin at 1, four half stitches.
2. Twist pairs 1 and 2 twice, cross, half stitch, pin at 2, four half stitches.
3. Twist pairs 4 and 5 twice, cross, half stitch, pin at 3, four half stitches.
4. Twist pairs 3 and 4 twice, cross, half stitch, pin at 4, four half stitches.
5. Twist pairs 2 and 3 twice, cross, half stitch, pin at 5, four half stitches.

Continue to work in the same manner, following the diagram. The number of half stitches at the pins varies in these laces. More stitches may be used. Sometimes a simpler ground is worked, and when heavier threads than the traditional fine linen type are used, this version may prove more satisfactory. Instead of making four half stitches after sticking the pins, make two. This ground is shown in the illustration, which was made with 20/2 linen thread.

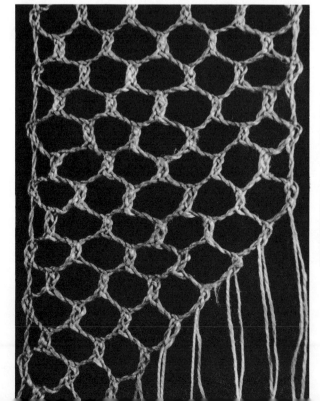

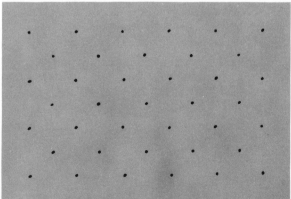

Pricking pattern for Brussels ground.

Maiden's Net (point de vierge)

Lightly pencil in or draw in ink on your pricking the diamonds shown in the diagram. Hang on two pairs of bobbins at each point at the top of the pattern.

1. Twist pairs 2 and 3, cross, pin at 1, half stitch.
2. Twist pairs 1 and 2, cross, pin at 2, half stitch.
3. Twist pairs 3 and 4, cross, pin at 3, half stitch.
4. Twist pairs 2 and 3, cross, pin at 4, half stitch.
5. Twist pairs 1 and 2, cross, pin at 5, half stitch.
6. Twist pairs 6 and 7, cross, pin at 6, half stitch.
7. Twist pairs 5 and 6, cross, pin at 7, half stitch.
8. Twist pairs 7 and 8, cross, pin at 8, half stitch.
9. Twist pairs 6 and 7, cross, pin at 9, half stitch.
10. Twist pairs 5 and 6 once, cross; twist pairs 3 and 4 once, cross. Twist pairs 4 and 5, cross; pin at 10, half stitch.
11. Twist pairs 3 and 4, cross, pin at 11, half stitch.
12. Twist pairs 5 and 6, cross, pin at 12, half stitch.
13. Twist pairs 4 and 5, cross, pin at 13, half stitch.
14. Twist pairs 3 and 4 once, cross. Twist pairs 2 and 3, cross, pin at 14, half stitch.
15. Twist pairs 1 and 2, cross, pin at 15, half stitch.
16. Twist pairs 3 and 4, cross, pin at 16, half stitch.
17. Twist pairs 2 and 3, cross, pin at 17, half stitch.
18. Twist pairs 1 and 2, cross, pin at 18, half stitch.
19. Twist pairs 10 and 11, cross, pin at 19, half stitch.

Continue working on the diagonal as above.

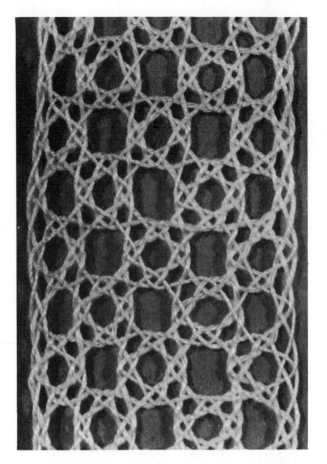

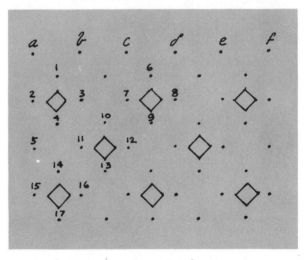

Pricking pattern for point de vierge.

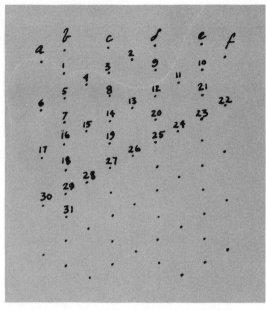

Pricking for round Flemish mesh.

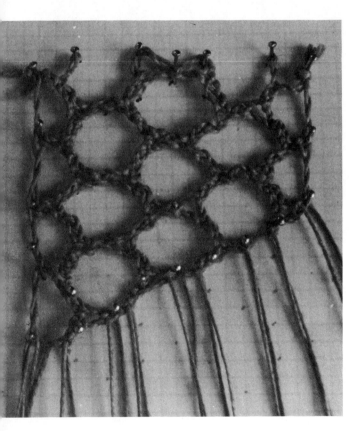

This mesh is also known as *maille ronde flamande, runde flandrische masche,* or *maglia rotonda di flandre.* It is worked on a hexagon-triangle pricking. Progress is diagonal, alternating left to right, then right to left. In making this mesh watch for pairs that may have come uncrossed. Hang two pairs of bobbins at *a, c, d,* and *f.* Hang on one pair at *b* and *e.*

1. Twist pairs 2 and 3 twice, whole stitch, pin at 1, twist, whole stitch.
2. Twist pairs 5 and 6 twice, cross, pin at 2, half stitch.
3. Twist pairs 4 and 5 twice, whole stitch, pin at 3, twist, whole stitch.
4. Twist pairs 3 and 4 twice, cross, pin at 4, half stitch.
5. Twist pairs 2 and 3 twice, whole stitch, pin at 5, twist, whole stitch.
6. Twist pairs 1 and 2 twice, cross, pin at 6, half stitch.
7. Twist pairs 2 and 3 twice, whole stitch, pin at 7, twist, whole stitch.
8. Twist pairs 4 and 5 twice, whole stitch, pin at 8, twist, whole stitch.
9. Twist pairs 6 and 7 twice, whole stitch, pin at 9, twist, whole stitch.

Continue to work diagonally in the same manner.

A simpler version of this ground is shown in this diagram. It is worked on the same pricking, but there is only one twist between pins and only one whole stitch around each pin. The sample was worked in 10/2 linen thread. Bobbins are hung on as above.

1. Twist pairs 2 and 3, cross, pin at 1, half stitch.
2. Twist pairs 5 and 6, cross, pin at 2, half stitch.
3. Twist pairs 4 and 5, cross, pin at 3, half stitch.
4. Twist pairs 3 and 4, cross, pin at 4, half stitch.
5. Twist pairs 2 and 3, cross, pin at 5, half stitch.

Round Flemish Mesh

255

6. Twist pairs 1 and 2, cross, pin at 6, half stitch.

7. Twist pairs 2 and 3, cross, pin at 7, half stitch.

8. Twist pairs 4 and 5, cross, pin at 8, half stitch.

9. Twist pairs 6 and 7, cross, pin at 9, half stitch.

10. Twist pairs 8 and 9, cross, pin at 10, half stitch.

11. Twist pairs 7 and 8, cross, pin at 11, half stitch.

Continue to work in the same manner.

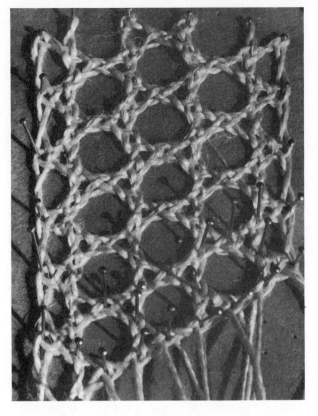

Simple round mesh.

Raccroc Stitch

Raccroc stitch is used to join strips of Brussels ground or *vrai réseau*. Make strips of ground with the usual two pairs of bobbins at each pin across the top of the mesh except for the first and last pins, at which only one pair is hung. Position the strips of ground next to one another so that they are one mesh apart. Hang two pairs of bobbins between the strips and make a plait, the same as for Brussels ground, to correspond to the pattern of the mesh. Twist one pair of the bobbins in pattern to work to the right and twist the other pair to work to the left. Make sewings into the twisted pairs at the edge of the strips of ground at each side to correspond to the upper end of the plaits lying within the horizontal row in which the joining is being made. Then twist each pair of bobbins being used in the raccroc twice and sew again to the adjacent edge pair, this time at a point corresponding to the lower edge of the row of plaits. Then twist each of the pairs being used for the raccroc the same number of times as required for the ground mesh. Join the pairs after twisting and again plait in pattern.

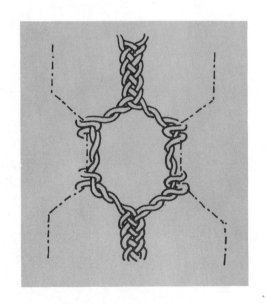

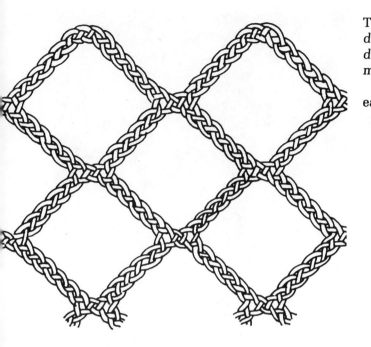

This lace filling is also called *La maille carée de Valenciennes, maglia Valenciennes qua-drangalare,* and *viereckige Valenciennes masche.*

To begin, hang four pairs of bobbins onto each head pin.

1. Twist pairs 3 and 4, cross, five half stitches. Twist pairs 5 and 6, cross, five half stitches. Whole stitch pairs 4 and 5, pin at 1 in center of stitch. (For round mesh twist pairs 3 and 6.)
2. Twist pairs 1 and 2, cross, five half stitches. Twist pairs 3 and 4, cross, five half stitches. Whole stitch pairs 2 and 3, pin at 2 in center of stitch. (Round mesh: twist pairs 1 and 4.)
3. Twist pairs 7 and 8, cross, five half stitches. Twist pairs 9 and 10, cross, five half stitches. Whole stitch pairs 8 and 9, pin at 3 in center of stitch. (Round mesh: twist pairs 7 and 10.)
4. Twist pairs 5 and 6, cross, five half stitches. Twist pairs 7 and 8, cross, five half stitches. Whole stitch pairs 6 and 7, pin at 4 in center of stitch. (Round mesh: twist pairs 5 and 8.)
5. Twist pairs 3 and 4, cross, five half stitches. Twist pairs 5 and 6, cross, five half stitches. Whole stitch pairs 4 and 5, pin at 5 in center of stitch. (Round mesh: twist pairs 3 and 6.)
6. Twist pairs 1 and 2, cross, five half stitches. Twist pairs 3 and 4, cross, five half stitches. Whole stitch pairs 2 and 3, pin at 6 in center of stitch. (Round mesh: twist pairs 1 and 4.)

Continue to work on the diagonal in the same manner, following the numbered sequence in the diagram.

For contemporary work, when this mesh may be worked in larger threads, fewer half stitches between the pins may be needed. In one sample, made with 20/2 linen thread, three half stitches were made between pins after the initial twist and cross.

For Valenciennes round mesh leave the stitches slack around the pins. Sometimes a second twist is made in the outer pairs.

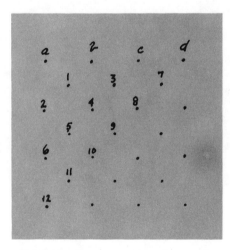

Pricking for square and round Valenciennes mesh.

Making a branched sprig, veined leaf, or similar effect presents certain problems in the manipulation of bobbins. To make this type of figure, progress with cloth stitch tape or other stitch down the central stem until you come to the first branching point. Here, discontinue making the stem, drop off two pairs of bobbins, and with the remaining bobbins work laterally to the end of the first side branch or vein.

When you reach the end of this vein, you must return the bobbins to the central stem in order to continue. This can be done by working each pair of bobbins back to the stem, making sewings into each pinhole along one side of the vein until the pair has been brought back into position alongside the pairs that were previously dropped off. You should begin with the pair of bobbins farthest from the side along which the rope sewing will be made, carrying the bobbin under the other bobbins until it is in the correct position to be sewn into the first pinhole. When all the pairs of bobbins have been worked back to the stem, you will see that you have built up a ridge along one side of the cloth tape branch or vein.

The returned pairs of bobbins increase the width of the side branch, so, although you dropped off two pairs of bobbins in turning away from the stem, the two sections, stem and branch, now appear equal in width. When all the bobbins are back in position at the stem, pick up the dropped pairs and continue to work the stem until you have reached the next branching point.

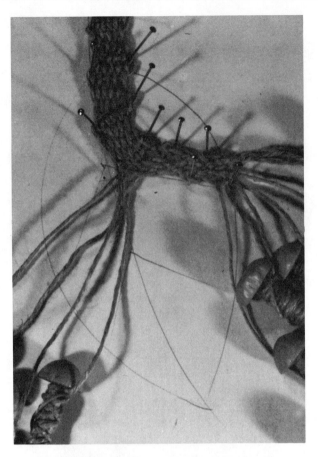

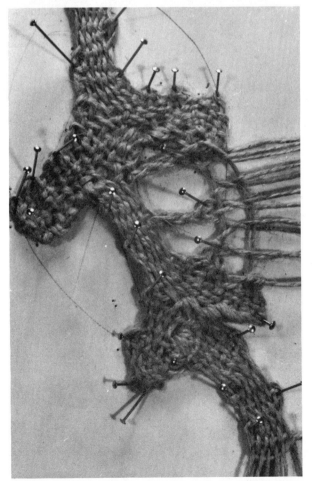

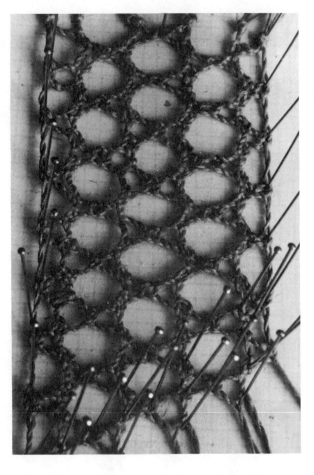

For the rose ground also known as *point de mariage*, *Scandanavian ground*, *gelosia* and *tulle double*, a hexagon-triangle pricking is used. Hang two pairs of bobbins at each head pin except for the second pin from each end. Hang one pair on these pins. Notice that work procedes alternately left to right and right to left on the diagonal. Holes develop around the pins, because an extra twist is given to the enclosing pairs before the last half stitch. There are two twists between pins at all points. The sample was worked in 20/2 linen thread.

Rose Net Ground

1. Twist pairs 2 and 3 twice, cross, pin at 1, twist, half stitch.
2. Twist pairs 5 and 6 twice, cross, pin at 2, twist, half stitch.
3. Twist pairs 4 and 5 twice, cross, pin at 3, twist, half stitch.
4. Twist pairs 3 and 4 twice, cross, pin at 4, twist, half stitch.
5. Twist pairs 2 and 3 twice, cross, pin at 5, twist, half stitch.
6. Twist pairs 1 and 2 twice, cross, pin at 6, twist, half stitch.
7. Twist pairs 2 and 3 twice, cross, pin at 7, twist, half stitch.
8. Twist pairs 4 and 5 twice, cross, pin at 8, twist, half stitch.
9. Twist pairs 6 and 7 twice, cross, pin at 9, twist, half stitch.
10. Twist pairs 8 and 9 twice, cross, pin at 10, twist, half stitch.
11. Twist pairs 7 and 8 twice, cross, pin at 11, twist, half stitch.

Continue to work diagonally in the same manner.

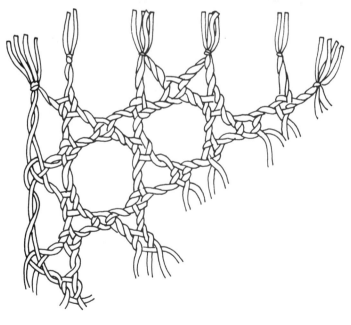

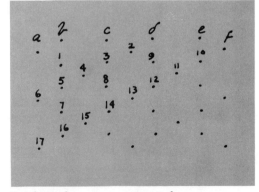

Pricking for rose net ground.

Binche Filling

This sample was made with eighteen pairs of bobbins, 20/2 linen thread, and a diagram on graph paper having ten squares per inch. Points on the pattern are two squares apart. Hang one pair of bobbins at *a, b, c, d, e, f, g, h, j, k, l, m, n, o, p,* and *q,* two pairs at *i.*

1. Twist pair 9 twice, cross with right thread of pair 8, pin at 1, half stitch.
2. Twist pair 10 twice, cross with left thread of pair 11, pin at 2, half stitch.
3. Twist pair 8 twice, cross with right thread of pair 7, pin at 3, half stitch.
4. Twist pair 7 twice, cross with right thread of pair 6, pin at 4, half stitch.
5. Twist pair 10 twice, cross with the left thread of pair 11. Twist pair 11 twice, cross with left thread of pair 12, pin at 5, half stitch.
6. Twist pair 12 twice, cross with left thread of pair 13, pin at 6, half stitch.
7. Twist pairs 9 and 10 three times, whole stitch. Twist pair 8 three times, cross with left thread of pair 9, half stitch. Twist pair 11 three times, cross with right thread of pair 10, half stitch. Whole stitch pairs 9 and 10. (To keep threads separate you can pin temporarily at 7 if you think it will help.) Twist pair 7 three times, cross with left thread of pair 8, half stitch. Twist pair 12 three times, cross with right thread of pair 11, half stitch. Whole stitch pairs 8 and 9, 9 and 10, 10 and 11; pin at 7. (The pin can be temporarily put under the last cross to keep threads separate, but it should be replaced later to the center of the spider.)
8. Whole stitch pairs 7 and 8, pairs 11 and 12, 8 and 9, 10 and 11, 9 and 10. Twist pair 6 twice, cross with right thread of pair 5, pin at 8.
9. Twist pair 6 twice, twist pair 7 three times, cross, twist twice, cross, pin above last cross at 9, half stitch.
10. Twist pair 7 twice, twist pair 8 three times, cross, twist twice, cross, pin above last cross at 10, half stitch.
11. Twist pair 8 twice, twist pair 9 three times, cross, twist twice, cross, pin above last cross at 11, half stitch.
12. Twist pair 13 twice, cross with left thread of pair 14, half stitch, pin at 12, above half stitch.

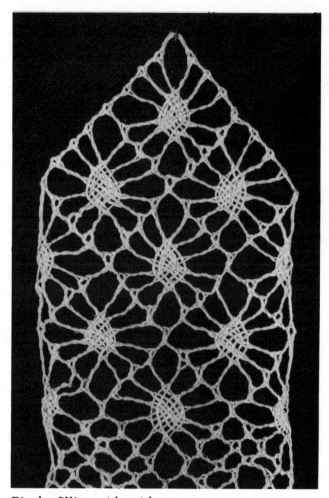

Binche *filling with spiders.*

13. Twist pair 13 twice, twist pair 12 three times, cross, twist twice, cross, pin above last cross at 13, half stitch.

14. Twist pair 12 twice, twist pair 11 three times, cross, twist twice, cross, pin above last cross at 14, half stitch.

15. Twist pair 11 twice, twist pair 10 three times, cross, twist twice, cross, pin above last cross at 15, half stitch.

16. Twist pairs 9 and 10 twice, cross, twist twice, cross, pin above last cross at 16, half stitch.

17. Twist pair 5 twice, cross with right thread of pair 4, pin at 17, half stitch.

18. Twist pair 4 twice, cross with right thread of pair 3, pin at 18, half stitch.

19. Twist pair 3 twice, cross with right thread of pair 2, pin at 19, half stitch.

20. Procedure at point 20 is the same as at point 7. Work continues to repeat, with the exception of the ommission of point 12, through point 28. The half-motif at the outer edge of the sample begins at point 29.

29. Twist pairs 1 and 2 three times, whole stitch. Twist pair 3 three times, cross with right thread of pair 2, half stitch. Whole stitch pairs 1 and 2. Twist pair 4 three times, cross with right thread of pair 3, half stitch. Whole stitch pairs 2 and 3, pairs 1 and 2, pin at 29.

30. Whole stitch pairs 3 and 4, 2 and 3, 1 and 2. Whole stitch pairs 2 and 3, 1 and 2. Twist pair 5 twice, twist pair 4 three times, cross, twist twice, cross, pin above last cross at 30, half stitch.

31. Whole stitch pairs 3 and 2, 2 and 1. Twist pair 4 twice, twist pair 3 three times, cross, twist twice, cross, pin above last cross at 31, half stitch.

32. Twist pair 3 twice, twist pair 2 three times, cross, twist twice, cross, pin above last cross at 32, half stitch.

33. Twist pair 2 twice, twist pair 1 three times, cross, twist twice, cross, pin above last cross at 33, half stitch.

At 34, 35, 36, and 37 twist the left-hand pair twice, cross with the right pair, pin. The procedure repeats the diagonal edge of the left side, but in reverse. Point 38 repeats 7 and 20.

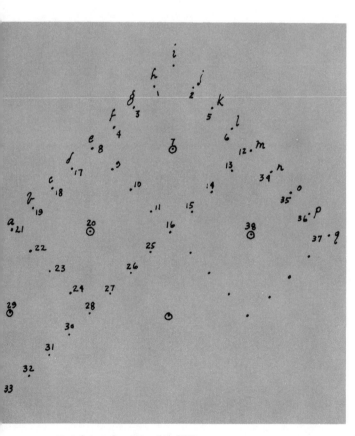

Pricking for Binche filling.

Bud Devices

Although variations of this filling stitch can be made, directions for only one are given below. Fillings of this sort can be seen in the laces shown in the illustrations. The sample was made with 20/2 linen thread without a pricking.

1. Whole stitch pairs 8 and 9, pairs 7 and 8, pairs 9 and 10, pairs 8 and 9. Pin at 1.
2. Whole stitch pairs 6 and 7, pairs 5 and 6. Twist pair 8 once, whole stitch pairs 7 and 8, pairs 6 and 7.
3. Whole stitch pairs 10 and 11, pairs 11 and 12. Twist pair 9 once, whole stitch pairs 9 and 10, pairs 10 and 11.
4. Twist pairs 8 and 9 once; whole stitch pairs 8 and 9, pairs 7 and 8, pairs 9 and 10, pairs 8 and 9. (At this point a pin can be stuck below last crossing of 8 and 9 to keep threads in order, if desired.)
5. Twist pair 5 twice; whole stitch pairs 4 and 5, 3 and 4. Twist pair 6 twice; whole stitch pairs 5 and 6, pairs 4 and 5. Pin at 2.
6. Whole stitch pairs 2 and 3, pairs 1 and 2. Twist pair 4 once; whole stitch pairs 3 and 4, pairs 2 and 3.
7. Twist pair 7 twice; whole stitch pairs 6 and 7. Twist pair 5 once; whole stitch pairs 5 and 6. Twist pair 8 twice; whole stitch pairs 7 and 8, pairs 6 and 7.
8. Twist pairs 4 and 5 once, whole stitch pairs 4 and 5, pairs 3 and 4, pairs 5 and 6, pairs 4 and 5. (A pin can be temporarily stuck between pairs 4 and 5 to keep threads in order, if desired.)
9. Twist pair 12 twice; whole stitch pairs 12 and 13. Twist pair 11 twice; whole stitch pairs 11 and 12, pairs 13 and 14, pairs 12 and 13. Pin at 3.
10. Twist pair 10 twice; whole stitch pairs 10 and 11. Twist pair 9 twice; whole stitch pairs 9 and 10. Twist pair 12 once; whole stitch pairs 11 and 12, pairs 10 and 11.
11. Whole stitch pairs 14 and 15. Twist pair 13 once; whole stitch pairs 13 and 14, pairs 14 and 15, pairs 13 and 14.
12. Twist pairs 12 and 13 once; whole stitch pairs 12 and 13, pairs 13 and 14, pairs 11 and 12, pairs 12 and 13. (Pin may be stuck between last crossing of 12 and 13 to keep order, if desired.)

Pricking for bud devices.

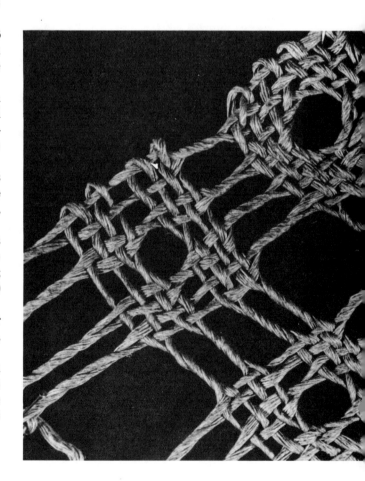

13. Twist pairs 8 and 9 twice; whole stitch pairs 8 and 9. Twist pair 10 twice; whole stitch pairs 9 and 10. Twist pair 7 twice; whole stitch pairs 7 and 8, pairs 8 and 9. Pin at 4.

14. Twist pair 6 twice; whole stitch pairs 6 and 7. Twist pair 8 once; whole stitch pairs 7 and 8. Twist pair 5 twice; whole stitch pairs 5 and 6, pairs 6 and 7.

15. Twist pair 11 twice; whole stitch pairs 10 and 11. Twist pair 9 once; whole stitch pairs 9 and 10. Twist pair 12 twice; whole stitch pairs 11 and 12, pairs 10 and 11.

16. Twist pairs 8 and 9 once; whole stitch pairs 8 and 9, pairs 7 and 8, pairs 9 and 10, pairs 8 and 9. (Pin may be stuck between the last crossing of pairs 8 and 9 to keep order, if desired.)

17. Twist pair 1 twice, twist pair 2 once, whole stitch pairs 1 and 2, half stitch pairs 1 and 2. Twist pair 3 twice; whole stitch pairs 2 and 3, pairs 1 and 2.

18. Twist pair 4 twice; whole stitch pairs 4 and 3, pairs 3 and 2, pairs 1 and 2. Pin at 5.

19. Twist pairs 4 and 5 twice; whole stitch pairs 4 and 5. Twist pair 3 twice; whole stitch pairs 3 and 4. Twist pair 6 twice; whole stitch pairs 5 and 6, pairs 4 and 5. Pin at 6.

20. Twist pair 2 twice; whole stitch pairs 2 and 3. Twist pair 1 twice; whole stitch pairs 1 and 2. Twist pair 4 once, whole stitch pairs 3 and 4, pairs 2 and 3.

21. Twist pair 7 twice; whole stitch pairs 6 and 7. Twist pair 8 twice; whole stitch pairs 7 and 8. Twist pair 5 once; whole stitch pairs 5 and 6, pairs 6 and 7.

22. Twist pairs 4 and 5 once; whole stitch pairs 4 and 5, pairs 3 and 4, pairs 5 and 6, pairs 4 and 5.

Bud filling.

Mechlin Ground

Make *Mechlin* ground (also called *le réseau Malines, Mechelner grund,* and *fondo di Malines*) on a diamond pricking. Hang two pairs of bobbins on at each head pin. Work progresses diagonally.

1. Twist pairs 2 and 3, cross, pin at 1, three half stitches.
2. Twist pairs 1 and 2, cross, pin at 2, three half stitches.
3. Twist pairs 4 and 5, cross, pin at 3, three half stitches.
4. Twist pairs 3 and 4, cross, pin at 4, three half stitches.
5. Twist pairs 2 and 3, cross, pin at 5, three half stitches.
6. Twist pairs 1 and 2, cross, pin at 6, three half stitches.
7. Twist pairs 6 and 7, cross, pin at 7, three half stitches.

Continue to work diagonally in the same manner. Directions for the making of *Mechlin* grounds vary. Some call for two twists between pins. Others call for fewer than three half stitches after the pin.

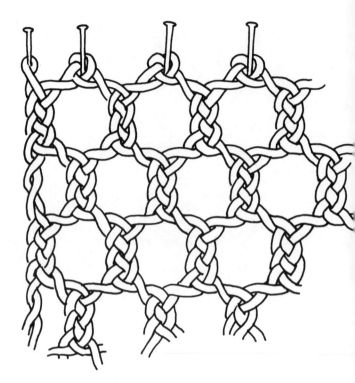

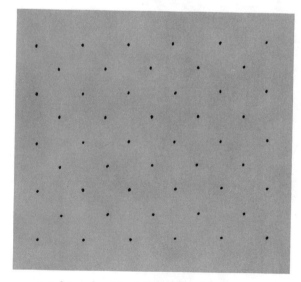

Pricking for Mechlin ground.

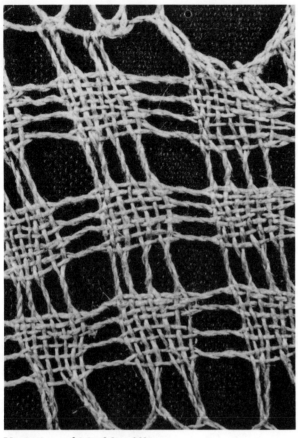

Variation of Mechlin filling.

This delicate filling stitch is found on several laces, with *Mechlin* among the oldest of them. It is a combination of cloth stitch with simple twists. Although the directions for the stitch seem complicated, once the technique has been tried its simplicity will be apparent. One whole stitch encloses each pin. Twice-twisted threads separate clusters of four cloth stitches. Numerous variations of this stitch can be tried. A lozenge of more than four cloth stitches can be used. The shape of the unit need not be a lozenge. The number of twists that make the bars between the units can be more or less than two. A great many variations can be found in old laces.

In working this filling the unit shape of the design is best disregarded. It will be most easily worked if rows of single points are worked diagonally as shown in the diagram. If units of four points are worked, there is more chance for threads to uncross or untwist, causing errors.

The sample was worked in 20/2 linen. The graph paper used for the diagram had ten squares per inch. To begin work, hang two pairs of bobbins on at points *a, b, c, d, e,* and *f.*

1. Cross pairs 2 and 3, pin at 1, half stitch.
2. Twist pair 1 once, twist pair 2 twice, cross, pin at 2, half stitch.
3. Twist pairs 4 and 5 twice, cross, pin at 3, half stitch.
4. Twist pair 3 twice, do not twist pair 4, cross, pin at 4, half stitch.
5. Twist pairs 2 and 3 twice, cross, pin at 5, half stitch.
6. Twist pair 1 once, do not twist pair 2, cross, half stitch.
7. Cross pairs 6 and 7, pin at 7, half stitch.
8. Twist pairs 5 and 6 twice, cross, pin at 8, half stitch.
9. Cross pairs 4 and 5, half stitch.
10. Twist pair 4 twice, do not twist pair 3, cross, pin at 10, half stitch.
11. Cross pairs 2 and 3, pin at 11, half stitch.
12. Twist pair 1 once, twist pair 2 twice, cross, pin at 12, half stitch.

Continue to work on the diagonal, maintaining blocks of four whole stitches separated by bars consisting of two twists.

Mechlin Filling

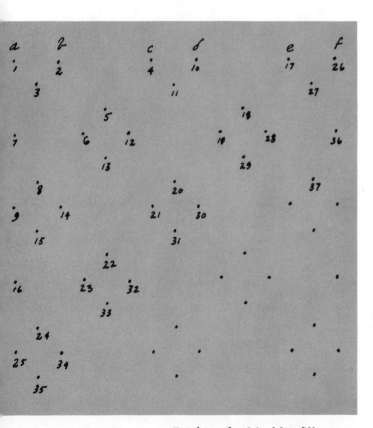

Pricking for Mechlin filling.

Tulle or Lille Ground

Make this ground on a diamond pricking with two pairs of bobbins hung on to each head pin. Procedure from pin to pin is the same as in *torchon* and Dieppe grounds, but there is no whole stitch made around the pins. Instead, cross the threads and stick a pin under the crossing. You can make one or more twists between pins. Only one twist makes a very fragile ground. Two twists more often are used. Three may make a very wiry ground.

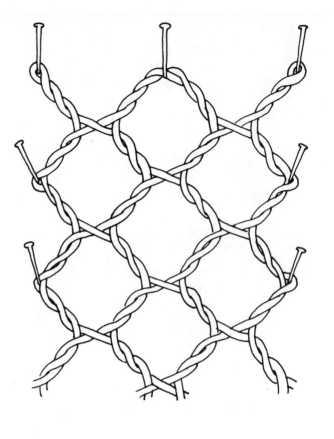

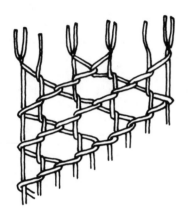

So-called three-thread version of tulle *or Lille.*

Star Mesh

This ground may also be called *double ground, point double, point de Paris, fond chant, fond clair, point de six, eternelle, Chantilly, Englesche grond, dentelle de Grammont, trenne, kat stitch,* and *wire ground.*

Work this ground on a diamond pricking with two pairs of bobbins at each head pin. In the working it is the same as rose net except that, since the pricking is simpler, no pins are stuck at some of the points where they are used in rose net. Also, between whole stitches, there often is only one twist rather than two. Where no pin is used at a whole stitch the stitch draws up tightly. Thus, star mesh is more angular and open than rose net.

Some confusion arises in the use of the term *fond clair,* which by some authors designates a Lille or *tulle* ground.

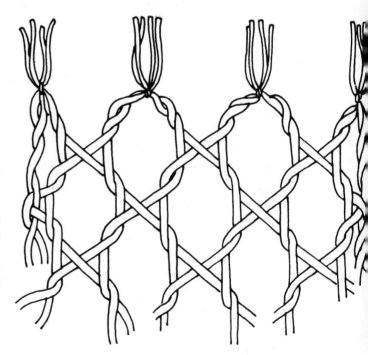

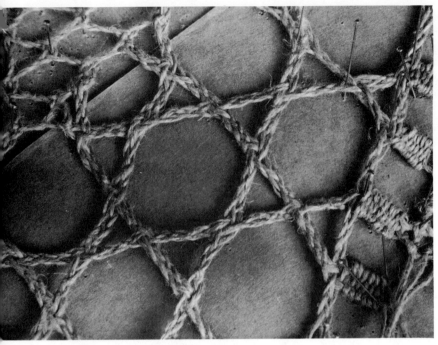

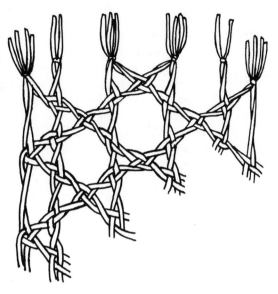

Fond chant *or* kat *stitch.*

Detail of star-hexagon patterned
plaiting, showing crossings of plaits
made with whole stitches using
doubled threads.

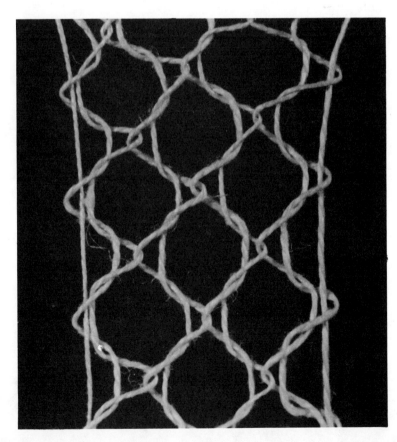

Two-thread ground.

Diamond Filling

In Milanese and many laces earlier than Honiton, geometric fillings made of matting stitch and twists in many designs can be found. In Honiton lace, areas having matting stitch, square dots, seeds, leaves, and other similar devices are said to contain leadworks or cutworks. Diamond filling is a simple version of this type of filling. It can be varied by altering the spacing, the number of passes in making the leadworks, or the number of twists made in pairs before and after the leadworks are made. Two pairs of bobbins are needed at each point along the top row.

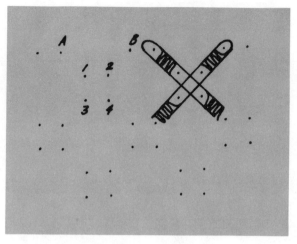

Diagram for diamond filling.

1. At *a* pick up pairs 1 and 2, twist twice (or the desired number of times), make a leadwork, (see page 00) twist each pair twice. Pin at 1 between twisted pairs. Observe the number of passes made by the worker in making the leadwork and make all other leadworks with the same number of passes.
2. At *b* twist pairs 3 and 4 twice, make a leadwork, twist pairs twice. Pin at 2 between the pairs.
3. With pairs 2 and 3 make a whole stitch. Twist pair 2 twice; whole stitch pairs 1 and 2. Twist pair 4 twice; whole stitch pairs 3 and 4. Twist pairs 2 and 3 twice; whole stitch pairs 2 and 3. Arrange pairs 1 and 2 around pin 3.
4. Arrange pairs 3 and 4 around pin 4.
5. Repeat from 1.

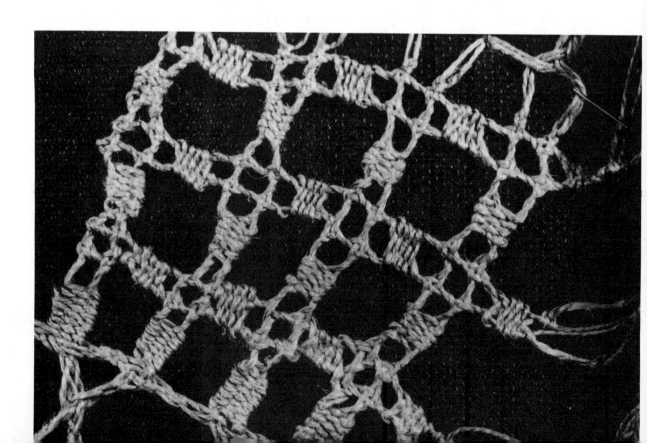

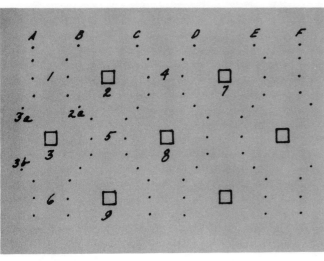

Diagram and pricking for toad in a hole.

Toad in a hole is a decorative filling composed of alternate sections of cloth stitch and lead-works, seen frequently in Honiton. It appears on the cuffs shown on page 193. It can be worked in horizontal rows, but the diagram has been numbered for diagonal working, which is usually the best procedure from the standpoint of keeping the bobbins in order as work progresses. Push the pins well down into the pillow so as not to interfere with the making of the leadworks. To make a sample as shown, hang on three pairs of bobbins at *b*, *c*, *d*, and *e*. Put two pairs at *a* and *f*. The spacing between pins depends upon the size of the thread in use and the effect desired. The filling can be very open, with more twists and plaits between sections. The cloth stitch areas can be worked either very densely, or they can be very loose. Any of these changes will alter the appearance of the filling considerably.

1. Plait pairs 1 and 2 twice; plait pairs 3 and 4 twice. Make cloth stitches between pinpoints in section 1.
2. Twist pairs 5 and 6 three times each. Make a leadwork (matting stitch area, see page 00) in section 2.
3. Plait pairs 3 and 4 twice; twist pair 5 three times. Whole stitch pair 5 with pairs 3 and 4, which have been plaited. Pin at 2a in the center of the whole stitch. Twist pair 6 three times.
4. Plait pairs 1 and 2 twice. Pin at 3a. Twist pair 1 five times. Temporarily secure the pair between the twists at 3b. Twist pairs 2 and 3 three times. Make a leadwork at 3.
5. Continue to work the squares as above in the order shown in the diagram.

Toad in a hole filling.

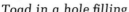

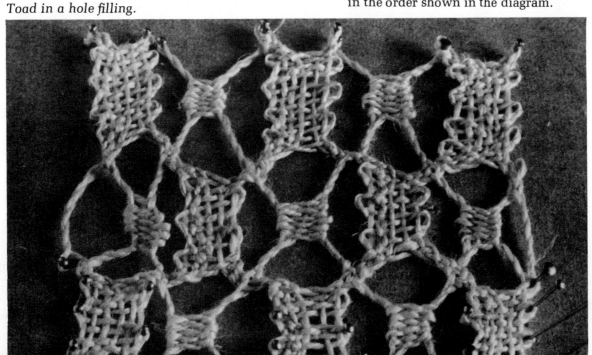

Double Pin Variation

The pricking for this interesting ground is an arrangement of small squares. It can be varied by using twists rather than whole stitches and by varying the scale. The sample was made with 20/2 linen thread. Hang two pairs of bobbins at points *a*, *b*, *c*, and *d*.

1. Twist pairs 3 and 4, 5 and 6; cross. *Twist pairs 4 and 5, whole stitch; twist pairs 3 and 4, whole stitch; twist pairs 5 and 6, whole stitch; twist pairs 4 and 5, whole stitch. Twist pairs 3 and 4, cross, pin at 1, half stitch.
2. Twist pairs 3 and 4, cross, pin at 2, half stitch. Twist pairs 1 and 2, cross. Twist pairs 2 and 3, whole stitch; twist pairs 1 and 2, whole stitch; twist pairs 3 and 4, whole stitch; twist pairs 2 and 3, whole stitch.
3. Twist pairs 1 and 2, cross, pin at 3, half stitch.
4. Twist pairs 5 and 6, cross, pin at 4, half stitch.
5. Twist pairs 3 and 4, cross, pin at 5, half stitch.
6. Twist pairs 5 and 6, cross, pin at 6, half stitch.
7. Twist pairs 2 and 4, cross, pin at 7, half stitch.
8. Twist pairs 7 and 8, cross. Twist pairs 6 and 7, whole stitch; twist pairs 5 and 6, whole stitch; twist pairs 7 and 8, whole stitch; twist pairs 6 and 7, whole stitch. Twist pairs 5 and 6, cross, pin at 8, half stitch.
9. Twist pairs 7 and 8, cross, pin at 9, half stitch.
10. Twist pairs 5 and 6, cross, pin at 10, half stitch.

Repeat the pattern from*. Bring bobbins into position at margins by plaiting. Keep the number of plaits (optional) equal between margin pins.

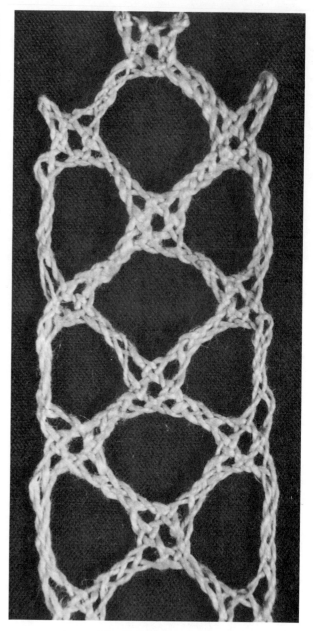

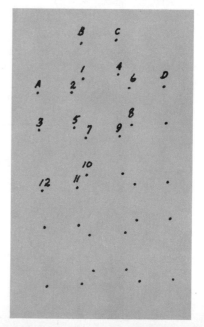

Pricking for double pin variation.

270

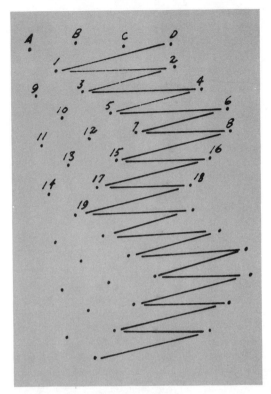

Diagram and pricking for Torchon edge with half stitch zigzags.

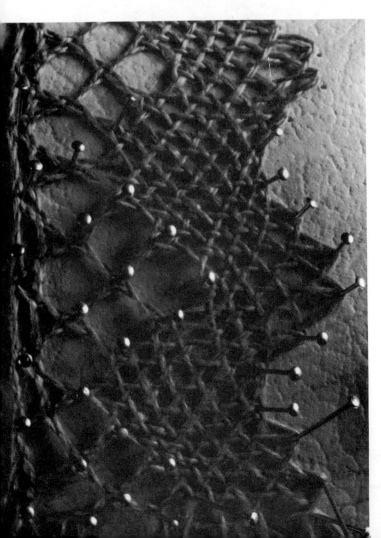

Torchon
Edge
with
Half-
Stitch
Zigzags

This is one of the simplest of *Torchon* edgings, combining *Torchon* net with half stitch. Since most nets, among them *Torchon*, develop along a diagonal, zigzag motifs are easily worked into them. This edge is worked in half stitch, but it could also be worked in whole stitch or a combination of whole and half stitch. For the sample, 20/2 linen thread was used. Make a pricking according to the diagram. Hang 3 pairs of bobbins at *a* and *b*, two pairs at *c* and *d*.

1. Twist pairs 3 and 4, cross, pin at 1, half stitch.
2. Twist and cross all pairs, in order until pin 2 is reached. (4 and 5, 5 and 6, 6 and 7, etc.) Pin at 2.
3. Work right to left, making half stitches with each pair until pin 3 is reached (4 pairs left of pin). Pin at 3, enclosing pin with second half stitch. Leave the left pair hanging.
4. Twist and cross pairs 5 and 6, make half stitches with all pairs until point 4 is reached. Pin at 4, half stitch.
5. Make half stitches with each pair until point 5 is reached. Pin at 5, half stitch.
6. Twist and cross pairs 6 and 7; continue making half stitches to point 6. Pin at 6, half stitch.
7. Make half stitches with each pair until point 7 is reached. Pin at 7, half stitch.
8. Half stitch beginning with pairs 6 and 7 until point 8 is reached. Pin at 8, half stitch. Work left to right in the next row, making half stitches. Drop the work at the crossing of pairs 6 and 7.
9. The half stitch area is dropped at this point and the net resumed. Twist pairs 2 and 3, whole stitch. Twist pair 1 twice, pair 2 once, whole stitch pairs 1 and 2. Pin at 9, twist pairs 2 and 3, whole stitch both pairs left of pin.
10. Twist pairs 3 and 4 once, pin at 10, half stitch.
11. Twist pairs 2 and 3 once, whole stitch. Twist pair 1 twice, twist pair 2 once, whole stitch. Pin at 11, pair 1 left of pin.
12. Twist pairs 2 and 3 once, whole stitch. Twist pairs 4 and 5 once, cross, pin at 12, half stitch.
13. Twist pairs 3 and 4 once, cross, pin at 13, half stitch.
14. Twist pairs 2 and 3, whole stitch. Twist

pair 1 twice; twist pair 2 once, whole stitch, pin at 14, keeping pair 1 left of the pin. Twist pairs 2 and 3, whole stitch.

15. At this point the half stitch area is resumed. Twist pairs 5 and 6, cross, pin at 15, half stitch.

16. Work right, making half stitches until pin 16 is reached. Pin at 16, half stitch.

17. Work left, making half stitches, ending with pairs 4 and 5. Pin at 17, half stitch.

18. Twist and cross pairs 5 and 6, half stitch to the right until point 18 is reached. Pin at 18, half stitch.

19. Work half stitches to the left, ending with pairs 4 and 5. Continue working in pattern.

Torchon Edge with Half-Stitch Shells and Spiders

When the various techniques that are combined in *Torchon* edgings like this one have become familiar, you will need little help in reproducing the pattern, but it is helpful to know in what order to work the parts of the design. Here the work begins with the *Torchon* ground, (each pin enclosed in a whole stitch, one twist between each whole stitch.) Work the lace according to the numbered diagram through point 20.

21. Pick up the last pair of bobbins on the right. Work left with half stitches to 21. Cross with the right pair of bobbins at d, which has been twisted once. Pin at 21, half stitch.

22. Work right with half stitch to point 22, pin at 22, twist once.

23. Work left with half stitches to point 23, pin at 23, half stitch.

24. Work right with half stitches to point 24, pin at 24, twist once.

25. Work left with half stitches to point 25, pin at 25, half stitch.

26, 27, 28, 29, 30, 31, 32, 33, and 34. Continue working in half stitch as above. Pick up one pair at 27, drop one pair at 29, 31, 33, and 34, finishing the shell by working extra pairs into the pin at 34.

35-41. Continue Torchon ground, dropping off one pair on the right in each row for

Torchon edge with half-stitch shells and spiders.

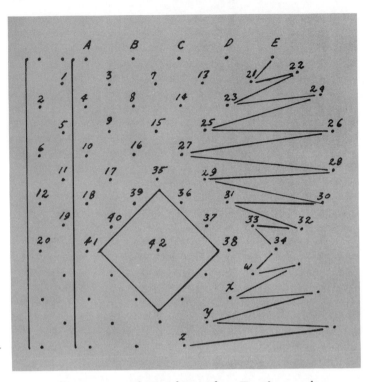

Diagram and pricking for Torchon edge with half stitch shells and spiders.

the spider.

42. Complete upper half of spider, (directions on page 246), pin at 42. Finish lower half of spider, leaving pairs in position to continue net ground on left and leaving points w, x, y, and z free to be picked up when the second half-stitch shell is made.

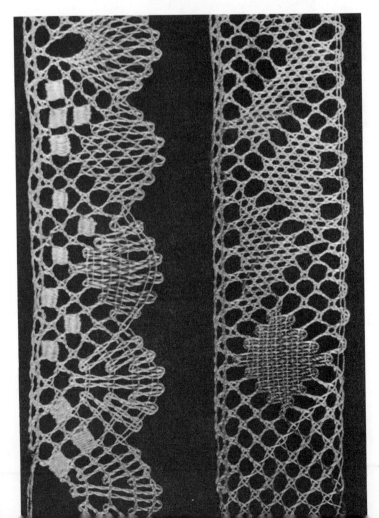

Sample strips with techniques characteristic of torchon: leaves, fans, square dots, spiders, and half stitch zigzags. Courtesy: Mary McPeek.

Fans

A pretty and familiar edge used in *Torchon* lace is the fanned edge, which may be worked in several variations. The most common variety has twists in both the radiating and the arcing pairs of threads. Hang two pairs of bobbins at 1 and whole stitch them around the pin. The pair on the left becomes the outside passive pair. The pair on the right is the working pair. Hang one pair on at each additional point across the top of the figure: *a*, *b*, and *c*. With the workers make whole stitches with the passives at *a*, *b*, and *c*, twisting both passives and workers once before making each whole stitch. (If desired, workers may be twisted more than once.) Work the fan according to the numbered diagram, pinning at each numbered point, making twists and whole stitches with each set of passives as the workers come to it. Pull up each whole stitch carefully so that the spacing will be even. This is a necessary precaution, because not every whole stitch is pinned in place, as in most of the previous processes.

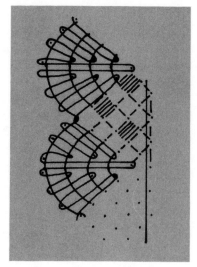

Working diagram for fans.

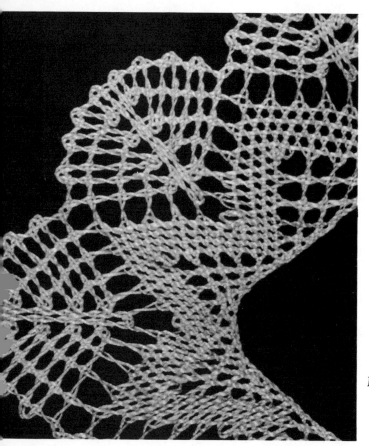

Pricking for fans.

Detail of the finished lace.

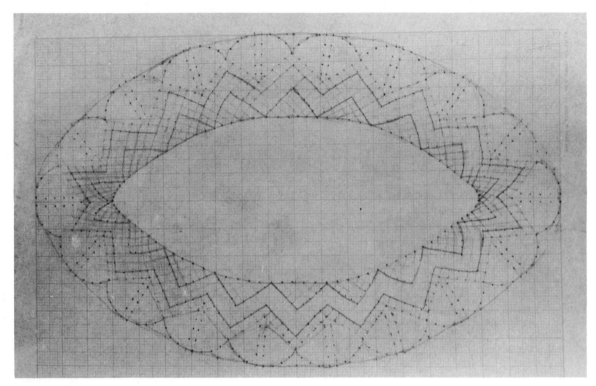

Diagram for lace edge with fans, zigzags. Note changes of scale as the design is modified to fit a pointed oval.

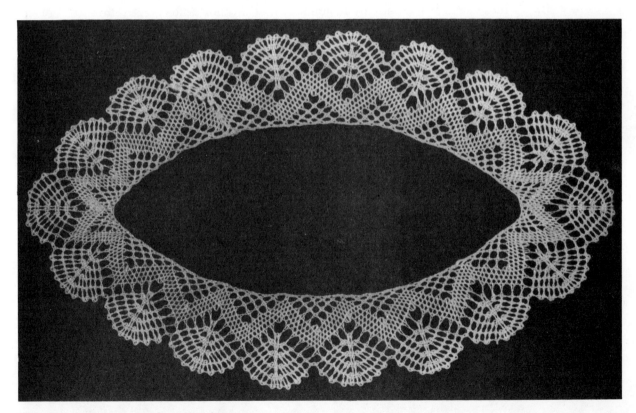

The finished lace made according to the pattern in the photo above. Courtesy: Mary McPeek.

Mixed Laces

After 1835 entirely hand-made laces gradually disappeared. Machine-made tulle was available, and a machine could produce mesh grounds a thousand times as fast as could a lacemaking expert. *Appliqué de Bruxelles* enjoyed enormous popularity, because many more people could afford to own this partially machine-made lace than had ever been able to buy other types made entirely by hand.

The common denominator in all the lace types of the nineteenth century was the idea of mixing techniques. In addition to the machine-made ground meshes, lacemakers could work with a variety of premade tapes, some hand made and some machine-woven.

The idea of making motifs or tapes separately and then applying them to a lace ground was not new. Among the famous antecedents were *Milan au lacet*, or *mezzo punto*, and Genoese braid laces. In the Southern Netherlands mixed laces needle-made motifs on bobbined meshes, were being made as early as the eighteenth century. Most of these laces were made by techniques that did not differ greatly from the construction method used later, when laces were made of machined parts, except that they were entirely hand made. Later others were hand made except for the ground. When both tapes and ground were premade by machine, all that remained for the lacemaker to do was to join parts, add fillings, and either sew on a ground or work *guipure* bars between the parts.

Doily of bobbin tape lace. United States, c. 1900. Linen. Square: 9½ inches. Courtesy: Art Institute of Chicago. Gift: Mrs. Floyd Raymond Stevenson.

Flounce of needle-run pattern on machine net. Italy, early 19th century. Courtesy: The Metropolitan Museum of Art. Gift of Dr. Lucia E. and John L. Heaton in memory of Eliza Putnam Heaton, 1919.

*"To Touch" (detail), by Virginia Bath.
Needle lace and machine lace. Lace
can be made on a home sewing
machine by darning between stretched
threads or across openings. The work
should be secured in a frame or hoop,
and the stitching should be made following the machine instructions for
darning.*

Patterns and Designs for Mixed Laces

Tape laces, appliquéd laces, and all the lace experiments of the nineteenth century are the textile artist's equivalent to collage and assemblage. They were made in the same years that produced the astonishing silk patchworks sometimes called crazy quilts. Both the laces and the coverlets often failed because of an excessive richness, but it is equally true that at times both were surprisingly successful, the sum of their parts exceeding their individual elements.

Lace in Ireland

Because of the dress edicts, lace was not much worn in Ireland until Charles I lifted apparel restrictions and English fashions began to be adopted. Then the Irish demand for lace created a market that had to be supplied by importers. Since most people could not afford to buy expensive imported lace, there was some pressure for a national industry. A school was founded by the Dublin Society in 1731; it continued for forty-three years. Under the sponsorship of Lady Arabella Denny, children in public care were taught to make lace.

After 1820 Carrickmacross laces were made, usually with Italianate patterns. One of the earliest schools for Carrickmacross was established at Ahan. Limerick laces began in 1829. Then famine in Ireland from 1846 to 1848 spurred the establishment of lace industries in many parts of the country. With the assistance of the government and concerned women of means, needle-made, embroidered, and crocheted imitations of the laces of Belgium, Italy, Spain and Greece were undertaken. Straight bobbin techniques also were taught in the schools.

In Carrickmacross, county of Monaghan, imitations of old point laces were made with appliqué on net or bride grounds. Old point techniques were taught at Belfast in Jane Clark's school. In county Fermanagh, Lady Erne's establishment taught bobbin lacemaking of the straight *Valenciennes* type as well as tape lacemaking and tatting. Crochets were made in Ross and in Cork, where Miss Susanna Meridith opened a school of crochet; another important center was at Limerick.

Irish point, also called *Curragh point*, was principally made at Youghal but it was manufactured at other places as well: New Ross, Kinware, Waterford, Killarney, and Clonakilty. *Curragh point* imitated the designs of Brussels point lace. A simpler form of the lace was made by working twisted bars and motifs over bobbin net and then cutting away the excess net.

The entire design was first marked out on colored paper, and each of the separate motifs was pricked on a parchment ground. An outlining *fil de trace* was couched onto the pattern and stitches were made in the paired holes of the pricking. Most of the familiar lace stitches were used in making the motifs and fillings. Buttonhole stitch was used for the solid sections. The laces had fancy fillings from Brussels, Venice, and Barcelona laces. Outlines were then made with fine buttonhole stitch in dainty single lines, sometimes with picots, or over-cords for a raised cordonnet.

When the separate sections were completed, they were laid on the original drawing, face down, and joined with twisted or buttonholed bars. Where bars were sparse or unsubstantial, net was put over the area, overcast to the edges of the motifs, and then cut away behind fancy fillings. For the finest lace, a hand-made mesh ground was used instead of machine net.

Border and insertion of cut and embroidered muslin on machine-made net. Ireland (Carrickmacross), last quarter of the 19th century. Courtesy: Victoria and Albert Museum, London.

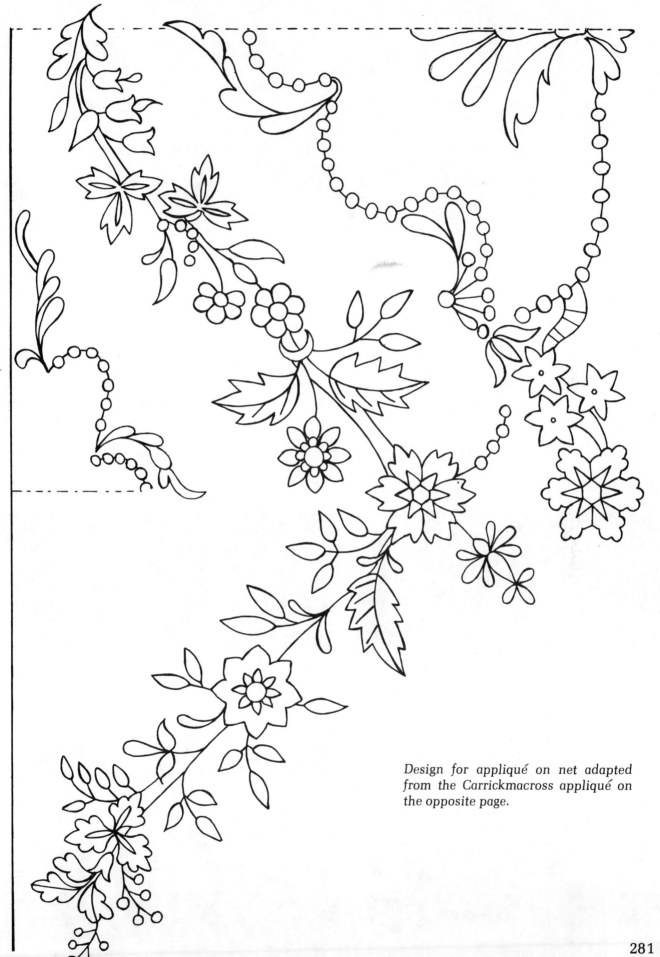

Design for appliqué on net adapted from the Carrickmacross appliqué on the opposite page.

281

Carrickmacross appliqué began with a piece of net stretched in a frame over glazed fabric. Over these was put cambric or muslin having a transfer of the pattern of the lace to be made. A *fil de trace* outline was couched over the contours of the motifs drawn on the muslin and then closely overcast, the worker taking care not to catch the glazed cloth base into the stitching. Openings were cut into motif centers at some points, and fancy fillings or picoted bars were worked into them. When the lace was complete and off the frame, the net behind the fillings was cut out with special scissors. The rest of the net served as a *réseau* for the lace after excess cambric was cut away.

A similar lace, though not as rich, was made at Limerick. Limerick appliqué was made of cambric or net over net. The work was stretched in a frame and a *fil de trace* was laid over a pattern on the upper cloth, or in the case of net on net, over a pattern under the net. Outlines were overcast, openings were cut and filled, and finally, the excess of the upper layer was cut away.

Carrickmacross guipure began with a design drawn on muslin or cambric, which was framed over smooth cloth. A *fil de trace* was couched over the outlines of the pattern and closely overcast. Openings were cut into the muslin centers of motifs. The edges of the openings were buttonholed and filled with wheels and other fancy needle-made *jours*. Sometimes the openings were filled with handmade net, which afterwards had darned patterns run into it. Motifs were joined with buttonholed and picoted bars, and the lace was removed from its backing. Then the muslin or lawn was carefully trimmed close to the overcast edges of the motifs, removing all the fabric but that needed to fill solid portions of the design.

Since the outer edges of the motifs were not buttonholed, but overcast, this lace was not as sturdy as those with buttonholed edges. However, the overcast edges were considered more dainty. The lace is not washable. As in much needlework of the nineteenth century in the British Isles, the favorite subject matter was a combination of rose, thistle, and shamrock.

Handkerchief of tambour and run net embroidery. Ireland (Limerick), first half of 19th century. Courtesy: Victoria and Albert Museum, London.

Border of tambour and run net embroidery. Ireland (Limerick), first half of 19th century. Courtesy: Victoria and Albert Museum.

Pattern derived from border design on
opposite page.

Tambour Laces

Tambour is an embroidery made early in China, India, Persia, and Turkey, and later in Saxony and Switzerland. It was introduced into France in the time of Louis XIV, and it is said that Madame de Pompadour liked it. *Tambour* lace was made in England after 1820. It was worked on a net ground in the same manner as it had previously been worked as embroidery on a solid ground. In the United States, tambour embroidery and lacemaking were favorite pastimes from 1780 until 1860.

Limerick *tambour* was worked in a *tambour* frame with a tambour needle. The effect of the stitch made with the hooked needle is almost identical to that of the chain stitch in embroidery. Floss threads were used. Designs included harps and shamrocks, patterns that were less complicated than Brussels *tambours*, which had the flowers and scrolls seen in other Flemish laces. Isle of Wight *tambours* had simple scrolling patterns in thick thread.

Tambour was combined with other stitches on net as well as on cambric and muslin. The stitch also was used for rugs, upholstery, and hangings, for which it was worked in silk or wool. *Tambour* braids were used to decorate garments, a Levantine idea. In Turkey *tambour* work was combined with crochet in *Oyah* (bebilla) lace.

Shawl of tambour. *England or Ireland, 19th century. Courtesy: Royal Ontario Museum, Toronto.*

Curtain, borders, and small cover of tambour on machine net, filet. France, 19th century. Courtesy: The Metropolitan Museum. Gift of Mrs. Nuttall, 1908.

Embroidered Net

The region of Luneville in France, in the department of Lorraine, produced fine white lace and excellent embroideries on tulle. Similar work was done at Lierre and Limerick. In Sicily and Spain, embroidered net laces were made with heavier threads in colored silk on silk, in imitation of bobbin-made *blonde* laces. In Northamptonshire, laces made at Lille began to be copied on hand-made grounds in the eighteenth century. In the Isle of Wight, Wiltshire, and the South Coast, laces were also made on machine net. Thick fillings were darned in and outlined with doubled thread.

In the States during the 1820s and 1830s, wedding veils and scarves were made by working fillings into machine-made nets. As in *tambour* work, there was much use of eyelets on embroidered nets; both used the same stitches. However, in *tambour* the chain stitch predominated, while in the darned nets the fancy fillings were most important. Both black and white versions of the nets were made. Each variety had its separate name, taken from its needle or bobbin lace prototype.

White embroidery on muslin had been popular in Mexico from about 1710 until 1840. A technique called *Spanish lacework* continued to be made in shawls and lace veils. These fashions were introduced into the United States from Mexico via New Orleans and were worn throughout the southern states. Veils were about a yard square. Shawls were about double that size. The net used to make them was a heavier fabric than the fragile net used for other laces, because it had to carry the weight of very heavy embroidery.

Border motif from the scarf on the opposite page.

288

Pattern for embroidery on machine
net, adapted from a scarf in the collection of the Buffalo Historical Society.

Ruffle of straw on tulle. France, c.
1890. 4¾ inches wide.

The lace was made over an inked design on paper or cloth. Sometimes areas to be filled were marked with red chalk. The cloth parts of the pattern were darned. It is easy to see why the designs have the block-spot distribution of pattern that was almost universally used. If worked in the hand, it is far more convenient to work with several small spots of design each on a little piece of paper than to work on a single large sheet of paper with a large composition. The same type of work also was mounted in a frame for the embroidery. An unfinished example of such work can be seen at the Metropolitan Museum of Art in New York.

All-white or all-black embroidered net laces were most popular in the United States, but other colors were used also. Silver on black was not unusual. Orange patterns on white were more unique. Multicolored patterns were less out-of-the-ordinary. Silk and cotton flosses were used for the embroidery.

Fischu of needle-run pattern on machine net. Ireland (Limerick), first half of 19th century. Courtesy: Victoria and Albert Museum, London.

Tape Laces

In the nineteenth century tape laces were called modern point laces. In different localities the same lace was given different names. *Dentelle Renaissance*, as tape laces are still called in Belgium, was introduced in 1885. It usually has only one filling stitch. The braid edges are overcast, and the bars are simple twists with an occasional wheel where eight points converge. Two such laces are *Battenberg* and *Branscombe point*. The former was made in the United States and the latter was an English lace; nevertheless, the two laces have much in common. Battenberg was often used as an edging for a piece of embroidery. The usual filling included rosettes or wheels and Sorrento bars made with Number 100 thread. Prepared rings were used frequently.

Doily. Bobbin tape lace, called Renaissance. *Belgium (Brussels), contemporary. Made for mass sale.*

Handkerchief. Bobbin tapes on net, called Princesse. Belgium (Bruges), contemporary. Made for mass sale.

Damascene lace differs in having hand-made Honiton sprigs as its motifs. Its bars are twisted. Like the other tape laces, it was worked over a smooth cloth pattern. Edges of braids were similarly overcast. The only decoration in addition to the Honiton sprays were occasional wheels or rosettes. In Honiton itself, many wedding garments with bobbin-made sprays on net were also made.

The tape lace known as *guipure* lace was made entirely of tapes joined with *brides.*

Louis Quinze lace was made with a coarse linen braid that had a straight edge and was woven in many widths. The braid is called *Louis Treize,* and it was worked into patterns that are symmetrical and formal, often with two symmetrical continuous braid motifs alternating in a border design. The bars of *Louis Quinze* lace are twisted, not buttonholed. Like the other laces mentioned, it is of *guipure* type.

Huguenot lace, on the other hand, was made on a net foundation. Its patterns consisted of twining stems with buds, rosettes, and leaves. Strips of muslin were folded and gathered in zigzag fashion in the manner of Marie Antoinette rosettes and sewn securely with a ring over the center.

Spaced braid work was a point lace that had no fillings. Varying types of braids were joined in rows with picoted bars. Cords were buttonholed over the edges of some of the braids, particularly those along the edge of the lace. Usually the edge braids were plain.

Corded laces sometimes had loops along the edges. To make the edges, the worker pinned a loop to the pattern, taking care not to twist the thread. He did not remove the pin until a lace knot had secured it. A lace knot was a buttonhole stitch worked tightly at the base of the loop, after which buttonholing of the edge cord continued. Then the pin could be removed.

A typically Victorian eccentricity was a stock foundation, made of whalebone and normally not intended to be exposed, that was covered with velvet ribbon to make a framework for fancy wheels. The spaces between the whalebone were filled with about twenty radiating threads, and wheels were woven in colored silks.

Cream colored tapes and nets were perennially popular. In the early twentieth century a grayish tinge was in vogue for a while. Fancy tapes as decorative as lace insertions were used for straight runs on stocks and collars.

Grapes were a popular feature of tape lace designs, their solid, raised circular form making a nice contrast to the serpentine courses of the tapes. Sometimes the grapes were buttonholed over rings. Showier versions were made over buttons.

Below: Design adapted from an 18th-century continuous braid lace, for use with bobbin tapes. Right: Neckline design derived from a pattern book of Paganino, for use with bobbin tapes.

One early twentieth-century set of trousseau laces included a wired rose with a jewel-dewdrop at the center, which was "poised" on a velvet bow and was "perfectly bewitching, when used in the hair." Jeweled rosettes were also used as danglers to be hung from belts or collars. The little flowers, hung from a cord, were centered with buttonholed rings and small stones. One method of stiffening ornamental flowers that were not to be wired consisted of dampening them slightly with cooled water in which rice had been boiled. An ivory knitting needle was used to shape petals while the lace was damp.

A great many different types of braids were made for use in tape lace. The braid called *Honiton braid*, which was used for Imitation Honiton, was a series of connected ovals that could be cut apart to make petals or leaves. *Duchesse braid* had open meshes along the sides and fancy openwork patterns running down the center of some versions. Russian braids, Bruges pull braids, and others had cords running down the center or along one or both edges that could be pulled to gather the tape evenly. These cords were threaded in a needle and drawn up wherever the pattern required. Marie Antoinette tapes had plain or looped edges and were made in various widths. Dutch lace braid, like Marie Antoinette, was rather plain, but it had a serpentine, regularly spaced design that gave the tape a scalloped edge. These tapes were loom-woven, as was Indian tape, which was woven in twill rather than plain weave, and was quite stiff. Lacet braids had looped edges.

For other laces, cords rather than tapes were used. These were backstitched firmly onto the pattern and buttonholed in rows to make designs. The ground was composed of bars and rings, both buttonholed. The heavy effect of the lace was relieved by the addition of picots at the center of the bars.

Each tape seemed to suggest a certain usage. With *Duchesse* tapes small wheels and rosette bars were used frequently as were crackle stitch (irregularly placed bars) and rings. Bruges pull braids were made into rosettes, a smaller circle laid over a larger one, both gathered full enough to lie flat and sewn securely into place. Marie Antoinette braids also were made into rosettes with cords used for stems, their ends carefully finished for a neat effect.

Of course, tapes were often combined. For example, in making medallions with Honiton and point (plain) tapes, the fancy Honiton (series of ovals) might be laid between two straight-edged point tapes. To join the three tapes, the worker overcast the point braid up to a position where a bar was needed. He carried the thread used for the overcasting from the point tape side to the Honiton braid side, inserted the needle and carried it back to the point side, twisting the second pass of thread around the first to make a corded bar. On the point side the thread continued in overcasting stitch to the position of the next bar, and the procedure was repeated.

Honiton ovals were used to make flowers. Two pairs and one single oval made a five-petaled flower. The tape was sewn down and a ring worked at the flower center. Stems were cords cut and arranged with as few exposed ends as possible and neatly sewn to the ground. Leaves were single ovals of Honiton braid arranged in series or as called for in the pattern.

Brussels net was very fine and was widely used for the mesh grounds. It was available seventy-two inches wide; hence it was appropriate for shawls and similar large articles. Silk net was made in England and elsewhere for use in the making of embroidered blonde laces. Sometimes the nets were stiffened for work. Arabian net was substantial and was used for items that were to have jewels applied to the tapes. Another interesting type of fabric was woven. Called Scotch gauze, it was intended for embroidered mesh grounds. The fabric was loosely woven and fine; its threads could be drawn up into regularly spaced groups with overcasting or other stitches, producing a mesh for embroidery quite like those used for lace, and without withdrawing any threads.

Techniques for Making Mixed Laces

Mixed laces require no tools or materials that cannot be acquired easily. Only if one insists upon having traditional tapes for tape laces is there difficulty, and these can be had from a few sources by mail. Other tapes can be used, and each new material will suggest its own use.

Laces made on net, whether appliquéd or embroidered, are interesting work. The heavy silk net that was used in the nineteenth century is no longer available, but other nets can be used. For large scale work stiff net like that used in the samples on pages 304 to 309 is useful. Designs can be darned in quickly. The appliqué on page 281 was worked on silk illusion, a very fine net, much more fragile than the type originally used. The design was adapted from a Carrickmacross appliqué in the Victoria and Albert Museum.

Bobbin tapes for lacemaking presently available for sale.

297

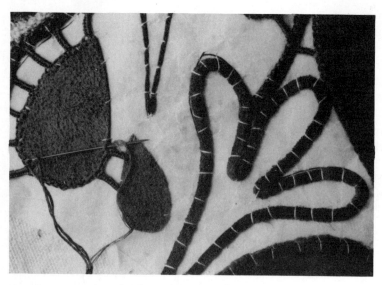

Suede tapes couched to base at the beginning of work on suede guipure jacket.

Shaping of dart, to be closed when jacket parts are assembled. Edges of dart are not buttonholed until assembly.

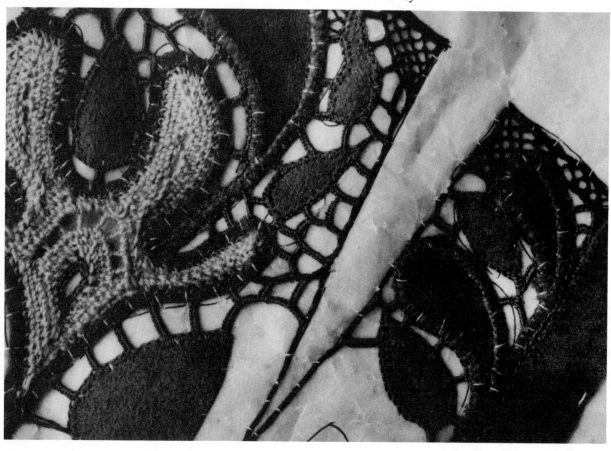

Jacket by Virginia Bath. 1973. Combined tape and appliqué lace, guipure ground. Suede, velveteen, silk, wool.

Details of jacket.

Tape Laces

The foundation used for tape lace was usually a piece of glazed material basted onto a piece of heavy paper that had been crumpled to take out its stiffness and then smoothed for work. Twentieth-century tape lacemakers occasionally used oil cloth as a foundation for the lacemaking. Sometimes the work was stretched in a frame. Tape laces were usually worked wrong side up. If net was applied, it was added after motifs were finished, sewn into picots and along edges.

Tapes were sewn securely to the cloth; basting was not sufficient. The braids were backstitched firmly along the outer edges of curves to assure ample fullness in the tape. In making turns, some tapes were lapped. Curves requiring gathers could be worked neatly when the tape was equipped with a pull thread. Corners were mitred.

Opinions differed about how a tape lace should be pressed. Some suggested a hot iron and damp cloth. Others insisted that pressing should only be done dry. There was general agreement that the laces should be dry cleaned and not laundered. With laundering, many of the tapes went limp, and restoring them to their former designs was impossible. In any case, the laces, however pressed, were ironed before they were removed from the pattern, sometimes with a wet cloth underneath.

A familiar feature of tape lace is the little buttonholed ring. These rings could be purchased, but they were also made by winding fine thread around a needle or pencil until a ring of sufficient thickness was created. The ring was then closely buttonholed. Purists insisted that rings should not be used on clothing.

Detail of tape lace. Detached petals over petals made from bobbin tape.

Gown (detail). Mixed guipure. Belgium, 19th century. Detail shows main motifs of needle-made lace with raised rings and cordonnets and secondary motifs of bobbined tape. Joining bars are bobbin-made.

Tape lace in the process of construction. Note pen drawing on wrapping paper.

Embroidery on Net

The nets used for lacemaking can be of fine silk with small meshes, as they were in the past, or the more contemporary, large-meshed versions that are available today. Whatever net is used, the important requirement is that the thread used for embroidery upon it should fill it sufficiently without causing it to pucker. The textures of the thread and net should be compatible. *Perle coton* (pearl cotton), generally available, is a traditional material, as are silk and cotton floss. Linen, when not too tightly twisted, makes a nice effect. For larger nets wool and acrylic yarns can be used, the softness that is sometimes objectionable in weaving and embroidery being appropriate in this work. In deciding what threads to use, take into account whether you want the final fabric to be stiff or to drape softly.

Partly finished segment of appliqué on net.

Entire segment completed, with excess organdy cut away.

Preparing the Foundation for Embroidered Net

Trace the design for the lace onto tracing cloth or heavy, dark paper. Then carefully baste the net to the foundation, keeping it smooth and basting within the design (in areas clear of pattern) as well as around the edges of the net. In making the embroidery, the first step should be the darning of the contours of motifs. Work these by simply following the outlines of the drawing under the net. When the meshes of the net are rather large, you will find that you cannot follow the lines exactly, but the angularity of the lines you do embroider will give your line-drawn pattern the character associated with run nets.

You will not always want to outline the motifs of your pattern with a row of stitching. Sometimes you can achieve a good, bold effect by darning the motifs without an outline. The direction in which you work darning stitches will effect the result also. If you include horizontal, vertical, and diagonal darning, the light will effect the thread used in different ways. Even when the darning is made with woolen threads, this light-vulnerability is quite apparent in the finished product.

Starting and ending embroidery must be done with care. A reef knot onto a bar of the mesh usually can be tucked under the stitching. If you run out of thread in the middle of a solid filling, you can knot another thread onto the end of the first thread and work it to the back. In a filling, where there is no place to conceal a knot, it is better to end threads at the beginning or end of a row. With some threads it is possible to weave in the threads without knotting, a preferred procedure that is not always practical.

Laces made by embroidery on net are often called *run net laces* because the motifs are made for the most part with running or darning, stitches. Many of the pieces have solid areas made by darning in silk or cotton floss, which gives them an appearance much like that of the *blonde* laces. Other pieces may have only an outline of the motif run in. These pieces may have many fancy fillings or they may have a simple but more open filling within the darned contour.

Darned areas can be made most easily by simply following a tracing under the work, but repeated geometric patterns may require thread-counting. Fillings are always thread-counted.

Fillings for Embroidered Nets

Cross Filling

To make a solid filling of cross stitches, work one half of each stitch across the row from left to right. Cross each stitch crossed from right to left in the second row. Don't skip any rows of meshes. Only three horizontal rows of mesh threads are covered with two rows of cross stitch. In each successive row, bring the needle up just under the cross of the stitch above. This stitch covers the mesh very densely, and it is as handsome on the back as on the front. You might want to use the back of the stitch for the face of your work if the texture fits your design.

Cross stitch filling.

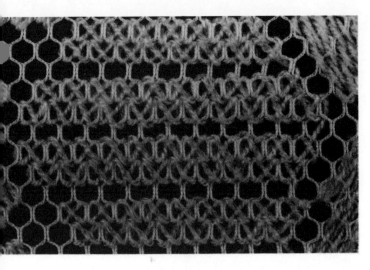

Cross stitch may be used for stripes as well as for solid areas of texture. Two rows of cross stitches followed by a skipped row of meshes will make a strong, striped effect.

Cross-Stripe Filling

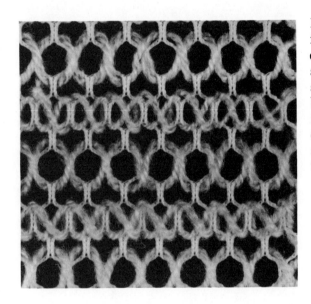

For a more delicate, intricately textured filling, make one row of cross stitches, skip a row of meshes, and then make a row of wider cross stitches. To make the larger crosses, work the slanting stitches around the junctions of the bars instead of working them over bars of the meshes. The row will look like a stripe of eyelets. Skip a row of meshes and make another row of cross stitches as you repeat the two rows of the pattern.

Fancy Cross-Stripe Filling

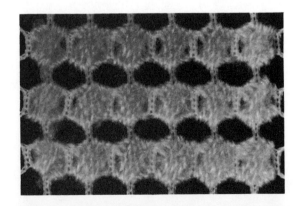

Work three stitches in each direction in each mesh along a horizontal row. Skip the next row and repeat the pattern.

Triple-Cross Filling

Dotted Filling

Work dotted filling back and forth, varying the stitch in alternate rows. From left to right, slant the overcasting stitches to the right on the top of the work and make three stitches in every second mesh. From right to left, slant the overcasting stitches to the left, with one stitch on top of the work in each second mesh.

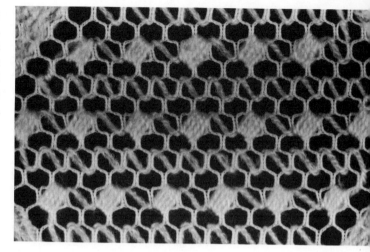

Reverse-Dot Filling

In this filling open dots appear against a background of solid stitching. In the first row of meshes, work four rows of darning stitch. In the second row of meshes, wrap the thread four times between two bars and carry it to the next pair of bars and wrap it similarly between them. Always pass the thread under the work when moving from one pair of bars to the next. The third row is like the first, and the fourth is like the second.

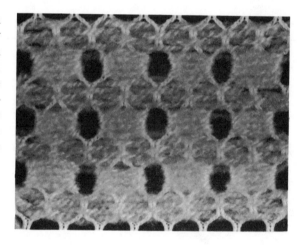

Star Filling

Make this simple, pretty filling by passing the thread horizontally under two bars of the mesh, then dropping down to the next row and passing the thread under two bars of that row, making sure that the first of the two bars lines up directly under the last of the two bars in the upper row. Then pass the needle under the next two bars on the upper row and drop it to the lower row again for the repeat. In the return journey, make the upper row of horizontal stitches through the same bars as the lower stitches of the row above. Thus there is a double stitch in every horizontal row.

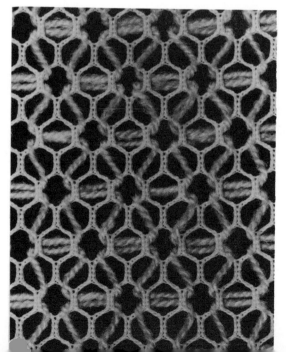

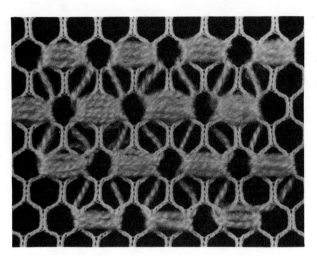

This filling is similar to star filling, but the oblique, rather than the horizontal, stitches are made on the back of the work. In making the horizontal stitch, carry the thread between the bars three times, making three stitches in the upper row of stitches in each journey.

Star-Bar Filling

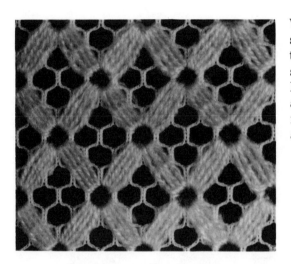

Work this bold filling by making three or more stitches around three bars in an oblique direction. Alternate the direction of each set of stitches so that a zigzagged row is produced. In the second passage of the thread across the area being filled, position the zigzags to form a row of lozenges in combination with the row above. Repeat the pattern in following rows.

Lattice Filling

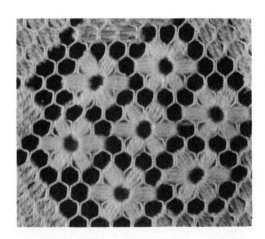

Make little blossoms or stars by making three or more stitches by wrapping the thread between two bars in every mesh surrounding the one that is selected as the bud center. The direction of the stitches should be like spokes of a wheel. Arrange the little motifs in various ways to make either solid or open fillings.

Bud Filling

Lozenge Filling

Select a mesh that is to be the center of the lozenge, and wrap the thread twice or more times diagonally in two directions. Fasten the thread on the back of the work. Leave a row of mesh all around the center mesh, plus one more at the center above the two meshes above it, and a similar mesh below, making a diamond. Make a row of wrapped stitches around the diamond, or lozenge, alternating horizontal and diagonal stitches in each mesh, so that a zigzagged effect is produced. These lozenges can be arranged in various ways for an allover filling.

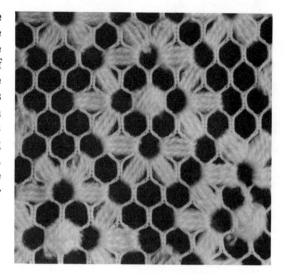

Satin Diamond Filling

The satiny effect of these diamond, or lozenge, shapes is the result of the fact that threads radiate around a central mesh-center. Tie the thread on at the center mesh, and make each stitch from the center to a mesh on the contour of the figure. With the other stitches, it describes a diamond shape.

Woven Filling

To produce this effect of weaving, work two rows of darning stitch in alternate diagonal rows. To make the opposite diagonal rows, carry darning stitches over, then under, the stitches of the first rows. The spacing of this ground can be varied. Motifs can be added in open spaces between the rows of stitching.

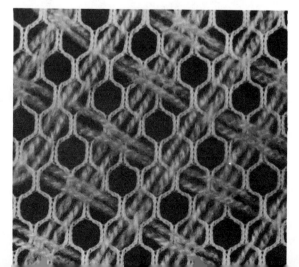

If you are using a thread heavier than that of the mesh for the fillings, you can achieve a dainty effect by wrapping the thread (as in overcasting) around the bars of the mesh in a vertical direction.

Vertical Zigzag Filling

When you are using a thick thread for the mesh embroidery, you can make a heavy filling by passing the thread in darning stitches through every mesh around an open center mesh. Work the thread around the circle as many times as needed to form a substantial ring. Then pass under the work to the next center mesh and repeat the process.

Continuous Circles Filling

Especially effective in heavy threads, this filling can be worked in several variations. Work the stitch from left to right. Pass the thread under the vertical bar below the horizontal row being worked. Then carry it across the vertical bar next in line and above the horizontal row, pass it under the vertical bar, bring it to the front, and pass it under the next vertical bar below the horizontal. Turn the work upside down and repeat the same pattern for the second row. Each row is the same, but the work is turned for alternate rows so that work is always progressing from left to right.

Loop Filling

Suppliers

Many of the materials needed for lacemaking (and all the materials required for needle lacemaking) can be purchased in department stores or yarn shops. Tools and special threads and yarns can be purchased from the following dealers.

Arachne Webworks
2390 N.W. Thurman
Portland, Oregon 97210

Boye Needle Company
916 Arcade
Freeport, Illinois 60132

Coulter Studios
118 East 59th Street
New York, New York 10022

Dryad
Northgates
Leicester LE1 4QR
England

Frederick J. Fawcett, Inc.
129 South Street
Boston, Massachusetts 02111

Greentree Ranch-Countryside Handweavers
163 North Carter Lake Road
Loveland, Colorado 80537

Handcrafts from Europe
1201 Bridgeway
Sausalito, California 94965

The Handweaver
1643 San Pablo Avenue
Berkeley, California 94702

Kessenich Looms and Yarn Shop
7463 Harwood Avenue
Wauwatosa, Wisconsin 53213

Lily Mills
P.O. Box 88
Shelby, North Carolina 21850

Macrame and Weaving Supply Company
63 East Adams
Chicago, Illinois 60603

Magnolia Weaving
2635 29 Avenue W.
Seattle, Washington 98199

The Needlewoman
146 Regent Street
London W1
England

Northwest Handcraft House Ltd.
110 West Esplanade
North Vancouver, British Columbia

Robin and Russ (Warp and Weft)
533 North Adams Street
McMinnville, Oregon 97128

Royal School of Needlework
25 Princes Gate
Kensington, London SW7
England

School Products Company, Inc.
1201 Broadway
New York, New York 10001

Serendipity Shop
1523 Ellinwood
Des Plaines, Illinois 60016

Some Place
2990 Adeline Street
Berkeley, California 94703

Spin It, Weave It Studio
840 Leland Place
El Cajon, California 92020

Straw into Gold
5533 College Avenue
Box 2904
Oakland, California 94618

Toika Finnish Loom Company
Box 2
Millwood, New York 10546

Yarn Depot, Inc.
545 Sutter Street
San Francisco, California 94102

Old Pattern Books

Pattern books for lacemakers first appeared between 1525 and 1527. There was a great demand for patterns before printing presses expedited the issue, but the patterns were made by hand. In an undated book, sometimes said to have been published in 1527, Colonia's *Il Burato*, designs for that technique, actually identical to *lacis* except for the difference in the construction of the openwork ground, appeared. Paganino's book of "transparent" designs also appeared about that time. The date is given by E. Ricci as 1525.

Ein New Modelbuch by Jorg Gastel, was printed at Zwickau in 1525. Peter Quentell's (Quinty, and in later edition, Quintell) *Eyn New Kunstlich* appeared in Cologne in 1527, the same year that Paganino's *De rechami* was published in Venice. These books combined designs for embroidery and *lacis*.

Until this date no patterns for laces free of a ground fabric had appeared, but in 1530 a book by Taglienti included designs for *punto in aria*, a technique that radically changed the style of designs for lace, bringing in free-flowing scrolls and naturalistic effects, although in Italian lace the forms of nature were stringently stylized. (Lefébure says that Antonio Taglienti's 1528 *Essempio de ricami* showed *punto in aere*.)

Few designs have been devised that are more beautiful or more appropriate for network and other lace techniques than those published in the pattern books of the sixteenth and seventeenth centuries. Fortunately, a number of these books were reissued in Venice in the 1870s by F. Ongania. Therefore, many libraries are supplied with copies of works by famous sixteenth-and seventeenth-century designers, and their books can still be used as design references. The following is a list of some of these books with notes about the kinds of designs they contain.

Libro primo de rechami, by Paganino, originally published in Venice in 1527. In addition to geometric patterns for network, this volume contains naturalistic branch and leaf designs and also characteristically Italian eagles, sirens, urns, and masks. Grapecluster designs are much in evidence, and there are some patterns derived from Persian textiles. There are four books. One shows an interesting illustration of a woman at work at four steps of the needle lacemaking process: (1) tracing a drawing from which, presumably, she will later make a pricked pattern, (2) pouncing (working color through the holes of her pricking onto the cloth), (3) inking the pounced design (presumably), and (4) working at framed lace.

Essemplario nuovo, by Giovanni Tagliente, originally published in Venice in 1531. Tagliente's book has many designs for network and needle lace. Among the motifs are naturalistic flowers and acorns and handsome strapwork patterns, some of Persian derivation. More typically Italian are the double-tailed mermaids and all sorts of fantastic and naturalistic animals: anteaters, snakes, lobsters, flies, griffins, dragons, unicorns, and other animals and insects. The book shows separate motifs within small, individual squares, several to a page. Animals and many floral motifs are handled in this way. Among other designs, the familiar three-dimensional ribbon appears. There are many small geometric patterns for network, the most interesting of them ingeniously interlocked motifs.

Opera Nova Universal, by Vavassore, published originally in Venice in 1546. Vavassore's book has scrolling leaf patterns, many of them oak leaves, as well as birds (some of them heraldic) and monstrous animals. It also has a wealth of rich, symmetrical interlaced and stepped patterns and some fancy, script-like alphabets.

Opera Nova, by Matio Pagan, published originally in Venice in 1546. This book has patterns for cutworks as well as decorated lacis in geometric and synthetic floral designs. There are many fine designs showing interlaced strapwork, some very complicated.

L'Honesto Essempio, published by Matio Pagan in 1550, has patterns for needle lace and network. Among the designs for work on *lacis* are some interesting strip patterns with oak leaves, branches, and birds.

Pretiosa Gemma delle Virtuose Donne, by Isabella Catanea Parasole, published in Venice in 1600-1601 (two books). These books contain designs for needle and bobbin lace as well as for network. Patterns for *mezzo mandolina* (see page 19) are included. Many of the border patterns have scrolls and birds, and some of Parasole's designs, as well as some of the other designers' works, seem to have been retained in the Greek island embroidery of a later date. Unlike some of the other designers, the author seems to have understood techniques very well. In network designs, she shows which areas are to be worked in open stitches and which in cloth stitch. Of all the designers Parasole seems to have best understood the technical problems of the lacemaker. Her patterns sometimes indicate exact stitches to be used, while the designs of others often left much to the imagination and decision of the worker. She includes non-square devices in some of her network designs and also in some of the designs for needle lace.

La Vera Perfettione, by Giovanni Ostans, published originally in Venice in 1567. Masks, grotesque figures and animals as well as playing cherubs cavort among the densely foliated scrolls and urns in Ostans' designs. There are some patterns showing two scrolling strips joined at the end with a pendant device that must have been intended for neck openings or other similar slits. The net patterns feature stars, straps, grape leaves, and acorns.

This much-abbreviated list of pattern books for lace should give some insight into the order of appearance of the various lace techniques. The first patterns were intended for the decoration of *lacis* and gauze grounds with embroidery. Then the cutworks and *punto in aria* patterns appeared. Not until 1559, with the issuing of *Le Pompe Opera*, did bobbin laces become important. Madame Paulis gives the date of *Le Pompe* as 1557 and Froschower's book (see Bibliography), published in Zurich, as 1560, but Dreger, Palliser and Strange say that the latter book was earlier. Froschower wrote that Venetian merchants had brought laces of their city to Switzerland since 1535. Many of the same patterns appear in both books, designs for both plaited and denser cloth laces. It was left to the lacemaker to figure out what the paths of the various plaits would have to be in order to achieve the designs, which were, in many cases, passementerie-like.

In England pattern books were rare in the sixteenth century, but among those used was a favorite, *New and singular patternes and workes of Linnen*, printed in London in 1591 by J. Wolfe and Edward White for Adrian Poyntz. An English version of the Vinciolo pattern book also appeared in 1591.

Bibliography

Ashley, Edgar L. "Spanish Blonde Lace." *Antiques*, New York, August 1922.

Backer, Stanley. "Yarn." *Scientific American*, Vol. 227, No. 6, New York, December 1972.

Bainbridge, Mabel Foster. "A Lacemaker's Pilgrimage in Devon." *Bulletin of the Needle and Bobbin Club*, Vol. 5, No. 2, 1921.

Barbour Bros. *Imperial Macramé Lace Book*. New York: W. Martin, 1877.

Bird, Junius and Bellinger, Louisa. *Paracas Fabrics and Nazca Needlework*. Washington, D. C.: The Textile Museum, National Publishing Co., 1954.

Caplan, Jessie F. *The Lace Book*. New York: The MacMillan Co., 1932.

Carlier de Lantsheere, Antoine. *Les dentelles à la main*. Paris: Librarie des arts décoratifs, 1906.

————. *Les duchesses anciennes et modernes*. Brussels: Vromant & Co., 1910.

————. *Trésor de l'art dentellier*. Brussels and Paris: G. van Oest et Cie, 1922.

Caulfeild, S. F. A., and Saward, Blanche C. *Dictionary of Needlework*. London: L. Upcott Gill, 1885.

Cole, Alan. *Ancient Needlepoint and Pillow Lace*. London: Arundel Society, 1875.

————. *On Means for Verifying Ancient Embroideries and Laces*. (Cantor lectures). London: W. Trounce, 1895.

Channer, C. C. *Lacemaking Point Ground*. Revised by M. Waller. Northgates, Leicester: Dryad Press, 1970.

Christie, Mrs. A. H. *Samplers and Stitches*. London: Batsford Ltd., 1920.

Cunnington, C. Willet, and Cunnington, Phillis. *Handbook of English Costume in the Seventeenth Century*. London: Faber & Faber Ltd., 1953.

Daniels, Margaret Harrington. "Early Pattern Books for Lace and Embroidery." *Bulletin of the Needle and Bobbin Club*, No. 17, 1933.

De Arzadun, Carmelo. "Las Industrias Artísticas Femeninas y La Composción Ornamental." *Trabajo*. Montevideo, 1920.

De Caro, Carmen Baraja. "El Encaje en España." *Editorial Labor, S. A.*, Barcelona and Buenos Aires, 1933.

De Dillmont, Therese. *Encyclopedia of Needlework*. Mulhouse, France: D. M. C. Library, n. d.

Despierres, Mme. Gérasime. *Histoire du Point d'Alencon depuis son origine jusquà nos jours*. Paris: Librairie Renouard, H. Laurens, Successeur, 1886.

Emery, Irene. *Primary Structures of Fabrics, An Illustrated Classification*. Washington, D. C.: The Textile Museum, 1966.

Groves, Sylvia. *A History of Needlework Tools and Accessories*. London: Country Life, 1966.

Haberlandt, Prof. Dr. M. *Textile Volkskunst aus Öesterreich*. Vienna: Hofkunstanstalt J. Lowy, 1912.

Hague, Marian. "Comparisons in Lace Design." *Bulletin of the Needle and Bobbin Club*, Vol. 29, Nos. 1 and 2, 1945.

Hanč, J. "Modern Czechoslovakian Lace." *Creative Art Magazine*. June 1929.

Harbeson, Georgianna Brown. *American Needlework*. New York: Bonanza. First edition, Coward McCann, 1938.

Harcourt, Raoul. *Textiles of Ancient Peru and their Techniques*. Seattle: University of Washington Press, 1962.

Harris, William Laurel. "Laces and their Affiliation with Architecture." *American Architect*. November 1917.

Hauglid, Roar. *The Native Arts of Norway*. Oslo: Mittet & Co., 1953.

Hawkins, Daisy Waterhouse. *Old Point Lace and How to Copy and Imitate It*. London: Chatto and Windus, 1878.

Head, Mrs. R. "A Note on Lace Bobbins." *Connoisseur*. London, November 1904.

———— . *The Lace and Embroidery Collector; a guide to collectors of old lace and embroidery*. New York: Dodd, Mead & Co., 1922.

Henneberg, Alfred von, freiherr. *Stil und technik der alten spitze*. Berlin: Ernest Wasmuth, 1931.

Hrdlicka, J. *Dentelles de Vienne*. Paris: A. Calavas, 191-.

Huish, Marcus. *Samplers and Tapestry Embroideries*. London: Longmans, Green & Co., 1913.

Holme, Charles. "Peasant Art in Italy." *The Studio Ltd*. London, n. d.

Ingram, Caroline Patience. " 'Point Compte' or Lace Netting." *Connoisseur*. February 1922.

Ionides, H. E. "Bebilla." *Embroidery*. London, June 1936.

Jackson, Mrs. F. Nevill. *A History of Handmade Lace*. London: L. U. Gill, and New York: Charles Scribners' Sons, 1900.

Johnstone, M. T. "Ragusa, the Mystery Spot in Lace History." *Bulletin of the Needle and Bobbin Club*, Vol. 10, No. 1, 1926.

Jones, Mary Eirwen. *The Romance of Lace*. London: Staples Press, 1951.

Jourdain, M. "Alencon." *Connoisseur*. Vol. XIV, March 1906.

———— . "Milanese Lace." *Connoisseur*. September 1906.

———— . "Gold and Silver Lace." *Connoisseur*. January and February 1907.

———— . "Mechlin and Antwerp Lace." *Connoisseur*. Vol. XIX, October 1907.

———— . "Brussels Lace." *Connoisseur*, Vol. XX, March 1908.

———— . *Old Lace, A Handbook for Collectors*. London: B. T. Batsford, 1908.

Kay-Shuttleworth, R. B. "Hollie Point." *Embroidery*. London, December 1933.

———— . "Lace II. How Did Lace Begin?" *Embroidery*. London, Autumn 1955.

———— . "Lace III. Needlemade Lace." *Embroidery*. London, Autumn-Winter 1955.

Kellogg, Charlotte. *Bobbins of Belgium*. New York and London: Funk and Wagnalls, 1920.

Kendrick, A. F. *Catalogue of the Burying Grounds of Egypt*. London: Victoria and Albert Museum, Her Majesty's Stationery Office, 1920.

King, Donald. *Samplers*. Victoria and Albert Museum, Her Majesty's Stationery Office, 1960.

Kybalová, Ludmila. *Emilie Paličková*. Prague: Nakladatelstvi Československých Výtvarných Umělců, 1962.

Laprade, Mme. Laurence de, *Le poinct de France et les centres dentelliers au XVII et au XVIII siècles*. Paris: L. Laveur, 1905.

Lawrence, William. "Hollie Point." *Embroidery*. London, December 1933.

Lefébure, Ernest. *Broderie et Dentelles*. Paris: Picard & Kaan, n.d. New York: G. P. Putnams' Sons, 1899. London: Grevel & Co., 1899.

Levetus, A. S. "Modern Austrian Lace." *International Studio*. February 1903.

———— . "The State Schools for Lacemaking in Austria." *International Studio*. November 1906.

———— . "A Revival of Lacemaking in Hungary." *International Studio*. December 1910.

Lord, Katherine. "Filet Lace." *Palette and Bench*. Syracuse, New York, October 1909.

Lord, Priscilla Sawyer, and Foley, Daniel J. *Folk Arts and Crafts of New England*. Philadelphia and New York: Chilton Books, 1965.

Lovett, Eva. "An Italian Lace School in New York." *International Studio*. October 1906.

Lowes, Emily Leigh. *Chats on Old Lace and Needlework*. London: T. F. Unwin, 1908.

Mahin, Abbie C. "Pusher Lace, an Early Machine-made Fabric." *Bulletin of the Needle and Bobbin Club*. Vol. 6, No. 2, 1922.

———— . "The Lace Trimmed Bonnets of Bohemia." *Bulletin of the Needle and Bobbin Club*, Vol. 4, No. 2, October 1920.

314

Maidment, Margaret. *A Manual of Handmade Bobbin Lacework*. London: Sir Isaac Pitman & Sons Ltd., 1931.

May, Florence. *Catalogue of Laces and Embroideries*. New York: The Hispanic Society of America, 1936.

——— . *Hispanic Lace and Lacemaking*. New York: The Hispanic Society of America. 1937.

Mezzara, Paul. "Le Filet Brodé." *L'Art et Décoration*. Tome XXIV, July-December 1908.

Middleton, George. "Imitations of Handmade Lace by Machinery." *Bulletin of the Needle and Bobbin Club*, Vol. 22, No. 2, 1938.

Mincoff-Marriage, Elizabeth. *Pillow Lace, a Practical Handbook*. New York: E. P. Dutton and Co., 1907.

Moore, Mrs. Hannah. *The Lace Book*. New York: Tudor Publishing Company, 1937.

Morris, Francis. *Antique Laces of American Collectors*. New York: William Helburn Inc. (for the Needle and Bobbin Club), 1926.

——— . "Lace Bobbins." *The Bulletin of the Needle and Bobbin Club*, Vol. 1, No. 1, December 1916.

Ostaus (Ostans), Giovanni. *La vera prefettione del disegno di varie sorti di recami*. Originally published in 1557. Venice: F. Ongania, 1878.

Overloop, Eugene van. *Dentelles anciennes des musées royaux des arts décoratifs et industriels à Bruxelles*. Brussels: Van Oest et Cie, 1912.

——— . *Dentelles anciennes de la collection Alfred Lescure*. Brussels: G. van Oest. 1914.

——— . *La dentelle, guide du visiteur*. Brussels: Dreeson & De Smet, n. d.

Pagan, Matio (Pagani, Mathio). *L'honesto essempio del vertuoso desiderio*. Originally published in 1550. Venice: F. Ongania, 1878.

Paganino, Alexandro. *Libro primo de rechami and libro secondo, libro terzo*. Originally published in Venice: F. Ongania, 1878.

Palliser, Mrs. Bury. *A Descriptive Catalogue of the Lace and Embroidery in the South Kensington Museum*. London: Her Majesty's Stationery Office, 1871.

——— . *Histoire de la Dentelle*. Paris: Firmin-Didot, 1901. Revised by M. Jourdain and Alice Dryden. New York: Charles Scribners' Sons, 1902.

Parasole, Signora Elisabetta Catanea. *Pretiosa gemma delle virtuose donne*. Rome: 1615. Venice, F. Ongania, 1879.

——— . *Teatro delle nobili et virtuose donne*. Rome: M. Bona, 1616. Venice: F. Ongania, 1891.

Paulis, Mme. L. *La dentelle au fuseaux*. Brussels: Lamertin, Librairie-Editeur, 1921.

——— . "Le Pompe." *Bulletin of the Needle and Bobbin Club*, Vol. 6, No. 2, 1922.

——— . "Note on the Lace Industry in Belgium in the Nineteenth Century." *Bulletin of the Needle and Bobbin Club*, Vol. 7, No. 1, 1923.

Pollen, Maria Margaret. *Seven Centuries of Lace*. New York: The MacMillan Company, 1908. London: W. Heineman, 1908.

Pond, Gabrielle. *An Introduction to Lace*. London: Garnstone Press, 1968.

Powys, Marian. *Lace and Lacemaking*. Boston: Charles T. Branford Company, 1953.

Quicherat. *L'histoire du Costume en France*.

Ricci, Elisa. *Old Italian Lace*. Vols. 1 and 2. London: W. Heinemann. Philadelphia and New York: J. P. Lippincott Company, 1913.

Romana, Lucretia. *Ornamenti nobili per ogni gentil matrona*. Preprinted Venice: F. Ongania, 1876.

Sera, Domenico da. *Opera nova*. Originally published in 1546. Venice: F. Ongania, 1879.

Schuette, Marie. *Alte Spitzen*. Berlin: Richard Carl Schmidt & Co., 1914.

Schwab, David E. *Story of Lace and Embroidery*. New York: Fairchild Publications, 1951.

Sharp, A. M. *Point and Pillow Lace*. New York: E. P. Dutton & Co. London: John Murray, 1899.

Simpson, Isabel A. (Carita). *Lacis, practical instructions in filet brodé or darning on net.* Philadelphia: J. B. Lippincott Company. London: S. Low Marston & Co. Ltd., 1908.

———. "Lacis." *Embroidery*, Vol. IV, No. 4, September 1936.

Six, Jan. "Notes on Early Dutch Lace." *The Bulletin of the Needle and Bobbin Club*, Vol. 16, No. 1, 1932.

Somerhof, Hazel Dunning, and Whiting, Gertrude. *La révolte des passemens.* New York: Select Printing Co. (for the Needle and Bobbin Club), 1935.

Taglienti, Giovanni Antonio. *Essemplario nouva.* Originally published in Venice in 1531. Venice: F. Ongania, 1879.

Taxhina, Maria José. "Lace." *Textile Conservation*, edited by Jentina E. Leene. Washington, D. C.: Smithsonian Institutions, 1972.

Townsend, Gertrude. "New England Needlework before 1800." *Bulletin of the Needle and Bobbin Club.*

Trendell, P. G. "Sixteenth Century Lace." *Embroidery.* June, 1933.

Urbani de Gheltof, G. M. *A Technical History of the Manufacture of Venetian Laces (Venice-Burano).* Translated by Lady Layard. Venice: F. Ongania, 1882.

Van der Meulen-Nulle, L. W. *Lace.* Netherlands: Van Dishoeck, Van Holkema & Warendorf N. V., 1964. New York: Universe Books, Inc., 1964.

Vavassore, G. A. *Opera nova . . .* Originally published 1546. Venice: F. Ongania, 1878.

Vecellio, Cesare. *Corona delle nobili et virtvose donne.* Originally published 1600. Venice: F. Ongania, 1879.

Verhaegen, Pierre. *La dentelle belge.* Brussels: Office de publicitée. J. Lebìque et Cie, 1912.

Vinciolo, Federico. *Les singuliers et nouveaux pourtraicts.* Paris: Iean le Clerc, 1603. New York: Dover Publications, Inc., 1971.

Wardle, Patricia. *Victorian Lace.* New York and Washington: Frederick A. Praeger, Publishers, 1969.

Warren, Mrs., and Pullen, Mrs. "Treasures of Needlework." *Embroidery,* 1934.

Walterstorff, Emilie von. "Swedish Textiles." *Amanuensis at the Nordiska Museet.* Nordiska Museet, 1925.

Wheeler, Candace. *Development of Embroidery in America.* New York: Harper and Bros. 1921.

Whiting, Gertrude. *A Lace Guide for Makers and Collectors.* New York. E. P. Dutton & Company, 1920.

———. "The Tercentenary of Colbert, the Great Patron of the French Lace and Textile Industries." *Bulletin of the Needle and Bobbin Club*, Vol. IV, No. 2, October 1920.

———, and Somerhof, Hazel Dunning. *Revolte des Passemens.* New York: Select Printing Company (for the Needle and Bobbin Club), 1935.

Worndel, Gertie. "Danish Drawnwork Lace of the Eighteenth Century." *Embroidery,* June 1938.

Zoppino, Nicolo. *Essemplario . . . .* Originally published 1530. Venice: F. Ongania, 1878.

"Exhibition of Binche and Val Laces." *Bulletin of the Needle and Bobbin Club,* June 1917.

"The Lace Industry in Belgium." *Bulletin of the Needle and Bobbin Club,* June 1917.

"Some Notes on Stitches—Their History, Names, and Localities." *Embroidery.* March 1937.

Weldon's Encyclopedia of Needlework. London: Waverley Book Co. Ltd., n. d.

Acknowledgments

A number of people gave valuable assistance in the assembling of material for this book. I am indebted particularly to artists Bucky King, Pittsburgh, Pennsylvania, Mary McPeek, Ann Arbor, Michigan, Brigita Fuhrmann, Andover, Massachusetts, Marie Vănková, Prague Czechoslovakia, Kaethe Kliot, Berkeley, California, and to Mary Lou Keuker, historian, Beltsville, Maryland, for suggesting artists who might be represented, for making demonstration material for the book, or for other services. For assistance in obtaining museum material thanks are owed to Miss Jean Mailey, Associate Curator in Charge of Textiles, members of the staff of the Textile Study Room and Photograph Services of the Metropolitan Museum of Art, New York; to Mr. Larry Salmon, Curator of Textiles and Miss Anne Rowe, Assistant Curator of Textiles, Museum of Fine Arts, Boston; to Mrs. K. B. Brett, Curator, Textile Department, Royal Ontario Museum, Toronto; to Mr. David Owsley, Curator of Decorative Arts, Museum of Art, Carnegie Institute, Pittsburgh; to Miss S. M. Levey, Research Assistant, Textile Department, Victoria and Albert Museum, London; to Mrs. Christa Mayer Thurman, Curator of Textiles, Art Institute of Chicago; and to Ms. Barbara Killway, Curator, Museum of Contemporary Crafts, New York.

As always, I had the daily aid and support of Russell G. Bath.

Adapted designs and other drawings, as well as demonstration samples and photos were made by the author unless otherwise indicated.

Book design by Mary Ann Simmonds and Karen Yops

Index